FINES WILL BE C

**Approaching Social Theory**

# Approaching Social Theory

E. Ellis Cashmore and
Bob Mullan

*Cartoons by Mick Davis*

Heinemann Educational Books

## Acknowledgement

We would like to thank our colleagues, Colin Bell, Martin Hollis and Dave Podmore, for commenting on an earlier draft of this book.

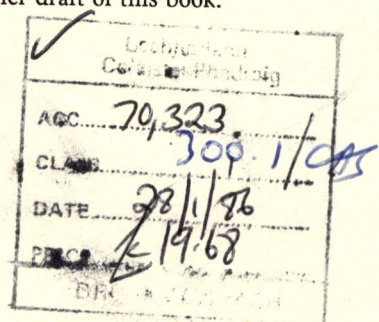

Heinemann Educational Books Ltd
22 Bedford Square, London WC1B 3HH
LONDON EDINBURGH MELBOURNE AUCKLAND
HONG KONG SINGAPORE KUALA LUMPUR NEW DELHI
IBADAN NAIROBI JOHANNESBURG
EXETER(NH) KINGSTON PORT OF SPAIN

© Ernest Cashmore and Bob Mullan 1983
First published 1983

**British Library Cataloguing in Publication Data**
Cashmore, E. Ellis
    Approaching social theory,
    1. Social sciences
    I. Title        II. Mullan, Bob
    300         HB85

    ISBN 0-435-82167-9
    ISBN 0-435-82168-7 Pbk

Phototypesetting by Georgia Origination, Liverpool
Printed in Great Britain by Biddles Ltd, Guildford, Surrey

# Contents

*Acknowledgement* — iv

*Introduction* — viii

## Part One: Behaviourism

**1 Man Machine** — 1
 Body and soul — 1
 Pavlov's dogs — 5
 Experiments with Albert — 9
 Changes from without — 13

**2 Plastic People** — 16
 The reinforcer — 16
 Inside the Skinner box — 22
 The technology of behaviour — 24
 Demons and goblins — 30

**3 Exchange and Reward** — 35
 In the market — 35
 *Quid pro quo:* Homans — 40
 Blau power — 42
 Individualism — 46

*Theory into Action: Sex, Violence and the Media* — 51

## Part Two: Interactionism

**4 Action Man** — 57
 The importance of meaning — 57

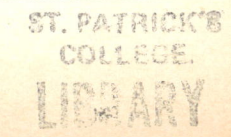

|   |   |   |
|---|---|---|
|   | A matter of interpretation: Weber | 62 |
|   | Ironies | 65 |
|   | The pragmatists | 68 |
| 5 | **The Selves** | 76 |
|   | Explorations of consciousness | 76 |
|   | All in the mind: Cooley | 79 |
|   | The definition of the situation | 84 |
|   | Mead's social theory of mind | 87 |
| 6 | **Society as Process** | 97 |
|   | Disembodied society | 97 |
|   | Roles and identities | 103 |
|   | Back-stage with Goffman | 108 |
|   | Society as a house of cards | 113 |

*Theory into Action: Sexual Deviance* — 123

## Part Three: Structuralism

| | | |
|---|---|---|
| 7 | **Social Wholes** | 129 |
|   | Greater than the sum of the parts | 129 |
|   | The organic model | 133 |
|   | The anthropologists | 140 |
|   | Building sight: Marx and Engels | 144 |
| 8 | **Psycho-structures** | 154 |
|   | Of madness and majesty | 154 |
|   | Schemes of thinking: Piaget | 160 |
|   | The innate blueprint | 165 |
|   | Universals | 171 |
| 9 | **Mistrust of Consciousness** | 180 |
|   | Systems | 180 |
|   | GST: the manic drive for unity | 186 |
|   | The Two Marxisms | 187 |
|   | Power-knowledge: Foucault | 195 |

*Theory into Action: The Capitalist State* — 202
*Epilogue* — 205
*Bibliography* — 209
*Index of Names* — 225
*Title Index* — 230
*Subject Index* — 232

# Introduction

Reality is not as it seems. All social theory takes this as its starting point. Appearances are superficial, deceptively superficial. So a real understanding of the nature of man and his relationships to his environment and other men must probe beneath the surface of appearances. In other words, social theory needs to go beyond the obvious.

Many people are interested in the sorts of fundamental questions social theory tries to answer. Questions such as whether men are naturally wild and feral creatures when stripped of the veneer of civilization – 'The Lord of the Flies effect'; or whether they are manipulated like puppets in a theatre or 'programmed' from birth. In sum, what are the kinds of influences to which men are subjected, to what degree are they affected by them and what are the results of the influences on their thoughts and behaviour? All social theory, in some way, attempts to tackle such issues; all theory tries to reach beyond the misleading appearance of men and present reality as an alternative version.

When it comes to social theory, people tend to talk in terms of good and bad theories, but these judgements usually refer to the theory's utility rather than its truth or falsity. Social theory is, to echo John Rex from 20 years ago, 'an imperfect and incomplete attempt to explain', rather than a claim to absolute truth or objective knowledge (1961, p. 2). For this reason, we believe *in* theories rather than simply believe them. Adherence to social theories is frequently a matter of intellectual or moral commitment. There is often nothing to choose between theories: they purport to explain – however incompletely – some facets about the relations of people with society. One theory is not necessarily better than another, it is simply that different theories concentrate on different facets, making differing assumptions and using different techniques.

No theory then can aspire to true explanation of social reality, or a true portrait of the types and extents of social influences or the individual. The nature of social reality, as we will show, simply does not lend itself to such

I'm just a vision on your TV screen
just something conjured from a screen
seen through your X-ray eyes
a see-through scene
the image is no images
*it's not what it seems.*

Siouxsie and the Banshees

*Mirage* by Sioux, Severin, McKay & Morris, Polydor, Pure Noise Chappell, 1978.

an analysis. We construct theories about reality. That reality doesn't somehow impose itself on our senses; we slice it up with concepts, then fit the pieces together to form a theory, or version, of reality. Merely observing the world is insufficient as Jonathan Turner illustrates:

> '... people watched apples fall from trees for centuries, but real understanding [sic] of this phenomenon came only with the more abstract concept of gravity, which allowed for many similar occurences to be visualized and incorporated into a theoretical statement that explained much more than why apples should fall from trees' (1982, p.4).

Theorizing is a creative process of imposing concepts on reality and, in each of the sections of this book, we show how broadly similar concepts have been aligned in such a way as to constitute what we call strains of theory. Our preference for the term strain is based on the conviction that there are three main tendencies of discourse in social theory, each tendency being internally related by basic theoretical assumptions that affect the type of questions used and the concerns considered by theorists working with them. We characterize each strain thus:

1. Concerns behaviour and the conditioning of human beings;
2. Is impelled by the attempt to reveal the consciousness underlying human interaction;
3. Strives to produce a notion of structure or system to denote the status of societies as distinct from individuals.

Two concerns surface time and again throughout the strains. One is: the extent to which man has the creative, ingenious capacity to control himself and his environment to some degree independently of constraints internal or external to himself. Those arguing for a large extent would say that humans have free will in their choice of thought and conduct and, therefore, in their propensities to construct social relations. If this is accepted, as it is by the strain of thought we depict as interactionism, then study should be directed to human consciousness and the meanings behind our actions.

If, on the other hand, this is rejected and the human is thought to be constrained either by psychic or social factors beyond his control, then a brand of determinism is espoused and attention is turned to the determinants of action. We refer to the theories in Part Three as structuralism. This term has become associated with a particular brand of French thought (which we do consider). However, there is unity between the general sense in which we use the term and the specific French form, as Anthony Giddens points out: 'both types of usage of the notion of structure, lead to the conceptual blotting-out of the active subject' (1976, p. 22).

Certainly, George Homans, one of the central figures in the first section, would not agree to the 'blotting-out'. In fact, he has made the case for social sciences to be 'bringing men back in' (1964a). Homan's theories are part of the strain of behaviourism, which depicts the human as a passive, uncreative respondent to stimuli in the environment. Again the individual is, if not entirely excluded from the scene, certainly neglected as a controller of his own destiny. The crucial determinants lie outside him, in the environment.

This flows into the second concern. If the active human subject is blotted out of the scene, then we have the problem of how to account for the sometimes rapid, other times glacial, changes in societies. If changes in societies are not caused by men's wills, what are they caused by? Social theory has to provide answers. Events, in the view of the social theorist, do not just happen mysteriously: there are mechanisms behind them that must be revealed. We believe that every social theory has, in some way, attempted to expose the mechanisms. Whereas the conventional argument is that all social theory hinges on the attempt to explain why humans live together in an ostensibly orderly fashion (i.e. 'the problem of order',) we propose that the more pressing question for theories is: how do societies change?

Some theorists, particularly some of those in Part Three, would contend that there is a logic of historical development, an inexorable progression over which humans have no control. At the other extreme, many would say that social change is unpredictable and subject to alterations of human thought; ideas are the propellers of change. Paul Rock sums up the interactionist view: 'Man's capacity to interpret the world allows him to transcend and synthesize contrasting facets into qualitatively new configurations. These configurations feed back into the world and present new possibilities of action, response and understanding' (1979, p. 55). Each of the theories we consider has an inbuilt conception of change as well as of order.

The reasoning behind the organization of the book has compelled us to deal somewhat cursorily with what some might regard as prominent theories, the most outstanding being critical marxism, which is considered as one of 'The two marxisms' of Part Three. Important as the individual contributions of critical theorists have been, we agree with David Held that: 'they have not, in my opinion, adequately demonstrated that critical theory has a special theoretical status' (1980, p. 399). Absent from the varied contributions is a *core* of concerns that might have otherwise distinguished them collectively as a distinct theory.

So, our book is not totally comprehensive (what book would aspire to be?) but by using the strain scheme of interpretation, we feel that we can incorporate the main figures in social theory and the important features of their works. This perforce means that there are omissions; not serious we feel, but omissions nevertheless. What we aim to provide, however, is both a text book and, perhaps more important, a method of understanding the nature of social theory. There is no attempt to locate the important theorists in their social contexts, nor an effort to expose the social conditions that underlay the rise of particular strains; there are already adequate introductions available from Lewis Coser (1977) for the former and Robert Nisbet (1970) for the latter.

Our sequence follows a sort of reductionist logic-in-reverse. In the first section we present a strain of thought in which humans are reduced and are seen as what they are when all other aspects are removed: living organisms. Man is examined as a biological entity inhabiting an environment over which he has no control and which supplies stimuli to which he responds. The contents of his head or of his interactions with others do not come under scrutiny: these are relegated to the realms of philosophy and conjecture. Scientific analysis does not try to penetrate deeper than visible flesh.

A quite different voluntaristic image of man emerges in the middle section: here he is much as the behaviourists see him in profile, but he gains new dimensions with the inclusion of active consciousness. No longer a mere respondent to stimuli, he defines his environment, reflects on it, establishes relationships with other humans and, in the process, actually makes society. This production is possible because of what goes on inside his head: society doesn't exist independently of man but is created by him in his conscious, imaginative, meaningful collaborations with others.

The essential creativity of man is blotted-out in Part Three, and here his actions are seen as rather inconsequential when confronted by the overarching and quite separate society. Defined as either a structure or a system, the social entity has a status that is independent of, and superior to, man and determines his actions. It imposes itself on humans and renders them incapable of making changes even if they intend them. Thus, consciousness and other subjective states are rendered insignificant in the analysis; what counts is the total structure. To simplify the strain images: in the first, man is a respondent, in the second a creator, in the third, insignificant.

Throughout this book, two concerns dominate: the freedom of man and his capacity to make changes. We argue that a grasp of these issues is vital to any understanding of social theory. The image of man, whether free and unconstrained or trapped by the necessities of his environment, the restrictions of his biology or the requirements of his society, lurks not too deeply beneath the surface of all social theory and it needs to be revealed.

Undergraduate students in sociology, psychology, anthropology or philosophy and all humanities subjects are frequently confronted by the monumental works of Marx, Freud, Weber and Mead as well as the works of other theorists. At the end of two or three years of study, the student might still be puzzled by the bewildering diversity in concerns of the theories of man. Why does Herbert Spencer crop up in the same course as Harold Garfinkel, or B. F. Skinner in the same as Michel Foucault? How can these writers all legitimately be said to be part of the same enterprise? By drawing on the fields of sociology, psychology, anthropology and philosophy, pulling together the uniting threads and organizing the material in terms of the three strains, we hope to provide some answers to questions such as these.

We also append each strain with an illustration of how the main theoretical thrust of each can be put into action research and used to inform practical endeavours.

Two issues of language arise. The first is due to the failure of English to provide suitable neuter words: we tend to use phrases such as 'action man' or 'man in society', not because we are sexist, but because the theorists we consider wrote in such a way and we, in the absence of alternatives, retain fidelity to their style. The other issue concerns the more obscure terms used by social theorists. (It will become apparent that many of the concepts we use in everyday language, like conditioning, self or structure, have different, often problematic, meanings when used in the three strains). We define them in the text and, where appropriate, give examples of their use. In some cases, this is stylistically clumsy, so we close each chapter with a short glossary of technical terms. In fact, we end this introduction with definitions of two of the crucial terms that will appear throughout this book.

## Technical Terms

**Determinism:** A philosophical doctrine which enters into social theory in many guises, but which has as its bedrock external forces impinging on human will or internal, possibly psychic, forces propelling humans to think and behave in specific ways. It follows that action is never spontaneous but always caused by factors beyond the individual's capacity to influence. 'Hard' determinists say that, given complete knowledge of external conditions, we could predict all action. 'Soft' determinists are less sure.

**Voluntarism:** The doctrine that human conduct is guided by the will of the individual and can never be fully determined by forces outside of his control. Central to this is the stress on the inviolability of free will which is an independent capacity of human beings to do as they please rather than react under compulsion. Underlying this is a strong opposition to determinists of any sort.

# Part One: Behaviourism

- Man Machine
- Plastic People
- Exchange and Reward

# 1

# Man Machine

**Body and soul**
The central theme of Ira Levin's novel, *The Stepford Wives*, concerns the possibility of constructing perfect humans – in this case wives – who are steadfast housewives, yet always immaculate in their appearance and attentive to their husbands' requirements. The wives are everything the normal chauvinist husband needs; and they never answer back!

The vision inspiring the novel is one which has intrigued and provoked many social theorists: that of reducing humans to their component parts as we might a machine. In its strongest form, as espoused by the French materialists of the eighteenth century, the vision sees all humans as animated machines. People like La Mettrie proclaimed that man is a machine, with his brain secreting thought as his stomach secretes digestive juices. *L'homme machine* as La Mettrie called it – or him – crops up elsewhere in literature, perhaps most famously in Mary Shelley's *Frankenstein* where a spare parts construction eventually takes on a life and will of its own. This really is the problem behind the whole vision: introducing human will, a will which so obviously seems the motor of human action. We can construct the most elaborate androids, but we can't build human will into them.

One way out of the problem is simply to deny that it's a problem at all: free will is an illusion. Certainly many modern sociobiologists like Edward O. Wilson would argue along these lines (1978). They would insist that human beings share a wide range of characteristics that have a complex, genetic foundation; these influence our entire lives in as yet unknown ways. We think we are acting as free and responsible persons only because it is a very complex procedure to trace back genetic origins and, therefore, predict future behaviours. In theory, however, this is entirely possible. Sociobiologists believe that all human behaviour is ultimately determined by genetic factors. In a different vein, Levin's manipulators made it possible to determine their wives' behaviour with sophisticated technology. In both extreme cases, the image of human beings minus free will is presented.

Before La Mettrie, another Frenchman, René Descartes, had struggled with the basic problem. He accepted the materialist conception of the human as a machine, claiming that all living processes like digestion, growth and reproduction could be explained in a mechanical fashion and that similar explanations can be offered for mental processes. Man, however, has an additional faculty that animals have not: souls. Descartes said that humans have a duality, a body and a soul that come into contact in the pineal gland at the base of the brain. This dualism of man is the feature that is essential to our understanding of the history of social theory. Both mind, or soul, and body were considered necessary to explain completely human behaviour. In Descartes' view, objects in the physical world affect the sense organs, which in turn send messages through the nerves to the brain. Two things then happen. First, in a purely mechanical way, the brain causes action by sending 'animal spirits' through the nerves to the muscles. This mechanical chain of effects eventually became known as a reflex arc. Secondly, at the same time the body makes contact with the mind at the pineal gland. This contact allows the mind to be aware of both kinds of the body's actions – reflex, involuntary actions as well as voluntary actions. All actions involve the same nerves and muscles, but voluntary actions originate in the mind, a nonphysical realm, and involuntary actions originate in objects in the physical world. Only humans possess the extra pathway that leads to voluntary action. Importantly, as Howard Rachlin points out, in Descartes' view, since much behaviour (including all animal behaviour) is 'as mindless as the behaviour of a stone, it can be considered subject to the same physical laws

---

### René Descartes (1591–1650)

French philosopher and mathematician, born in La Haye. After attending the Jesuit La Flèche, he went on to study law at Poitiers, graduating in 1616. Published his philosophical masterpiece *Meditations* in 1641, and three years later his *Principles* appeared, providing a full account of his metaphysical and scientific theories. The most influential aspect of his work is the theory of the human mind and its distinction from the human body – 'I think therefore I am.' Cartesian dualism, as his conception has become known, has exerted a profound influence on the philosophy and psychology of mind.

that govern a stone's behaviour. On the other hand, the actions of the mind are not subject to physical laws but are determined by other laws, unknown, and perhaps unknowable' (1970, p. 7).

The effect of Descartes' dualism was to divide up the study of behaviour, with involuntary behaviour being studied by physiologists specializing in the study of the body, whilst voluntary behaviour remained in the realm of philosophers. These two branches of study gave rise to two distinct methods of collecting psychological data. Edwin Boring, in his seminal work on the history of experimental psychology, notes that: 'put in its simplest terms the basic problem about the data of psychology is that: Does psychology deal with the data of consciousness or the data of behaviour or both?' (1957, p. 620).

In Descartes' time, the investigation of mind by studying behaviour alone was thought impossible; involuntary behaviour was not determined by the mind and voluntary behaviour (which was governed by the mind) was considered to be unpredictable, and guided by man's free will. The most that we can do, these philosophers contended, is to study the mind by looking inward. This method, called introspection, was thought to be reliable, for as Rachlin notes: 'the information carried from the body to the mind was considered to be orderly and to affect the mind in orderly ways' (1970, p. 8).

If we accept, for the moment, the notion that the mind can be examined by introspection and that the aspect of the examination is to determine the nature and origin of its contents, we can focus on another key question: what is the effect of experience on ideas and emotions? The question re-stated is not whether experience modifies our ideas, but to what extent it modifies our ideas. Descartes himself, while believing that experience had a role in how we think, held that our most basic ideas are innate – we are born with them. The position that holds that there are innate ideas, or that innate ideas are more basic and important than what is learned from experience, is called nativism. On the other hand, the perspective which denies the existence of innate ideas, or holds that the idea of innate ideas is relatively unimportant, is termed empiricism.

Rachlin argues that: 'by and large, the beliefs of most contemporary psychologists fall somewhere between extreme nativism and extreme empiricism' (1970, p. 10). We will leave nativism until later in the book when we discuss 'psycho-structuralism', and concentrate on empiricism, the extreme version that asserts that all, or almost all, ideas are due to experience, and which came to be known as British Associationism. The empiricists' basic axiom was that all knowledge must come from the senses. Man may be born with the capacity to acquire knowledge, but everything we know, they argued, comes from our experience. As Rachlin puts it: 'If we lived different lives, if our experiences were different, if we had been transported to a foreign land in infancy, then our knowledge would be different, and we would be, essentially, different people' (1970, p. 11).

This conception stood in complete contrast to all notions of innate ideas. The British empiricists, Thomas Hobbes and John Locke, argued that the human mind is no more than a blank tablet, or *tabula rasa*, that all sensations are drawn from experience in the physical world and, crucially, all ideas are the result of associations among sense impressions. These associations constituted what Rachlan calls the 'mental glue' holding together different sensations. In basic terms, the concept of association draws on the Ancient Greek idea that 'practice makes perfect'. If a person experiences two sensations in close proximity within a short period of time and then experiences the same two over and over again, he associates them in his mind – glues them into an idea. This, following Aristotle, was called the law of contiguity.

As a principle behind acquiring simple ideas and concepts this is fine, but there is a problem when it comes to more complex matters, as Daniel Robinson notes when he argues that the associationists failed to distinguish between (a) the process of acquisition of ideas and (b) the final composition of ideas. He gives the example of a pianist picking up his basic skills through association, but doing something more complex than this when playing the 'Moonlight' Sonata. In other words, it is not just a matter of experience.

In response, the early associationists would have argued that while the performance of the piece is complex and varied, it nevertheless may be reduced to a complicated series of associations between manifold sensations over a period of time and that, although it may not be practically possible to spell them out, technically it could be. The actual performance of the sonata illustrated a perfect correspondence between what the pianist did with his hands and the associations formed in his head. Thus there was a perfect symmetry of body and mind.

Chiefly trained in medicine and the biological sciences, people like Cabanis and d'Azyr led an intellectual movement which was to provide the mechanical model of man on which later behaviourists were to build. In France they became known as *Les Ideologues*, and set the foundations for the study of man based on pure, though not always simple, observation. Knowledge of human beings and, therefore, of societies in this perspective, derives not from introspection, nor by abstract theorizing, but by observation, the principle being that appearances are reality – an idea questioned by the theorists we'll meet in later sections.

Sharing this view were the early positivists, who stringently pursued the scientific method in all living spheres. They studied men in exactly the same way as they would animals, plants or, for that matter, stones. They were interested only in what was observable. This approach dovetailed neatly with one of the supposed implications of Darwin's theory: that all living creatures share a common biological heritage and that there was no sharp boundary separating higher animals from lower organisms.

The achievements of the functional psychologists with animals at the start of the twentieth century were impressive and, combining the principles of associationism and the approach of positivism with the central insight of Darwinism, led to a promising area of study which could be developed in relation to humans. Interestingly, however, the great pathfinding work which was to give the whole theoretical strain its biggest impetus came from a series of laboratory experiments with dogs – Pavlov's.

## Pavlov's dogs

At the turn of the twentieth century, the Russian physiologist Ivan Petrovitch Pavlov (1849–1936), whilst researching into the physiology of digestion, and through some incidental observations, considered that his research seemed to point 'to a new and promising area, but...[was]...uncertain about its scientific propriety' (Fancher, 1979, p. 295). The new idea was to study a class of responses that Pavlov initially called 'psychic secretions'. His earlier research had concerned itself only with innate or unlearned digestive responses that occurred in response to clear-cut and measurable physical stimuli, such as the salivation of a dog whenever powder or dilute acid was placed in its mouth. Pavlov noticed, however, that many digestive responses were learned, and occurred in the presence of psychological stimuli. The watering of a dog's mouth at the sight of its keeper as its customary mealtime approached was the clearest example. Pavlov knew that he had already developed procedures and an apparatus that could enable him to study and measure these psychic secretions with the same precision he had achieved on the innate responses. However as Raymond Fancher points out: 'he was worried by the nature of the scientific company he might have to keep if he plunged into this new venture...[and]...was disdainful of the introspection-based theories of academic psychology' (1979, p. 296).

The work of his colleague, Ivan Sechenov, offered a solution. His book *Reflexes of the Brain* argued that all behaviour could be accounted for in psychological terms. Acquired reflex processes in the cortex of the brain could presumably become superimposed on innate reflexes lower in the nervous system, thus exerting control over them. The cortical reflexes were thought to be the neurological underpinnings of such psychological phenomena as thinking, willing or deciding. In effect, what we conventionally think of as products of our free will are, deep down, only physiological processes. Spurred on by Sechenov's work, Pavlov considered that 'psychic secretions' could be interpreted as the result of new, cortical reflexes becoming attached to the neural circuitry of the basic digestive reflexes with which we are born. Fancher notes: 'From this new point of view, everything could be described in proper physiological

**Ivan Petrovich Pavlov (1849–1936)**
Born in Ryazan, he was the eldest of ten children. He enrolled in the Ryazan Theological Seminary in 1864 but left before graduation and studied at the natural science faculty at the University of St Petersburg and graduated in 1875. He then became a student at the Imperial Medico-Surgical Academy, where he graduated in 1879 with, unusually, eleven scientific publications. In 1884 he obtained a lectureship in physiology and was awarded a foreign travel fellowship for which he went to Leipzig and Breslau. He was given a chair in pharmacology in 1890, and in 1924 the Soviet Academy of Sciences established the Institute of Physiology under his direction. A Nobel prize winner.

terms, and embarrassing references to subjective psychological states could be dropped altogether.' For example: 'Psychic secretions could be renamed *conditioned* (or *conditional*) *reflexes* to emphasize their acquired and variable character; by contrast, the innate digestive responses could be called *unconditioned reflexes*' (1979, p. 296). Observed relationships between conditioned and unconditioned reflexes could form the basis of inference, not about vague psychological states, but about potentially observable physiological processes in the brain – a truly mechanical model of man. Pavlov formally banned all psychological terminology from his laboratory, threatening to sack anyone who discussed findings in subjective terms; he maintained he was not a psychologist but a physiologist studying the brain.

He discerned four basic components of the conditioned reflex: the unconditioned stimulus (UCS), the unconditioned response (UCR) the conditioned stimulus (CS), and the conditioned response (CR). Before any conditioning occurred, the unconditioned stimulus and response were united in the innate unconditioned reflex. For example, food in the mouth was an UCS which automatically elicited the UCR of salivation. The CS – say, the sight of the animal keeper or the sound of a tone in an experiment – originally failed to elicit any salivary response, but after it had been paired with the UCS a number of times, it elicited salivation even in the absence of the UCS. Pavlov expressed the relationships among the concepts 'objectively', not in mentalistic terms, but in terms of the magnitude of the unconditioned stimuli and responses, the number of pairings between the conditioned and unconditioned stimuli, the conditions under which the pairings took place and so on.

To illustrate, consider a simple Pavlovian experiment. The UCS was a certain amount of dilute acid on a dog's tongue, which had been shown by repeated trials to elicit a certain average number of drops of saliva as a UCR. The CS was a tone of a certain pitch and loudness, which was sounded a certain number of times and immediately followed each time by the acid. Then, in the crucial test trial, the tone was sounded but not followed by the acid. The dog salivated, and the number of drops was taken as a measure of the strength of its new conditioned reflex. As Fancher points out, within this simple design 'there was room for the systematic variation of many factors, and the precise calculation of many laws of conditioning' (1979, p. 306). For example, the interval between the CS and the US was varied, and it was found that the strongest and quickest CRs occurred when the interval was very short. If the CS followed the UCS, however – even by a very short interval – no CR at all could be produced.

There are other important 'laws of conditioning' as follows. Pavlov investigated the effect of a test stimulus that was somewhat different from the original CS. He discovered that a response did occur, but it was weaker than it would have been in response to the original CS. The more dissimilar the test stimulus was, the weaker the response. This phenomenon is known as 'generalization', since the subject generalizes its CR from one stimulus to other similar ones. In further tests, a dog was repeatedly fed following the sounding of a certain musical tone. On the first generalization trial a tone half an octave lower was sounded, and a substantial salivary response occurred. Thereafter, the two tones were sounded at random on different trials, with the original tone always being 'reinforced' by the immediate presentation of food, and the lower tone never being reinforced. Gradually, the generalized response to the lower tone decreased until it finally disappeared altogether. In Pavlov's terminology the conditioning procedures had led to a 'discrimination' between the two stimuli. That is, says Fancher: 'the animal has learned not only to respond positively to one stimulus, but also to inhibit the generalization of the response to a similar stimulus' (1979, p. 307).

A CR depends upon a UCS for its existence and that is precisely why Pavlov referred to the UCS as a reinforcer. Obviously, without the UCS, a CS would never develop the capability of eliciting a CR. Likewise, if, after a CR has been developed, the CS is continually presented without the UCS's following the CR, the CR gradually disappears. When the CS no longer elicits a CR, experimental extinction is said to have occurred. Again, extinction results when the CS is presented to the organism and is not followed by reinforcement. After a period of time following extinction, if the CS is again presented to the animal, the CR will temporarily reappear. The CR has 'spontaneously recovered' even though there had been no further pairings between the CS and the UCS (Hergenhahn, 1976, p. 166). Once a CS reliably elicits a CR, higher order conditionings can occur. This means that a neutral stimulus which accompanies a CS on a number of occasions can itself become a CS. An experiment conducted in Pavlov's laboratory is a simple example of this. Having established a sound as a CS for salivation, the sound was accompanied repeatedly by the presentation of a black square, after which the square evoked salivation in the absence of the sound.

In summary, he argued that unconditioned reflexes are mediated by connections between sensory and motor nerves at the spinal and lower brain centres of the nervous system. Conditioned reflexes supposedly occurred when neural pathways in the cortex became part of the circuitry, establishing connections between certain stimuli and responses that had not been interconnected before. As Fancher observes: 'crude evidence for the importance of the cortex was provided by animals whose cortexes were completely removed after they had already acquired a number of conditioned reflexes. These animals, who were kept alive by attentive keepers for up to four and a half years, retained their unconditioned reflexes. Their conditioned reflexes disappeared with their cortexes, however, and no amount of training could make them return' (1979, pp. 308-9). Outside the Soviet Union, Pavlov's influence has been felt mainly in American psychology. At first, as Gray argues, it was 'largely symbolic, providing an experimentally based vocabulary for a revolution in thought that was bound to occur anyway' (1979, p. 124). That revolution was known as behaviourism, and the early behaviourists led by Watson took from Pavlov the language of conditioned reflexes, but not his methods or theories (particularly concerning the brain).

A few general remarks are in order here. For some, the notion that the principles of conditioning, derived from the study of animals, can be used to alter and control human behaviour is a threat to their 'most cherished beliefs about the nature of Man' (Gray, 1979, p. 131). The term 'reflex' whether conditioned or not, calls forth the image of a slot machine; insert an appropriate stimulus and the corresponding response inevitably occurs. There is not, however, much in common experience that fits this image. Gray makes the point:

> We all know what it is to think about what to do, solve a problem, make a decision and so on. This kind of behaviour not only does not feel like a reflex, it is precisely in opposition to it that we recognize *as* reflex a blink of the eye or a sneeze in sudden sunlight. Tell us that both kinds of behaviour are reflex, and we feel puzzled. And, if we believe that there is a non-material world to which mind gives access, a world perhaps charged with spiritual significance, the puzzle may become outrage or panic. (1979, p. 132).

So what we are talking about is an illegitimate extension of the concept of reflex. The feeling that there is a fundamental difference between the intentional, willed behaviour we display when choosing to catch a taxi in order to see *ET*, as opposed to *The Return of the Jedi*, and an involuntary eye blink is soundly based. Indeed, both may be products of the activity of that physical system which is the brain; 'but they are surely products of a different order of complexity, and to call them both "reflex" obscures rather than illuminates this difference' (Gray, 1979, p. 134). This is not to say there is not evidence of classical conditioning occurring in human subjects, as we shall soon see.

### Experiments with Albert

Behaviourism, like many intellectual movements, did not come out of a clear sky, but there were many signs of it in the air before J. B. Watson issued his manifesto in 1913. But, as W. M. O'Neil puts it: 'it seemed that a thunderbolt was needed to make it rain. Watson volunteered to play Zeus' (1968, p. 132). Boring considers that the 'manifesto' provides an excellent example of the way in which movements start, for:

'behaviourism had both positive and negative conscious reasons for being brought forward and supported and there was also operative the unconscious positive influence of the *Zeitgeist*' (1957, p. 641). On the conscious positive side there was Watson's firm belief that behaviour in itself is interesting and important. He did not deny the existence of consciousness, he merely asked psychologists to ignore it and to deal with the more reliable data of behaviour. On the conscious negative side there was the protest against introspection. Watson considered that the technique, the description of consciousness, had resulted in no large interesting systematic body of knowledge. (In the final section we will see how an equally deterministic, yet totally unrelated group of theorists entertained the same mistrust of consciousness as a source of knowledge).

Watson in his manifesto of 1913, 'Psychology as the behaviourist views it', asserted in its opening paragraph that:

> Psychology as the behaviorist views it is purely objective natural science. Its theoretical goal is the prediction and control of behavior. Introspection forms no essential part of its methods, nor is the scientific value of its data dependent upon the readiness with which they lend themselves to interpretation in terms of consciousness. The behaviorist, in his efforts to get a unitary scheme of animal response, recognizes no dividing line between man and brute. The behavior of man with all of its refinement and complexity, forms only a part of the behaviorist's total scheme of investigation. (1913, p. 159)

Three features of the statement merit attention. Most importantly, Watson decreed that behaviouristic psychology must be purely objective, ruling out all subjective data or interpretations in terms of conscious experience. For Watson psychology became the 'science of behaviour'

---

### John Broadus Watson (1878–1958)

Born near Greenville, South Carolina. Received an M.A. from Furman University in 1899 and then went to Chicago to undertake postgraduate work. He worked in animal psychology and his Ph.D. was published in 1903, *Animal Education*. In 1908 he moved to John Hopkins University and worked with rats, monkeys and birds – 'homing mechanism of terns'. His paper of 1913 'Psychology as the behaviourist views it' was a landmark in the history of psychology, stressing as it did the need to study observable behaviour and to ignore consciousness. Following a 'scandalous' divorce he left academic life and went into advertising, successfully. He still wrote popular books on psychology, for example *Behaviourism* (1925), and was a crucial figure in sensitizing the American public to psychology.

rather than the traditional 'science of conscious experience'. Another striking feature of Watson's model was the new and highly practical set of goals it prescribed for psychology. 'Whereas traditional psychologies sought to describe and explain conscious states, Watson's goals were to predict and control overt behaviour' (Fancher, 1979, p. 319). Importantly, he, like others of his ilk, believed human behaviour and thought to be infinitely malleable and, therefore, programmable; man can be shaped.

What then were the principles of Watson's model? To begin with it must be appreciated that Watson's views shifted and changed, and so what we will illustrate are the basic ideas of his model. We have already seen what Watson considered to be the 'science of psychology', but it is important to repeat the point. Anything smacking of the 'mental' was anathema to Watson. It was as if, to him, the mental world were outside this rational world of ours, dwelling in the dark with ghosts and goblins. One may assume, Watson argued, the presence or absence of consciousness as one wishes; it does not affect the problems of behaviour one iota. Mentalistic terms implying consciousness, such as sensation, image, perception, thinking, willing, would be replaced by objective behavioural terms.

Watson at first differentiated between 'instinct' and 'habit' but later extended his argument that: 'the instincts are overlapped and obscured by later habits', arguing that innate factors are so completely overlaid by experience as to be negligible (Fancher, 1979, p. 324). So if both consciousness as a 'mover' of human behaviour, and the role of instincts are reduced in importance, what is left? What does make us behave?

Watson's argument was that, to reduce behaviour to its simplest terms, it is found that the acts of human behaviour always involve a stimulus that brings about a particular response. This stimulus is provided by something either in the environment or by movements of the muscles or by glandular secretions. The response follows upon the incidence of the stimulus. Thus, as Robert Watson puts it: 'the task of psychology is to study the laws of behaviour, such that, when given the stimulus, one may learn to predict the response, or, given the response, one may isolate the effective stimulus' (1971, p. 433).

Stimulus-response (S-R) units are, by an extension of their meaning in physiology, reflexes. And when Watson 'discovered' the work of Pavlov he considered that the conditioned reflex could become the foundation of a full-scale human psychology encompassing everything from habit-formation to emotional disorders. The S-R units were not to be analysed by a psychologist as minutely as by the physiologist. Rather, the interest was in larger segments of behaviour; what an individual would do in a given situation – say, with what hand the infant would reach for the peppermint stick or what his response would be to a loud noise.

So the 'unit' of behaviour was the conditioned reflex, and complex forms of behaviour were a combination of these units. Watson's explanation of psychological processes was to be of the descriptive variety, and he was to remain relatively neutral on questions of physiological detail and hostile on questions of mental referents.

To give a few examples of Watson's interpretation of psychological processes we can look at language and thinking. Watson considered language to be but the product of conditioned reflexes involving the laryngeal musculature. Thinking, he said, is nothing more than subvocal talking or muscular habits learned in overt speech that become inaudible as we grow up. After learning to talk by conditioning, thought is nothing more than talking to ourselves.

Watson's major process was conditioning and through this process anything could come to elicit a given response provided that it had been presented in conjunction with an unconditioned stimulus. By association, the previously neutral stimulus becomes the substitute for the unconditioned stimulus. To Watson, emotions were not matters of experienced states, but bodily reactions to specific stimuli. Watson directly applied Pavlov's conditioned reflex theory in his treatment of human emotions. His first step was to try and determine 'which aspects of human emotional response are innate – that is, what kinds of "emotional" behaviours may be observed in infants and what kinds of stimuli elicit those behaviours' (Fancher, 1979, p. 327). These would correspond to the Pavlovian unconditioned reflexes. On the basis of his observations, Watson concluded that there were just three kinds of unconditioned emotional response, which one elicited by a specific and surprisingly restricted range of stimuli. The three innate responses he referred to as fear, rage and love (sex).

As nearly as Watson could tell, these three responses, and the restricted range of stimuli that produced them, constituted the sum total of the innate human emotional predilections. Everything else, including such supposedly 'instinctive' emotional responses as fear of the dark or love of one's mother were interpreted as the result of conditioning. As Fancher puts it: 'All the complications and complexities of adult emotional experience were explained as nothing more than conditioned responses based on three relatively simple unconditioned emotional reflexes.' (1979, p. 328).

Entitled, somewhat disingenuously, as 'experiments with Albert', his most famous and controversial case history was an attempt to produce a conditioned fear response in an eleven-month-old child. The purpose of the experiment was to see if Albert could be conditioned to fear a white rat, a stimulus that initially evoked his interest and enjoyment rather than fear. The unconditioned fear stimulus subsequently paired with the rat was the sudden sound of a steel bar struck violently with a hammer just behind

Albert's head. Watson and Rayner described the first conditioning trial as follows:

1 White rat suddenly taken from the basket and presented to Albert. He began to reach for rat with left hand. Just as his hand touched the animal the bar was struck immediately behind his head. The infant jumped violently and fell forward, burying his face in the mattress. He did not cry, however.
2 Just as the right hand touched the rat the bar was again struck. Again the infant jumped violently, fell forward and began to whimper. (1920, p. 4)

After six similar episodes, Watson and Rayner noted the fully fledged fear response: 'the instant the rat was shown, the baby began to cry' (1920, p. 5).

Successive experiments to test Albert's capacity to generalize produced negative responses to such things as rabbits, cotton wool and even Watson's grey hair. Using the same principle involved in producing fear, Watson thought it possible to destroy such things as ignorance and superstition. Understanding the principles of behaviour, he thought, was the first step toward it. This leads to the final principle of behaviourism we are to discuss, namely its radical environmentalism; that is, the assertion that experiential factors are of overwhelmingly greater importance than hereditary ones in determining human behaviour.

Since, according to Watson, the innately given foundations of behaviour are so often obscured or modified by learned complications, Watson argued that one may safely disregard virtually all innate factors in accounting for individual differences in the behaviour of adults. The most significant factors affecting individual differences, Watson believed, were early experiences rather than innate predispositions. The major practical implication of this view, of course, is that an individual's character can be completely moulded if one exerts complete and proper control over the crucial developmental experiences. One of Watson's most quoted passages – in the tradition of Locke's *tabula rasa* – boldly proclaimed this belief:

> Give me a dozen healthy infants, well-formed, and my own specified world to bring them up in and I'll guarantee to take any one at random and train him to become any type of specialist I might select – doctor, lawyer, artist, merchant-chief and yes, even beggarman and thief, regardless of his talents, penchants, tendencies, abilities, vocations, and race of his ancestors. (1926, p. 10)

## Changes from without

Sigmund Koch distinguished two main phases of the post-Watsonian behaviourism, one from the 1930s to mid-forties which he termed 'neo-behaviourism'. The other formed in the late 1940s he termed 'neo-neobehaviourism'. Both phases, but particularly the latter, have been characterized, Koch argues, by extensive modification – 'attenuation', 'liberalization' – of the behaviourist position in respect of its methods and concepts (Misiak and Sexton, 1968, p. 335). R. B. Joynson talks of an 'evolution' which has tended to erode the more extreme features of the model, either through internal reform or external pressure. He adds that behaviourism has moved 'from pure stimulus-determination towards the admission of intervening variables' (1980, p. 7), which of course are often referred to as 'mediating processes'.

The movement tended to dilute Watson's original formulation, introducing contents of the mind, such as consciousness, to the programme, but always attempting to deal with them as one would do with physical entities – as if they were observable. The model of man favoured by the behaviourists is essentially passive and mechanistic. Only observable behaviour can be studied and explained. Change is from without; an environment has to be manipulated in order to bring about individual change. This holds true whether we are talking about Pavlov or Watson. Both assumed that man is no more than a machine, albeit a sophisticated one; he is a machine that responds to different stimuli lying outside him. It follows that he can be manipulated by making adjustments to the environment. The vision harboured by people like Watson was of a society in which our knowledge of human possibilities was such that we could change people without ever bothering about them individually; we could do it simply by adjusting their environment. Man is a reactor to his environment, rather than an active creator of it. Ultimately, he is determined by factors lying beyond his control; he has no innate creative capacities with which he can contribute to his own destiny. The dynamics of change lie outside him, probably unknown to him. Yet there lurks the intriguing, even eery, possibility that some men, scientists perhaps, have access to the kinds of knowledge needed to manipulate environments and, therefore shape human beings. That possibility is elaborated most spectacularly in the work of B. F. Skinner, to whom we now turn.

**Technical Terms**

**Concept:** An abstraction usually forming part of a more general theory. Differs from ideas or notions which are usually unscientific, in that concepts are more precisely defined and may lend themselves to analysis.
**Contiguity:** One of the laws of association which states that the brain tends to associate stimuli which occur close together in time or space.
**Dualism:** Associated with René Descartes, this is a theory concerning the fundamental types into which individual substances are to be divided. It asserts that substances are either material or mental, neither types being reducible to the other.
**Empiricism:** 'All knowledge is based on actual human experience' is the philosophical idea informing this approach. In total contrast to nativism (see below), people like John Locke and Thomas Hobbes rejected conceptions of the mind 'programmed' at birth and laid stress on the role of contacts with the

outside world in acquiring knowledge.
**Introspection:** The process of examining the contents of one's own mind by self-investigation.
**Mentalistic concepts:** Referring to the unseen inner workings of the human brain; totally rejected by behaviourists who insist on studying only directly observable phenomena.
**Model:** In the social sciences generally, an abstraction drawing together key elements of some social phenomena simply to facilitate understanding rather than to reflect accurately reality. Models are metaphors like social 'system' or the man 'machine'.
**Nativism:** A philosophical doctrine stressing the influence of genetic inheritance as opposed to learning or experience. Human behaviour is explained in terms of innate properties (i.e. those with which we are born) rather than what we experience throughout life.

**Reflex:** An involuntary, automatic, apparently mechanical, response of a human or animal to a stimulus.
**Reflex Arc:** The supposed physiological link between a stimulus and a response. The arc, sometimes known as the sensori-motor arc, is the unit of the nervous system establishing a connection between the situation with which an organism is faced and the motor response it makes.
**Tabula Rasa:** Latin for blank tablet, this term is popularly associated with the philosopher John Locke (1632–1704) who used it to describe the condition of men at birth. For Locke (and many others) the mind at birth is void and all later contents are put there by experience.
**Zeitgeist:** German, meaning the 'spirit of the times'. It is used to denote the prevailing social and political mood of an historical era, the conventional wisdom, current attitudes and so on.

## Further Reading

*Introduction to Modern Behaviourism* (1970) by Howard Rachlin is a summary of behaviourism with a particularly concise account of its philosophical antecedents.
*A History of Experimental Psychology* (1957) by Edwin G. Boring, simply the definitive history of psychology.
*Pavlov* (1979) by Jeffrey A. Gray is a clear and concise introduction to Pavlov.

## Advanced Reading

*Systems of Modern Psychology* (1979) by Daniel N. Robinson, pp. 1–142, is both an interesting and original account of behaviourism.
*Purposive Explanation in Psychology* (1972) by Margaret A. Boden is an extremely important, if difficult, work which focuses on the conceptualisation of 'purpose' in various psychological theories.
*Social Learning Theory* (1977) by Albert Bandura is an example of behaviourism modified so as to allow the inclusion of mediating processes or intervening variables (as they are sometimes called).

# 2
# Plastic People

**The reinforcer**
The possibility that people can be controlled, shaped and moulded to suit the requirements of science or even the whims of rulers has intrigued man for centuries. In literature, we find Frayn's *The Tin Men*, Zamyatin's *We*, Orwell's *1984* all exploring schemes to manipulate humans, but none perhaps as vividly as Huxley's *Brave New World* in which test-tube babies destined to be workers are 'programmed' with a lifelong distaste for books and flowers; they are electrically shocked as they crawl towards them.

The assumption on which this possibility rests is more or less the same one made by Pavlov, Watson and their followers: that man is a passive respondent to outside agents, which move him to react in ways that conform to others' demands. The image of what Isidor Chein calls 'Man the impotent reactor' is rich with promise for the theorist seeking means of shaping others' behaviour and thought' (1981, p. 385). Without doubt, the most prominent theorist in this field has been B. F. Skinner who, according to Leslie Stevenson 'carried on' Watson's programme: 'He sticks to the behaviourist methodology even more rigorously and eschews all reference to unobservable entities. He shows a similar faith in the programme of explaining all behaviour of animals and men as the effect of the environment upon them, an effect mediated by a few basic conditioning processes' (1974, p. 93).

The most fundamental premises of Skinner's model are, first, that organisms are active – they emit behaviours of various kinds; secondly, that when a behaviour occurs it has consequences that may affect the future of the behaviour – these consequences may either increase or decrease the likelihood that the behaviour will occur again; and thirdly, the consequences are determined by the organism's physical and social environments. Beyond these premises there are a number of assumptions that Skinner has made in developing his psychology, and which constitute

**Burrhus Frederic Skinner (1904– )**

Born in Susquehanna, USA on March 20. He received an M.A. from Harvard in 1930 and a year later received his Ph.D. He married in 1936, and at Harvard since 1931 has been research fellow, instructor, associate professor and finally professor of psychology in 1974. He was made Professor Emeritus in 1974. Was awarded Gold Medal of the American Psychological Association in 1971, and has received numerous honorary degrees. Considered by radicals to be a reactionary influence by his insistence that freedom is an illusion and that we are all controlled, his main publications are *Behaviours of Organisms* (1938), *Walden Two* (1948), *Science and Human Behaviour* (1953) and *Beyond Freedom and Dignity* (1971).

a framework characterized by practical applications. Robert D. Nye (1979, pp. 23–5) lists these as follows:

1 Behaviour is lawful; it is determined and controlled in systematic and consistent ways of genetic and environmental factors;
2 Genetic endowment determines certain aspects of behaviour, however environmental factors determine the many details of behaviour and can be observed and altered more directly;
3 The role of psychology is to discover the 'cause and effect' relationships between environmental factors and behaviour;
4 The best method for determining critical relationships is to control specific environmental conditions ('causes') and observe the resulting behavioural outcomes ('effects');
5 Studies of lower animals are useful in determining basic behavioural concepts that can then be tested out at the human level;
6 Behavioural concepts derived from the experimental study of relationships between environmental factors and behaviours can be applied to human problems;
7 It is unnecessary and misleading to speculate about feelings, thoughts, or other 'inner states' as *causes* of behaviour.

Skinner is particularly concerned with behaviours that have effects on the physical and social environments within which we live. Behaviours that operate on the environment to produce consequences, and are in turn affected by these consequences, are called operants. The consequences determine whether we do the same thing again; or try something new. Certain outcomes strengthen the types of behaviour that precede them while others do not. The multitude of consequences that we experience during our lifetime shapes us into what we are at any given point in time.

Skinner's concept of the operant comes from his critique of the reflex argument of Pavlov. Skinner acknowledges the significance of Pavlovian conditioning in explaining various reflexive type responses to initially neutral stimuli, but his main interest is in the more active, voluntary type responses that organisms make. As George Miller notes, Skinner points to the 'crushing difficulties' encountered in finding a stimulus for every response and so proposes instead to distinguish two classes of response, elicited and emitted (1969, p. 230). Responses elicited by known stimuli are respondents while operants are responses emitted without any known stimuli. In other words, the main difference is that in operant conditioning you examine and utilize the consequences that a particular behaviour generates.

In the Stan Barstow novel, *A Kind of Loving*, the central character, Vic, is initially attracted by the appearance of Ingrid, a secretary. His behaviour is under the direct control of its antecedents and is therefore respondent. After contact with her, his attraction diminishes and his contacts become less frequent; this behaviour is produced by the effects or consequences of his encounters, and is operant, that is, caused not by any identifiable stimulus (like Ingrid's appearance) but by the actual consequences of the encounters themselves. The term operant indicates that the consequences themselves constitute causes of future behaviours.

The most important of Skinner's concepts is reinforcement. If a piece of behaviour is reinforced, the probability is increased that the type of behaviour will be repeated in similar circumstances in the future. The concept is among the oldest of theories about the determinants of conduct. We find, for example, the powers of reward and punishment extolled in Plato's *Republic*, in Aristotle's *Politics*, and in virtually every ethical statement advanced in the modern age. And aside from these formal treatments, reinforcement theories have appeared latently in the: 'actions of parents, teachers, animal-trainers, and pet owners since remote antiquity' (Robinson, 1979, p. 115).

E. L. Thorndike's study of the behaviour of kittens in a puzzle box is a psychological classic in exploring this idea. A series of these boxes, open-slatted ones, each had a different 'combination' that, when learned, allowed the hungry kitten to escape from the box and to secure food placed outside it. The learning tasks for a kitten involved strings to pull, buttons to turn and levers to press. At first, the kitten's behaviour showed excessive activity, clawing all over the box and trying to squeeze through the bars. In this struggle the kitten happened to claw the string or button, and the door opened. In other words, the kitten carried on very actively and randomly until the successful act was hit upon. On repeated trials, gradually the erroneous, unsuccessful acts were dropped, one by one, in a process of trial and error. Ultimately, when the kitten was placed in the puzzle box, he would immediately claw the button or string or whatever and escape from the box. This learning, as expressed in the decrease of

---

**Edward Lee Thorndike (1874–1949)**

Born Williamsburg, Massachusetts, his father was a lawyer, then Methodist clergyman. He graduated in 1895 with a general degree from the Wesleyan University in Connecticut. Following a scholarship to Harvard he sampled many disciplines but after studying under William James he chose psychology. In 1897 he went to Columbia University and his doctoral study, a classic, was published in 1901, *Animal Intelligence*. He was appointed in 1904 to a chair in educational psychology at Columbia. He was the founder of scientific comparative psychology and through his 'laws of learning' brought British Associationism into the twentieth century.

errors and time, was gradual. Thorndike interpreted the results to mean that: 'practice stamped in correct responses and stamped out incorrect ones' (Watson, 1971, p. 426). The law of effect states that any act in a given situation producing satisfaction becomes associated with that situation, so that when the situation recurs, that act is also more likely to recur. Through the same process, a dog who begs finds himself rewarded with food and so learns to beg, as does a child who says 'please' and get rewards, or a crawling employee who continually agrees with his boss.

What must not be done is to equate 'reward' with 'reinforcement', as the two are not the same. Rewards may or may not strengthen behaviour. By Skinner's definition, reinforcement does strengthen behaviour; or if whatever is being done does not have that effect, reinforcement cannot be said to be occurring. Skinner's argument then is that our behaviour is affected by reinforcers such as money, compliments, public attention, sex, and approval from others. Our actions also are often reinforced by the direct environmental changes they produce: reaching for an object produces contact with it, approaching something brings us closer to it, and so on (Nye, 1979, p. 31). The effects of reinforcement during our lifetime moulds our behaviours along certain lines; the successful (reinforced) responses are the ones we continue to make while the unsuccessful responses tend to drop away.

A distinction that has to be drawn is between positive and negative reinforcement. When a response is strengthened by the addition of something to the situation it is a positive reinforcement; whilst when something is removed it is a negative reinforcement. It is particularly important to note that negative reinforcement refers to a process whereby behaviour is strengthened, not weakened. If we place our hand in a flame, we withdraw it quickly, so the behaviour of avoiding flames is reinforced. This term is often quite incorrectly confused with 'punishment'. Whereas negative reinforcement results in an increase in the probability of behaviour, punishment typically acts to suppress behaviour. As B.R. Hergenhahn points out, punishment involves either taking away what is positively reinforcing, or applying a negative reinforcer (1976, p. 102). Thus, punishment is either taking away something someone wants, like a Porsche, or giving him something he does not want, like a bicycle.

Skinner's main argument against the use of punishment is that it is ineffective in the long run. It appears that punishment simply suppresses behaviour and when the threat of punishment is removed, the rate with which the behaviour occurs returns to its original level. Other arguments against the use of punishment are enumerated by Hergenhahn: it causes unfortunate emotional by-products; it indicates what the organism should not do, not what it should do; it justifies inflicting pain on others; when in a situation where previously-punishable behaviour could be indulged in without being punished, it might excuse one to do so; punishment elicits aggression toward the punishing agent and others; the punishment often replaces one undesirable response with another undesirable response (1976, p. 104). The reason why punishment is nonetheless so extensively used is that it is, of course, rewarding to the punisher. If a teacher, through caning his pupils, elicits order in the classroom, then the consequences of his behaviour is rewarding.

Skinner suggests that negative reinforcement is a very influential determinant of behaviour – for example the car driver who obeys the speed limit to avoid prosecution. In Skinner's opinion, it is unfortunate that so much of our social behaviour is influenced by negative reinforcement. In an 'improved' society we would be: 'controlled more by *positive* reinforcement. In other words, instead of escaping and avoiding aversive stimuli, it would be better to be positively reinforced more of the time' (Nye 1979, p. 34). The emphasis then should be on positive reinforcement. One major reason for this, according to Skinner, is that the outcomes of positive reinforcement are more predictable than those of negative reinforcement. But more of this later.

When a reinforcement is removed from the operant conditioning situation, we produce extinction. We would be somewhat inaccurate if we argued that after extinction a response is no longer made; it is more accurate to say that after extinction, the response rate goes back to where it was before reinforcement was introduced. As Nye puts it: 'your friendly, good-natured neighbour may no longer give you a warm smile and a big hello if you have been too busy in recent weeks to be friendly in return' (1979, p. 42).

Already the broad analysis of Skinner's model has been described; indeed there is not much left:

> Some of the things we do are reinforced (either positively or negatively) and we continue them. Other behaviours have been punished and tend to be suppressed, at least under certain conditions. Still other behaviours have been extinguished and appear seldom or never. What gets reinforced, punished, or extinguished differs in various social settings. For example, aggressiveness may be reinforced in one society or family and punished in another. This helps to account for cultural and individual differences in behaviour patterns. (Nye, 1979, p. 50).

The finer details can now be briefly described. To begin with is the concept of generalization: many situations have similar stimuli, and it is in the presence of these stimuli that we respond in ways that have been reinforced in the past. Generalization provides the advantage of 'ready-made' responses in a variety of settings. Discrimination, on the other hand, refers to making different responses in various stimulus situations and is basically the opposite side of the coin from generalization.

Another important concept is that of shaping, which refers to the notion that most things we learn are the result of a gradual process. 'Each bit of progress made toward the final behavioural goal is reinforced, but we have to keep moving toward that goal in order to keep the reinforcers coming' (Nye, 1979, p. 53).

Once – if at all – a behaviour has been shaped, it can be maintained by various patterns or schedules of reinforcement. Depending on the particular schedule, we may respond slowly or rapidly, show long pauses between responses, persistently respond despite the fact that we haven't been reinforced in a long time, and display other variations in behaviour. The two broad categories of schedules are continuous and intermittent; with the former each response of a particular type is reinforced, with the latter reinforcement occurs less each time. Technically there are two major types of schedules of intermittent reinforcement: interval schedules are based on number of responses. And intervals between reinforcement can be fixed or variable. Nye offers an interesting example of how different reinforcement schedules might affect sexual activity:

> Suppose that you are on a variable-ratio schedule. In other words, there is always the chance that the next approach to your lover will be reinforced with sexual activity. Isn't it likely that your approaches will be much more frequent and constant than if a pattern has been established by which your sexual advances are reinforced only after a week-long interval has passed? This latter schedule is a fixed-interval schedule, and would very likely result in long pauses followed by increased seductive approaches around the end of the week. (1979, p. 62)

Finally, the concept of chaining helps explain how we carry out smooth sequences of behaviour; for Skinner complex behaviour patterns are made up of separate responses joined together in chains. Each response generates consequences that affect the next response in the chain. Now to see how Skinner puts these concepts into action.

## Inside the Skinner box

For Skinner the role of psychology is to discover the 'cause and effect' relationships between environmental factors and behaviour, and the best method for doing this is the 'experimental method'; and often using 'lower' animals. Following the eighteenth century philosopher David Hume (1711–1776), Skinner conceives of cause as 'constant conjunction', or in other words 'C is regularly followed by E' (Hospers, 1956, p. 287). Or, in still other words: that event is the cause of this one if events like that are regularly succeeded, in circumstances like these, by events like this. So, if every time a violent scene was shown on television, every person viewing ran amok in the streets, the showing of the scene would be said to be the cause of the unruly behaviour.

There are profound difficulties in establishing causal relations between phenomena in laboratory situations and these are compounded when the results are supposed to be applicable to human beings generally. Nevertheless, Skinner, in his most productive phase, devised and implemented experiments with animals, the results of which made Pavlov's earlier work look like a circus act. One of the important tools used was a direct descendant of Thorndike's puzzle box.

The Skinner box is a small soundproof chamber that provides an experimental space within which an animal – usually a white rat – can be studied. The animal can be isolated from interfering influences and subjected to specific conditions created by the experimenter. The operant behaviours that typically are studied are lever pressing by a rat or the pressing of a small disc by a pigeon. When sufficient pressure is applied to the lever or the disc, a food dispenser is triggered and a food pellet or grain (which serves as a reinforcer for lever pressing or key pecking) is made available. The animal's presses or pecks are recorded eletromechanically over a space of time, with the rate of response being the datum that is of primary interest. Various schedules of reinforcement can be produced by an experimenter to see how each condition affects the animal's response rate; such studies indicate how hard an animal will work under different conditions of reinforcement. A Skinner box programmed to provide intermittent reinforcement thus resembles a Las Vegas slot machine, according to Fancher.

> The rat in the box, like the slot machine player in Las Vegas, has no way of predicting accurately when the next reinforcement will come. But the occasional and irregular reinforcements they do receive nurture a constant hope that the 'next' response will be a rewarded one. Rat and player alike may become hooked, and respond long past the point of diminishing returns. (1979, p. 364)

By shaping procedures, Skinner has trained pigeons to play ping-pong, an effective example of the kind of highly complex responses that can be produced by the efficient use of operant conditioning. Furthermore, and obviously, Skinner believed that the principles found effective in shaping animal behaviour could also be applied to humans. Indeed, this is the subject of the next section of this chapter, but perhaps a few preliminary words are in order.

There is nothing peculiar in believing in certain similarities among living organisms and that behavioural processes found at one level may well apply at other levels. Two problems may operate though. Firstly, if experimentation is restricted only to 'lower' animals, statements can only

## 24  Behaviourism

be made about those animals; inferences to 'higher' animals are suspect. Secondly, and related, is the temptation to seek 'animal' roots to human behaviour. Robin Fox (!) for example argues that: 'once one gets behind the surface manifestations, the uniformity of human behaviour and of human social arrangements is remarkable... much of our behaviour and in particular our social arrangements can be seen as a variation of common primate and gregarious mammalian themes' (1970, p. 14). Here the keywords 'a variation' are made to carry an unreasonable load. It is illegitimate to assert, as David Kaplan and Robert Manners put it, that: 'locating, wounding and stalking a giraffe for two or three days in the Kalahari Desert is just a "variation" on buying a frozen rib roast in the nearest supermarket' (1972, p. 155).

Skinner would in fact agree to certain similarities, but for different reasons. Not for him similar roots, or oneness. Rather, both types of animal are susceptible to environmental shaping.

Can Skinner's model move from rats and table tennis-playing pigeons to the complex behaviour of humans? For example, what is the nature of human 'language' in this view. John Weigel argues that Skinner's approach to human language is simply an extension of his approach to the: 'non-verbal behaviour of rats and pigeons, with due concern for the enormous increase in complexity' (1977, p. 75).

The human's ability to talk to each other presented no particular problem to Skinner: he believed that language (verbal behaviour) can be explained within the context of reinforcement. Talking and listening are responses that are influenced by reinforcement just as is any other response. Any utterance, therefore, will tend to be repeated if it is reinforced. The inescapable conclusion is that humans can be manipulated to do things in exactly the same way as rats can be made to manoeuvre in mazes. And Skinner shows how.

### The technology of behaviour

In a variety of writings, Skinner discusses conditioning techniques and programmes for human societies. It hardly needs pointing out that most criticism of Skinner arises at the point of extrapolating from: 'experiments with pigeons to suggestions for social engineering for human societies' (Ions, 1977, p. 127). (Perplexingly, H. S. Terrace has recently argued that a variety of studies have, for the first time, revealed some phenomena that even the most elaborate stimulus-response theory cannot explain – for example, a pigeon's ability to form concepts and to memorize 'lists' of colours, and a rat's ability to remember where it recently found food (1982, p. 341).

The broad idea behind Skinner's 'social engineering' concern is quite simply environmental determinism; or as Vance Packard put it, people are seen as 'high on plasticity' (1978, p. 22). Skinner makes the point himself in his essay, 'Why I am not a cognitive psychologist', where he states that the appeal to cognitive states and processes is a diversion which could well be responsible for much of our failure to solve our problems: 'We need to change our behaviour and we can do so only by changing our physical and social environment. We choose the wrong path at the very start when we suppose that our goal is to change the "minds and hearts of men and women" rather than the world in which they live' (1978, p. 112). One is tempted to say, tell that to the Hare Krishnas.

The environmental determinism is, of course, simply an extension of the techniques of operant conditioning; through a variety of schedules of reinforcement, behaviour can be shaped. John Shotter (1975, p. 81) is quite correct in conceiving Skinner as a 'philosopher king' at heart, and, for example, in 1948 Skinner drew upon his experiment with rats to write a novel, *Walden Two* about a human utopia. Walden Two is a commune where everything, including work, is shared. Everyone is contented. Everyone is free of jealousy. Everyone's behaviour is substantially controlled by sound behavioural engineering principles. The founder of the commune, Frazier, is a man who talks a lot like Skinner. Below Frazier there are six planners. Through reinforcement, preferably positive, all significant behaviour that the Planners want to encourage or discourage is guided. Even in his utopia Skinner suggested that while everyone was conditioned to feel 'free', freedom itself is an illusion. Frazier continually denies that freedom exists at all: 'I must deny it – or my programme would be absurd.'

Frazier expresses the commune's rationale, and the paradoxical role of 'freedom' within it, in a conversation with a sceptical visitor. 'When a science of behaviour has once been achieved,' he remarks, 'there's no alternative to a planned society. We can't leave mankind to an accidental or biased control. But by using the principle of positive reinforcement – carefully avoiding force or the threat of force – we can preserve a personal sense of freedom'. The visitor interrupts, 'But you haven't denied that you are in complete control. You are still the long-range dictator.' Frazier responds, 'As you will. In fact, I'm inclined to agree.'

Skinner is both confident and ambitious. In 1976 in a new preface to *Walden Two*, he argued that what is needed is: 'not a new political leader or a new kind of government but further knowledge about human behaviour and new ways of applying that knowledge to the design of cultural practices' (1976, p. xvi). In *Beyond Freedom and Dignity*, first published in 1971, Skinner repeated his argument that behavioural freedom is a mirage, as man is already controlled by external influences, some of which are haphazard, some arranged. (Sartre, on the other hand, maintains that we are free, but keep pretending that we are not.)

## 26  Behaviourism

For Skinner, man's struggle for freedom is not due to any inner will to be free, but is simply a reaction to aversive stimuli in the environment. Skinner suggests that we are so preoccupied with the illusion of freedom that we are unprepared for the next step, which is not to free people from control but to analyse and change the kinds of control to which they are already exposed. Skinner has also pointed out that the doctrine of 'autonomous man' upon which so many institutions are based has deleterious consequences. Under this doctrine, we 'credit' a person more for good behaviour if we do not know the contingencies that produced it, than if we do. That is, a person who is perceived to do something good 'of his own free will' is more to be praised than one who does it because he has to. As Fancher notes, the: 'dark and obverse side of the position is that if a person is to be credited for good behaviour, then he must be *blamed and punished* for his freely produced bad behaviour' (1979, p. 369). In other words, one rarely emphasized consequence of the assumption that people are free is the requirement that punishment, or threat of punishment, must constantly be employed as negative reinforcers.

Since the autonomy of autonomous man is only apparent, the receipt of personal 'credit' for good behaviour seems to Skinner a very small recompense for the constant exposure to punishment. Further, his experiments show that behaviour may be more efficiently and effectively conditioned with positive rather than with negative reinforcement. Thus he argues that we should abandon our illusory beliefs in freedom, accept the inevitability of control, and set ourselves to designing environments in which people's behaviour will be directed toward socially desirable ends by the exclusive means of positive reinforcements.

Thus, for Skinner, freedom is the avoidance of painful conditions; freedom is not a possession, or indeed a 'state of mind'. David Cohen notes that Skinner accuses those who 'are responsible – if, of course, they can be fairly said to be responsible for anything – for the "literature of freedom", as it is misleading' (1977, p. 268). It is not quite clear what this literature is, but as Cohen once again observes: '*Hamlet* without free will is as worthwhile a dramatic proposition as *Hamlet* without the prince. *Macbeth* becomes ridiculous if he does not have the choice to kill or not to kill. The whole of literature almost is the literature of freedom' (1977, p. 268).

Radical consequences follow from Skinner's environmentalism – 'The nomad on horseback in Outer Mongolia and the astronaut in outer space are different people, but, as far as we know, if they had been exchanged at birth, they would have taken each other's place' (Skinner, 1971, p. 185). For if we have no choice we are not free and can neither deserve blame nor credit. It is the environment that did it tô us.

Skinner is misunderstood on many matters. For example, he does not favour punishment and therefore is not, as is often held, the obvious inspiration of Burgess's *A Clockwork Orange*. Of course, behaviour modification techniques have consciously been in use for some time. As Packard reminds us, an 'ardent people-programmer at the Camelot Behaviour Systems in Kansas suggests that husbands and wives can "reinforce" each other. They began by charting the number of times they smile at each other each day for a couple of weeks' (1978, p. 31). At the University of Michigan an experiment was carried out based on the premise that a sound marriage boils down to a balancing of reinforcement rewards. For example, the wife collected tokens for satisfying desires; three tokens for kisses, five tokens for 'heavy petting' and fifteen tokens for intercourse! (1978, p. 31).

More serious has been the use of behaviour modification techniques in the treatment of neuroses. Behaviour therapy is ostensibly a simple procedure; the therapist attempts to teach the patient new and more suitable ways of responding, through the knowledge of principles like reinforcement. One technique is 'systematic desensitization' and is based on two principles discovered in the course of work with animals. Firstly, the startle response to an alarming stimulus can be greatly diminished if the stimulus is initially introduced at such a low intensity that no startle ensues, and if it is then very gradually increased in strength. The animal is thus enabled to tolerate a very intense stimulus that, in the absence of training, would have produced a massive fear response. Secondly, it has been found that animals may overcome their fear of an object if they are induced to approach gradually closer to it by rewarding them with food or some other pleasurable experience (Sutherland, 1977, p. 167-8; see also Beech, 1969, and Kiernan, 1978). In other words, if Brahms turns you on but spiders don't, learn to appreciate spiders at a distance in a box first, while listening to Brahms.

A major difficulty with this procedure is that when the reinforcement is removed, behaviour may revert to the original pattern. Part of this problem is to do with the fact that behaviour therapy recognizes only the observables: 'there is no neurosis underlying the symptoms, only the symptom itself'. Indeed, Kathleen Nott remarked that a symptom 'is always of something' (quoted in Koestler, 1967, p. 350).

To recapitulate, Skinner emphasized that society, since it does control the behaviour of its members (whether or not this is acknowledged openly) needs to take seriously its responsibilities. He believes that the many problems of human conduct are too serious and complex to leave to chance or to antiquated and ill-formed concepts of freedom and dignity. He suggests that those who continually espouse the values of freedom and dignity generally miss the point that human behaviour is always affected by environmental factors; they confuse the issue by assuming that humans can somehow operate outside the cause-and-effect principles of conditioning. Environmental control is needed to foster behaviours that are both personally and socially advantageous, and programmes should be instituted to shape and maintain these behaviours. What are the criticisms of such an approach?

Vance Packard makes the point that trying to grasp the meaning of 'environment' as Skinner uses it can be as difficult as trying to 'grasp a greased pig' (1978, p. 37). Environment can be a physical set-up; a prevailing social pattern; or a person's life history. Max Black points out that one might reasonably gloss it as *'physical* environment' because this is the sense that Skinner needs, but he repeatedly renders his call for human conditioning persuasive by stretching the word to cover *persons*. Thus, 'setting an example' counts as changing the environment, and counts also, therefore, as controlling those influenced by the example. As Black adds: 'in this expansive sense, changing others and ourselves, by whatever means, will count as changing the "environment" ' (1973, p. 126).

Another sticky question that can be asked of Skinner is: if we are all controlled by our environments, and if we have no free choice, how can we 'decide' to follow his recommendations and put his suggested programmes into effect? As Black observes of *Beyond Freedom and Dignity*, the: 'spectacle of a convinced determinist *urging* his readers to save the human race is bound to be somewhat comic' (1973, p. 125). Skinner has attempted to answer such criticisms, but they never convincingly do away with the feeling that he is asking us to do something that is apparently in violation of his laws of behaviour.

Is behaviour conditioning dehumanizing? Well obviously it need not necessarily be so. Nevertheless the fundamental assumption of Skinner is that we can control all organisms, whether human or animal; and certainly the generalization can be made that: 'any person who senses that he is being manipulated will also sense that his personal integrity is being undermined' (Packard, 1978, p. 39).

Like Karl Marx, as we shall see, Skinner holds that human circumstances can and should be humanly formed. But the problem here for Skinner is, who operates the operant conditioning and on what principles? As Edmund Ions puts it: 'Skinner's proposals fail to meet the old problem, *Quis custodes ipsos custodiet?* Who are the guardians of the public weal who decide what contingencies will be reinforced, and what discouraged?' (1977). Skinner himself argues that 'no one person will emerge as the controller' (Cohen, 1977, p. 273) but many see him as politically naïve. He certainly makes a highly questionable assumption that it should be the aim of social engineering to produce a certain 'ideal' kind of society and individual. An alternative view is that the aim should be purely negative, that is to eliminate specific causes of human unhappiness – say poverty – and that to try to 'condition people according to some blueprint is to trespass upon what should be the area of individual choice', according to Stevenson (1974, p. 103). Packard adds: 'is life just a bowl of rewards?' He argues that, for example, 'would inquisitiveness disappear if school performance is linked continually to rewards?' (1978, p. 38).

Noam Chomsky sees Skinner's ideas as making it easier, and more respectable, for the state to exercise power over individuals. Chomsky also suspects Skinner of really finding ways to enshrine the *status quo*, keeping things as they are. But Skinner has personally argued for reform in the prison and education systems. Similarly, as sociobiologist Edward O. Wilson points out, Skinner is a radical environmentalist whose conclusions about human behaviour are quite similar to many 'left groups'. The political conclusions he has drawn are anathema to the left, but these conclusions are shaped in good part by: 'personal judgements lying outside the domain of scientific evaluation' (1978, p. 302).

What Skinner himself has not learned is the fact that many people do not want to use science to remedy their behaviour. What lingers is the sense of his political naïveté. Skinner's answer to who 'controls the controller' is 'countercontrol'. He is however vague about who is to exert the requisite countercontrol or restraint. Skinner notes: 'In a democracy, the controller is found among the controlled, although he behaves in different ways in the two roles' (1973, p. 172). Max Black adds, 'indeed he does, as the case of Joe McCarthy may remind us' (1973, p. 129). Black concludes:

> Faced with Skinner's skeleton design, we can only be reasonably sure that manipulation will be more congenial to an authoritarian than to an imperfectly democratic form of society – if only because dictatorships, as we know, pride themselves upon 'efficiency'. Mussolini boasted of making the trains run on time; a Skinnerian dictator may be expected to have all of us running on time. (1973, p. 129).

But all these political criticisms assume that the conditioning of humans is possible. To begin with there is the acute problem of reductionism. For example, controlled experiments on pigeons do not necessarily tell us anything fundamental about pigeons in an uncontrolled environment. In their natural habitat, living creatures prey or scavenge; there is an element of risk or uncertainty in every activity, says Ions (1977, p. 131). Further, operant conditioning is quite easy to understand, so long as we consider the behaviour of one individual at a time; when interactions are visualized, it becomes much more difficult. For example, take the case of two-person behaviour. The same behaviour (for example, person A getting rid of person B) may be negatively reinforcing to one and aversive to the other. Adding a third person, or more, enormously complicates the situation, so that it virtually defies analysis. Trained people can under proper conditions control, mould and restructure the behaviour of other people by operant conditioning techniques. Conditioning is most effective when the people to be shaped are in a controlled environment such as a prison or school. It works best when the desired change in behaviour is specific, and it works best with people who are not too advanced in learning. Permanent changes in behaviour are a problem, particularly following the removal of a reinforcement. Stuart Sutherland makes the general point that such attention was paid to the methods of 'brainwashing' used by the Chinese against American prisoners taken in the Korean war.

> 'Despite the fact that the Chinese had complete control over every aspect of these men's lives, at the end of the War only twenty-two American prisoners out of a total of four thousand and fifty elected to remain in China' (1977, p. 178).

Janet Radcliffe Richards, in *The Sceptical Feminist*, makes the observation that we cannot distinguish between the woman as she is now and what is supposed to be the 'true' woman by pointing at the way society has shaped her. It is, she adds: 'absolutely inevitable that the adult woman should be as she is partly as a result of social influence...[and]...we cannot say of social pressures *in general* that they turn the woman into something which is not her true self; on the contrary, they cannot be anything other than a contribution to what she actually is' (1982, p. 106). This, in fact, illustrates the crucial objection to Skinner, an objection that underpins much of the previous criticism and one which is always ready to raise its head. The objection is to Skinner's assertion that 'autonomous man', the 'homunculus' or 'inner man' of tradition, is a myth.

### Demons and goblins

Skinner considered that it is unnecessary, misleading and unscientific to speculate about feelings, thoughts, or other 'inner states' as causes of behaviour. As Robinson puts it, in Skinner's model: 'the abiding issues of consciousness, will, purpose, and inner struggles are swept away by the stubborn commitment to confine the discipline to directly observable behaviour' (1979, p. 131). The organism may be safely judged as 'empty', as a sort of 'black box' which emits behaviour under specifiable experimental conditions.

Jack Stranger notes that after a behaviouristic hiatus of over fifty years, American psychologists in the 1960s began to return consciousness to its former central position of concern (1978, p. 9; see also Ornstein, 1977). To take an easy definition of consciousness, we can say that to be conscious is to be aware, and consciousness is the state of being aware. Skinner on the other hand points out that to say a person is conscious of states and events in his body is simply to say that he is under the control of internal stimuli:

A boxer who has been 'knocked unconscious' is not responding to current stimuli... A person becomes conscious in a different sense when a verbal community arranges contingencies under which he not only sees an object but sees that he is seeing it. In this special sense, consciousness or awareness is a social product (1974, pp. 219-220).

This is related to Skinner's argument to 'abolish the autonomous man – the inner man, the homunculus, the possessing demon, the man defended by the literature of freedom and dignity' (Dennett, 1981, p. 57), an argument to which Daniel Dennett objected. In response, he reckoned Skinner conflated the concept of the human moral agent with ideas about men in the brain, 'demons of yore' and 'goblins', whereas many modern psychologists deduce inner states and drives without resorting to superstitions (1981, p. 57).

Skinner is totally uninterested in establishing, less still inferring, the intentions apparently guiding behaviour. Yet, it becomes tricky to explain some patterns of behaviour where intentions do seem to come into play, such as in creative endeavours, when an artist, a composer or a writer actually intends to produce something and doesn't seem to be responding to any observable stimuli. This is the gist of Arthur Koestler's critique of Skinner: 'how can scientific discovery or artistic originality be explained or described without reference to mind and imagination?' (1967, p. 13).

As Skinner must account for behaviour by citing past histories of similar stimuli and response, novel and innovative behaviour become problems to explain. An example. I am held up and asked for my wallet. This has never happened to me before, so the correct response cannot have been reinforced for me, yet I do the clever thing: I hand over my wallet. Why? Because, as Dennett puts it, it is perfectly clear that: 'what experience has taught me is that if I *want* to save my skin, and *believe* I am being threatened, I should do what I *believe* my threatener *wants* me to do' (1981, p. 67).

Shotter argues that whatever metaphysical notions one might have (like Skinner) about everything being caused by things external to them, people can cause (in an everyday sense of the word) at least some of their own motions: 'I can move my finger. I can do it, without being caused by anything else to do it, for no other reason than just to demonstrate that I can do it' (1975, p. 87). Indeed, people evidently and constantly act and feel in ways to which they have been conditioned, and the idea that anything so complex as a human being could be 'totally plastic and structureless is unintelligible', according to Mary Midgley (1980, p. 19). She notes that, for Skinner, abstract thinking is the product of a particular kind of environment, not of a cognitive faculty, so she adds, 'why can't a psychologist's parrot talk psychology?' (1980, p. 21).

A problem that faces Skinner is that there is not always correspondence between mental concepts and behaviour anyway. Why is one person angry one day when faced with a certain situation and not angry another day? Similarly, in the Skinnerian position there is precious little room for 'pretending'. In other words, no particular behaviour is essential to any given mental state. As Daniel Taylor states, in the extreme case, a man might be angry and yet conceal it completely (1970, p. 46).

In Skinner's externalization of laws, concepts such as motivation and emotion have been moved out into the environment. A 'motive', if it has any operational meaning at all, must refer to some property of a stimulus by which that stimulus gains control over behaviour. However, Skinner inevitably distorts what he is supposed to be explaining. His analyses can seem plausible only where they rely on concepts that he claims to disregard. As Midgley puts it, references to a conscious subject always slip in simply because language has been framed so as to contend with it: 'if all such references were really strained out, most descriptions of behaviour would become either misleading or unintelligible' (1980, p. 106). Midgley makes the point with an illustration of laughter: the behaviour of laughing is making a peculiar convulsive noise, like hyenas or kookaburras, yet human laughter is always guided by the laugher's intentions and the context in which he finds himself (1980, p. 107).

Much of the row over Skinner's exclusion of 'inner states' derives from his extensive use of external concepts which describe observable events. Yet, Dennett notices how mechanistic explanations may sometimes be quite compatible with intentional ones, and it may be that many of the differences between Skinner and his critics are just about words: 'It is not false to say that the [chess-playing] computer *figures out* or *recognizes* the best move, or that it *concludes* that its opponent cannot make a certain move, any more than it is false to say that a computer *adds* or *multiplies*' (1981, p. 64).

Our suggestion is that we can transpose the mechanistic model onto man, and concede that humans are pieces of highly sophisticated machinery, which are subject to very major influences from the environment. Yet they are also massively affected by other causes, like chemical ones inside the brain that determine disposition and behaviour. The chemical structure of the brain may, in turn, be modified by experiences in the environment. The two-way process still keeps man mostly determined by factors outside his immediate control, but does allow other than environmental influences into play.

Skinner's model is basically that of Watson and, before him, Pavlov and the associationists. Man is an uncreative vehicle that is built on mechanical lines and can be controlled by outside influences. He lacks facilities for conscious control over his destiny and is carried along by a stream of stimuli to which he responds. He is totally determined by his environment, including physical, and other human, objects. Social change is the result of rather haphazard, involuntary changes in the arrangements of stimuli – unless, of course, they are carefully monitored and controlled by a man of knowledge, like Frazier in *Walden Two*.

The peculiar attraction of the model is that it purports to explain all facets of human behaviour, even the most complicated ones; the ones it can't explain it dismisses as remnants of superstitious ages. It offers a comprehensive scheme for interpreting an endless range of human behaviour, and this scheme has been picked up by other theorists who have adopted the basic mechanistic model and elaborated the concepts of rewards and punishment to paramount importance in the conduct of social life. These theorists occupy the next chapter.

## Technical Terms

**Behaviour Therapy:** A form of therapy designed to remove the symptoms rather than causes of disturbance. This is based on the behaviourist principle of focussing on observable behaviour. Undesired behaviour is negatively reinforced, whilst desired behaviour is positively reinforced.

**Consciousness:** Human awareness of oneself and of objects in the environment. This is possible through introspection and perception.

**Environment:** Surrounding objects, regions or conditions, especially those having direct effects on a person's thought and behaviour. It is composed of both physical objects and living beings.

**Genetic Endowment:** The biological characteristics and properties with which one is born and which act as either constraints or facilitators of later mental and physical development.

**Operant Conditioning:** This form of conditioning, associated with Skinner, attempts to shape behaviour by reinforcing (negatively or positively) a response that is spontaneously emitted (i.e. without a recognisable stimulus), rather than elicited as in *Classical Conditioning* (associated with Pavlov and Watson).

**Philosopher-King:** Based on Plato's idea that people with particular types of knowledge are eminently suited to rule and therefore have power. Expertise yields power.

**Reinforcement:** The method chosen by behaviourists to guarantee, or at least increase, the likelihood, that a particular piece of behaviour will be repeated time and again. This is the basic method of conditioning.

**Walden Two:** Skinner's fictional work depicting a dubious Utopia in which people are totally controlled through the conditioning techniques pioneered by behaviourist psychology. Originally published in 1948.

## Further Reading

*What is B. F. Skinner Really Saying?* (1979) by Robert Nye, is a punchy, clear, and positive account of the corpus of Skinner's work.

*Beyond the Punitive Society* (1973) edited by Harvey Wheeler, is a collection of essays on Skinner's *Beyond Freedom and Dignity*, together with a reply by Skinner.

*Walden Two* (1976) by B. F. Skinner, is his only work of fiction.

## Advanced Reading

*Behaviourism and Phenomenology* (1964) edited by T. W. Wann, is a collection of papers concerned with contrasting theoretical bases of psychology, and includes pieces by Skinner and Koch.

*Science and Human Behaviour* (1953) by B. F. Skinner, is a technical account of his model.

*Brainstorms: philosophical essays on mind and psychology* (1981) by Daniel Dennett, contains the essay 'Skinner Skinned', which is both imaginative and lively.

# 3

# Exchange and Reward

**In the market**

Exchange, Anthony Heath notes, is by no means the prerogative of the economist and of the economic market: neighbours exchange favours; children, toys; politicians, concessions and so on. Heath adds that these social exchanges are not insignificant. Rather, the 'exchange of gifts and favours between friends, neighbours and kin are strong and enduring threads in the social fabric' (1976, p. 1). One estimate asserts that in Britain the cards exchanged at Christmas alone were worth £40 million in 1964, while over 4 per cent of consumer expenditure – about one third of what is spent on housing – was spent on gifts. Heath quite rightly points out that there are simply no estimates of the 'money value of the services exchanged by kin and neighbours in time of need or emergency but there can be little doubt of their importance, or that the welfare services of our society would be overwhelmed if they were to stop' (1976, p. 1).

The two leading contemporary 'exchange theorists', George Homans and Peter Blau, see processes of exchange everywhere. Homans has suggested that most social behaviour can be viewed as 'an exchange of activity, tangible or intangible, and more or less rewarding or costly, between at least two person', while Blau has added that 'social exchange can be observed everywhere once we are sensitized by this conception to it, not only in market relations but also in friendship and even in love' (Heath, 1976, p. 1).

The exchange theories of Homans and Blau appear to be 'curious and unspecified mixture of utilitarian economics, functional anthropology and behavioural psychology' according to Jonathan Turner (1974, p. 211). By contrast, early sociologists showed little interest in an exchange perspective, the sole exception being Georg Simmel. He was particularly interested in the ways and reasons people move from isolation to different forms of contact with each other; and like modern exchange theorists, he argued that their motive was to satisfy needs and pursue individual goals. Simmel also suggested that although the returns people receive may not be equal, their interactions are always characterized by some form of reciprocity, and should therefore be viewed as kinds of exchange (Wallace and Wolf, 1980, p. 165).

The quite diverse eighteenth century economic writings of men like Adam Smith, David Ricardo and Jeremy Bentham are nonetheless given the label of 'utilitarianism'. Contained in the writings were certain core assumptions about the nature of man and his relation to the marketplace. Exchange theory argues implicitly that these same assumptions or premises apply to behaviour that does not involve the exchange of material goods for money, the production of goods for sale, or the workings of the economy. For the 'classical' economists, men were viewed as rationally seeking to maximize their material benefits, or 'utility', from transactions or exchanges with others in a free and competitive marketplace. The assumption was that men would have access to relevant information and would consider the alternatives before weighing up the costs and benefits, always seeking to maximize their material benefits.

Exchange theorists recognized that rarely do men attempt to maximize profits, they are not always rational, their transactions with each other are not free from external regulation and constraint, and they do not have precise information of all available alternatives. They do, however, always seek to make *some* profit in transactions, engage in calculations of costs and benefits in social transaction, are usually aware of at least some alternatives and, despite constraints, compete with each other in seeking to make a profit in their transactions. Added to these reformulations is the assumption that economic transactions are merely a special case of more general exchange relations occurring among individuals in virtually all social contexts, together with the related assumption that men exchange other, non-material goods.

Economics, of a sort, supplied not only the basic propositions of exchange theory but also its limitations. Ruth Wallace and Alison Wolf notice that its users are generally 'not concerned with explaining the origins of people's beliefs, values and tastes, but take them as given and address themselves to the behaviour that follows' (1980, p. 171).

The importance of Skinner in this instance is self-evident. Homans, in particular, shared several of the behaviourists' bedrock assumptions not only about the nature of man, but of the ambitions of science: he was interested in observable, preferably quantifiable, data and so directed his gaze at human behaviour. Like Skinner and the others, Homans believed that a science of man could ultimately be reduced to the same principles of animal psychology. He rejected the validity of inner states and introspection as well as the grander concepts favoured by social theorists, such as capitalism, institutions or social forces. To Homans there is nothing apart from, or beyond, the individuals in society. So behavioural science should study them alone.

In particular, Skinner's ideas on reinforcement were to ring bells with Homans. Skinner's impressive results in shaping animals' behaviour by positive reinforcement with things like food or comfort and others negatively with electric shocks influenced Homans's view on people and convinced him that humans, like animals, modify their behaviour to maximize rewards and minimize punishments. If a husband, for example, continually returns home drunk and is slapped in the face by his wife as he walks through the front door, he will try another route. Entering through a downstairs window enables him to make his way neatly to bed and slumber – which is what he is seeking. The negative reinforcement of his wife's hand across his face increases the probability of his use of modified behaviour in taking the window route.

The beauty of these types of ideas for exchange theory is that they are totally complementary with those of economics, and this strengthens the claim that exchange principles can be applied to all aspects of social life.

There is also an anthropological influence on exchange theory. The work of Bronislaw Malinowski that is pertinent to us here, arose out of a critique of the analysis of cross-cousin marriage offered by Sir James Frazer. Frazer, on an examination of various kinship and marriage practices among primitive societies was at pains to explain why Australian aboriginals tended to marry either their mother's brother's children or their father's sister's children, that is, cross-cousins. In a manner clearly in the utilitarian mould, Frazer offered an economic interpretation of the predominance of cross-cousin marriage patterns. He invoked the 'law' of 'economic motives' since, in having no equivalent in property to give for a wife, an Australian aboriginal is generally obliged to get her in exchange for a female relative, usually a sister or a daughter.

In his *Argonauts of the Western Pacific*, based on research in the Melanesian Islands, Malinowski observed an exchange system termed the Kula Ring, a closed circle of exchange relations among individuals in communities inhabiting a wide ring of islands (1922, p. 81). What was distinctive in the closed circle was the predominance of exchange of two articles – armlets and necklaces – which constantly travelled in opposite directions. In one direction around the Kula Ring, armlets travelled and were exchanged by individuals for necklaces moving in the opposite direction around the ring. In any particular exchange between individuals, then, an armlet would always be exchanged for a necklace. In interpreting this unique exchange network, Malinowski was led to distinguish material (economic) from non-material (symbolic) exchanges: 'One transaction does not finish the Kula relationship, the rule being "once in the Kula, always in the Kula" and a partnership between two men is a permanent and lifelong affair' (1922, pp. 82-3).

While purely economic transactions could occur within the rules of the Kula, the ceremonial exchange of armlets and necklaces was observed by Malinowski to be the principal 'function' of the Kula. The motives behind the Kula were social psychological, for the exchanges in the Ring were viewed by Malinowski to have implications for the 'needs' of both individuals and society; he interpreted the Kula to meet the fundamental impulse to 'display, to share, to bestow [and] the deep tendency to create social ties' (1922, p. 175).

As well as the Kula Ring the potlach of the Tlingit and Haidi Indians of the American Northwest has similarly fascinated anthropologists. The potlach was a magnificent feast ostensibly celebrating some social event. On the occasion of, for example, a marriage, one chief would put on a display to press lavish gifts on his guests, including rival chiefs. The more magnificent the potlach, the more it increased the host's prestige and the more obligated to him his guests and rivals became. Consequently they were expected to play host in their turn. In this competitive gift, 'everything is conceived as if it were a war of wealth ... Whole cases of candlefish or whale oil ... are burnt, and the most valuable coppers are broken ... to level and crush a rival' whose prestige the host wishes to better, according to Mauss, whose work we will consider in Chapter Seven (1954, p. 18). A crucial aspect of such exchanges is the way they bind society together through mutual obligations and ties. Reacting to what he perceived as Malinowski's tendency to overemphasize psychological over social needs, Marcel Mauss reinterpreted Malinowski's analysis of the Kula. Through this he was to formulate the broad outlines of a collectivist view on exchange.

For Mauss, the critical question in examining complex exchange processes such as the Kula was: what is the principle whereby the gift received has to be repaid? And what force is there in the thing which compels the recipient to make a return? The force compelling reciprocity was, for Mauss, society (or the group), since it is groups and 'not individuals, which carry on exchange, make contracts and are bound by obligations' (Mauss, 1954, p. 3). This is precisely what Alvin Gouldner was later to term the 'norm of reciprocity' (1960).

Similarly, in 1949 Claude Lévi-Strauss emphasized that it is the exchange which counts and not the things exchanged; an exchange must be viewed in terms of its functions for integrating groups and society. He then contested the assumption that the first principles of human behaviour are economic. He also rejected psychological interpretations of exchange processes in that, unlike rats and pigeons, humans possess a cultural heritage of norms and values which sets apart their behaviour and organization into society from the behaviour and organization of animal species. In their view, human behaviour, unlike that of animals, produces complex patterns of activity that are over and above one individual and can, in fact, work to influence groups of individuals. This view will come to the fore in Part Three but, for the moment, we will consider Homans's individualistic interpretation of exchange.

From anthropology, then, the reciprocal human need to create lasting social ties through the exchange of items; from utilitarian economics, a model of man as rational, calculating and looking to maximize rewards; and, from behaviourism, an explanation of the moulding of human procedures through processes of conditioning. These were the main influences behind exchange theory, though there is an obvious sprinkling of the philosophical doctrine of hedonism, that the pursuit of pleasure and the avoidance of pain are the chief aims and, therefore, motivation of humans.

What about altruistic acts? The kidney donor? Certainly these activities entail loss and risk, something seemingly contrary to the exchange theorists' view of motivation. The usual way that this kind of problem has been handled is by recognition that the rewards involved in exchange theory can be of any type whatsoever. Thus the risks involved in giving a kidney (whilst one is still alive, note) may well be worth it for the gratitude and recognition that such an act might produce. So gain is not necessarily tangible. If everyone is seeking pleasure and avoiding pain, everybody will have to give as well as get, or as Skidmore puts it: 'there is always some cost involved in gaining reward. Cost is normally defined as the effort required to gain satisfaction, plus the potential rewards foregone as a result of the specific choice' (1979, p. 72). To an exchange theorist, if someone maximizes his reward and minimizes his cost, a profit is made. The donor loses a kidney, but profits from gratification. His profit is determined by comparing reward and cost – it is the difference between them. Frank Hahn and Martin Hollis make the point and their comments serve as a suitable summary to this section:

> In social exchange theory social life is seen very much as a market in varying states of co-operation and competition. The giving of gifts, for instance, can be interestingly explored on the assumption that recipients always reciprocate somehow to the same amount. The forming of friendships, the working of charities, the conduct of elections, the basis of coalitions, the stockpiling of weapons, the diplomacy of nations have all been treated as neo-Classical transactions. The medium of exchange varies from one realm to another but the constant aim of each agent is to enact his highest preference at lowest cost, calculated with regard to risk and uncertainty. (1979, p. 15).

### Quid pro quo: Homans

Uniting all the theorists in this chapter is the conviction that there is a *quid pro quo* motive in life: that men always want something for something and never give without at least the promise of receiving. Homan's version of exchange theory is, as we have seen, a synthesis of many intellectual traditions, but shining through them is a commitment to the view that man is ultimately determined by outside influences, whether other humans or the physical environment. Man himself attempts to be rational, calculating and hedonistic, but always responsive. This becomes clear when we consider the five axioms of Homans's theory, the first three of which are pure Skinner:

1 If a particular stimulus has, in the past, brought about the rewarding of an individual's activity, then a present, similar stimulus is likely to cause him to repeat that activity (or a similar activity) now (1961, p. 53);
2 If, within a given period of time, an individual's activity frequently rewards that of another, the more often the other will emit the activity (1961, p. 54);
3 If an individual receives a valuable unit of activity from another, he will more frequently emit the activity which is rewarded by that of the other (1961, p. 55);
4 The more often that an individual has, in the recent past, received a rewarding activity from another, the less valuable any future units of that activity becomes (1961, p. 55);
5 The more that distributive justice fails to realize an individual's expectations, the more likely he is to display the emotional behaviour we call anger (1961, p. 75).

The fourth proposition indicates the condition under which the first three fall into temporary abeyance, for, in accordance with the 'law of diminishing returns' in economic theory, for example, humans eventually define as less valuable the rewarded activities and begin to emit other activities in search of different rewards. So, having wined and dined a person, a man may gain his desired end – pleasure – but after several sub-

---

#### George Caspar Homans (1910– )

Born in Boston, Massachussets and educated at the University of Harvard. Became an instructor in sociology at Harvard 1939–46 with a spell of military service from 1941–5 when he was a Lt. Comdr. in the USNR. Became an associate professor at Harvard 1946–53 and in 1953 he obtained a chair in sociology. He also held temporary posts at Manchester and Cambridge. His *Human Group* appeared in 1950 with *Social Behaviour* appearing in 1967.

sequent procedures, he may feel that his expenditure beyond a certain point does not produce a proportionate yield; his response is to turn his wining and dining attentions elsewhere.

The final proposition introduces a set of conditions which qualifies the previous ones. As Turner notes, Homans, following Skinner's observation that pigeons reveal 'anger' and 'frustration' when they don't receive an expected reward, suspects that humans will probably reveal basically the same behaviour (1974, p. 236). Humans, however, unlike pigeons, engage in a series of implicit calculations before they emit the pigeon's type of anger: 'the most important of these calculations of "distributive justice" whereby, in accordance with an implicit formula, humans assess whether the rewards received from a situation are proportional to the costs incurred in it and the investments brought to it.' Distributive justice is thus an expected ratio of investments and costs to rewards and when this expectation is not realized, 'humans, much like their simpler animal counterparts in the Skinner box, get angry' (Turner, 1974, p. 237).

'Homans offers an image of society and social processes that is, if only intuitively, pleasing', writes Turner (1974, p. 257). For all its elaborations, the model is tight, logical, and allegedly self-explanatory. Homans claims his axioms hold not only for small groups but for societies too, though, as we have mentioned, emphasis is on the individual and the concepts of reward, cost, activity and so on keep the focus directly on the individual, or on a two-person group. Homans spends considerable time talking about his hypothetical characters, Person and Other, and how they get along with each other. However, he also does go beyond Person and Other to give an exchange of more complex patterns of social organization. Essentially, Homans argues that institutions are based on the same principles of exchange as small group behaviour, but that institutions are more complex networks of exchange. In the description of why this should be so, he provides a scenario of how patterns of social organization are created, maintained, changed and broken down. For Homans, the emergence of most patterns of social organization, whether at a group or institutional level, are 'frequently buried in the recesses of history', yet such emergence is typified by 'accelerating' exchange processes in which:

1 Men with 'capital' (reward capacity) 'invest' in the creation of more complex social relations that increase their rewards and allow those whose activities are organized to realize a 'profit';
2 With increased rewards, these other men can invest in more complex patterns of organization themselves;
3 Increasingly, these complex patterns of organization require, first of all, the use of generalized reinforcers, like money or barter, and then a framework of rules, regulations and guidelines to control activity;
4 With this basic organization, it then becomes possible to elaborate further

the pattern organization, creating the necessity for a differentiation of splinter groups that assure the stability of the generalized reinforcers and the integrity of the rules and guidelines;
5 With this differentiation, it is possible to expand even further the networks of interaction.

These complex patterns of social organization must never cease to meet the more basic or 'primary' needs of individuals. Institutions originally emerged to meet these needs, and thus these extended networks must ultimately reinforce man's more primary needs to eat, have shelter, derive physical satisfaction and so on. When these arrangements cease to meet the primary needs from which they ultimately arose, an institution is vulnerable and apt to collapse, particularly if alternative activities which can provide primary rewards present themselves. The fact that institutions of society must also meet primary needs sets the stage for a continual conflict between institutional elaboration and the primary needs of men. As one dominant form of institutional elaboration meets one set of needs, it may deprive men of other important rewards; this opens the door for deviation and innovation by those presenting these alternative rewards. In a bizarre way, Homan's formulations supply an explanation of revolutions: one set of institutional arrangements is developed to meet certain basic human needs, but succeeds in benefiting only some sections of the population whilst severely depriving others; the latter groups, in turn, will react against the lack of fulfillment of these needs.

### Blau power

Peter Blau, a contemporary of Homans, is often seen as adding to exchange theory; indeed, his theoretical eclecticism does offer 'something for everyone', and his intention to add more principles from economic theory to the social exchange model of man is of paramount importance. In common with Homans, Blau initially examines 'elementary' forms of social exchange with an eye to how they help in the analysis of more complex social processes. But Blau, unlike Homan, limits his notion of exchange to a particular type of association: exchange occurs only among those relationships in which rewards are expected and received from designated others, that is, other people whom the person regards as, in some sense, important and worthy. Blau employs the basic concepts of all exchange theories – costs, rewards, profit – but, as Turner puts it, he limits their application to 'relations with *others* from whom rewards are expected and received' (1974, p. 266).

Consistent with Homan's theory, social life is conceived to be a marketplace in which actors negotiate with each other in an effort to make a profit. Blau recognizes that unlike the simple 'economic man' of classical economics, humans rarely pursue only one goal, are frequently inconsistent in their preferences, virtually never have complete information of alternatives, and are never free from social commitments limiting the available alternatives. Also, in contrast with a purely economic model of life, social associations involve the exchange of rewards whose worth varies from transaction to transaction without a fixed market value, and whose own value cannot be expressed precisely in terms of a single accepted medium of exchange. It is difficult to put a price on some of the valued rewards in social exchanges; humour, for example, assumes different values for different people, and what might be rewarding in one exchange may be totally unrewarding in another.

Although Blau, unlike Homans, does not enumerate a formal set of 'principles', his work does contain a set of guidelines for the general process of human exchange. They are:

1  The more profit a person expects from another in emitting a particular activity, the more likely he is to emit that activity (this is straight from behaviourism);
2  The more a person has exchanged rewards with another, the more likely are reciprocal obligations to emerge and guide subsequent exchanges among those persons (like in the Kula ring);
3  The more the reciprocal obligations of an exchange relationship are violated, the more are deprived parties disposed to sanction negatively those violating the norm of reciprocity (for example, we establish an exchange relationship with a neighbour in which we give him a ride to work every morning and, to reciprocate, he buys the drinks in the evening; then, he begins to stay in during the evenings instead of going to the bar, thus violating the norm; so we might sanction him by 'forgetting' to pick him up on the occasional morning or charging him a 'fee' for the petrol used);
4  The more that expected rewards are forthcoming from the emission of a

---

### Peter Michael Blau (1918–    )

Born in Vienna, he went to the USA in 1939, and was naturalized. He graduated from Elmhurst College in 1942, and received a Ph.D from Columbia in 1952. Has taught at the universities of Wayne, Cornell, Chicago, where he was Professor of Sociology from 1963–70, and at Columbia 1970–78. He has researched in the UK and Netherlands, and in 1978 obtained a chair at SUNY, Albany. Was President of the American Sociological Association from 1973–74, and was decorated as a Bronze Star member of the Association. His major publications are *The Dynamics of Bureaucracy* (1955) and *Exchange and Power in Social Life* (1964).

particular activity, the less valuable the activity, and the less likely its continuing emission ('diminishing returns');

5   The more that exchange relations have been established, the more likely they are to be governed by norms of 'fair exchange' (so both parties come to see their exchange as fair and equal);
6   The less norms of fairness are realized in an exchange, the more are deprived parties disposed to sanction negatively those violating the norms (and remove or decrease the contribution to the relationship);
7   The more stabilized and balanced some exchange relations are among social units, the more likely other exchange relations are to become imbalanced and unstable.

Principles 4, 6 and 7 are most pertinent to our discussion. To begin with, Blau, in 4, has criticised Homans for assuming that the principle of 'distributive justice' can operate independently of group standards. As Blau notes: 'while all men undoubtedly have some sense of justice, the system of values and norms that prevails in a society is what gives their notion of justice its specific content and meaning' (1971, p. 68). In other words, the meaning of justice changes from one social context to another. Since Blau's exchange model is vitally concerned with the conditions under which conflict and change occur in social life, principle 4 becomes a crucial generalization. As Turner notes, in Blau's subsequent analysis, the 'deprivations arising from violating the norms of fair exchange are viewed as translated, under specific conditions, into retaliation against violators' (1974, p. 269). This concern with enumerating exchange principles that can account for conflict in social relations is underscored by Blau's final principle. This refers to the fact that all established exchange relations involve 'costs', and since most people must be engaged in more than one exchange relation, the balance and stabilization of one exchange relation is likely to create imbalance and strain in other necessary exchange relations. Take as an example a journalist who derives benefit from a series of relationships with sports stars, in the sense that he acts deferentially towards them, agrees with their views etc., whilst they, in return, acknowledge him as a friend, acquaintance and colleague-in-sport. The same journalist also has an exchange relationship with a junior reporter, who treats him with respect in exchange for tips and advice, but whose respect would greatly diminish if he saw him bowing and scraping to the sportsmen. Thus, by stabilizing his relationships with sports stars, our journalist creates a strain in his relationship with the trainee.

Turner puts it well when he states that, for Blau, 'social life is thus filled with "dilemmas" in which men must successively trade off stability and balance in one exchange relation for strain in others as they attempt to cope with the variety of relations they must maintain' (1974, p. 269).

Blau thus attempts to analyse how exchange acts become institutionalized into meshes of reciprocity. He also emphasizes the importance of actors aligning and realigning their behaviour to suit different partners in exchange networks in the pursuit of rewards. The stress on how exchange inevitably generates imbalances leads to his concern with the sources of conflict processes in a social network, and his concern with order leads him to see the positive functions of conflict.

As stated earlier, Blau limits his definition as to what constitutes an exchange relationship, and this can be seen as he outlines his discussion of elementary exchange processes. He asserts that people enter social exchange because they perceive the possibility of deriving rewards; Blau labels this perception 'social attraction'. People attempt to impress each other through 'competition', in which each actor reveals the rewards he has to offer in an effort to force others, in accordance with the norm of reciprocity, to give back an even more valuable reward. It is evident however, as interaction proceeds, that some people have more valuable resources to offer than others. This puts them in a unique position to extract rewards from all others who value their resources. It is at this point in exchange relations that groups of individuals become differentiated in terms of the resources they possess and the kinds of reciprocal demands they can make on others; and Blau conceptualizes four general classes of rewards that those with resources can extract in return for bestowing their valued resources upon others – money, social approval, esteem or respect, and compliance. For Blau, 'power' exists when one party can regularly, as Percy Cohen puts it, 'use a threat of punishment or withdrawal of facilities from another in order to gain compliance' (1968, p. 122). Power, then, involves exchange, whereas pure physical coercion does not.

As with Homans, Blau shares the view that the same processes that characterize face-to-face relations are typical of larger units. When the focus turns to power, for example, Blau demonstrates how relationships built on the basis of the exchange of rewards have in them the quality of power. This is what we call a micro-conception of power: the idea that power is not some facility in the hands of a small elite, but is generated through face-to-face relationships. It is a conception shared though interpreted in different ways, by theorists as diverse as Erving Goffman (see pp. 108–13) and Michael Foucault (see pp. 195–200).

Cohen paraphrases Blau's position on power: wherever human collectivities exist there will always be a need for some men to offer a potential lien on services and so on in return for immediate or foreseeable concrete benefits. This creates a need for power. Those who get power may have personal abilities, or they may control resources or inspire loyalties which make them desirable. One of the things they are able to give is approval, so that personal qualities may be a condition for obtaining power. But, in seeking power, men run risks of differentiating themselves from others and presenting themselves as enviable. Some men, the majority in fact, will prefer the benefits of approval by those who have power, and of their satraps who have less of it, to the possible benefits of power itself. (1968, p. 122).

Cohen asks of Blau's conception of power, 'how much power is actually created in this way?' Power does not only occur within small groups through spontaneous processes; often, power relationships do not result from free market-type relations but from conquest and domination. As Cohen puts it: 'it is not simply that men wait to be given power by those who need them to perform a necessary role ... in many cases men are only too ready to create the conditions in which they or others like them are "needed" ' (1968, p. 123). In other words, Blau recognized that many human 'needs' which men seek in the form of rewards are often artificially created by others;. For example, a multinational corporation might take root in a third world country and, through the establishment of industries and advertising media, actually create 'needs' for the native population – and perhaps their government as well – who are prepared to offer their labour in return for salaries and consumer goods which they might not previously have found necessary or rewarding. Power as conceived by Blau is something that emerges from personal exchange arrangements, rather than a political facility held by some, which can be used to control what people seek to take in terms of rewards from those exchanges. The things that people come to regard as rewards and costs can be severely affected by larger political powers.

**Individualism**

One way to tackle exchange theory is by looking at one of its central concepts. Turner notes that Homan's concept of value – or the degree of reinforcement of an activity – refers to literally any activity that a person defines, perceives or believes to be rewarding. Fine, but by defining the concept 'value' and by implication 'reward' in such a general way, Homans confronts the problem of 'how one knows what is valuable or rewarding to a person?' (1974, p. 245). Presumably, man can value anything, and as no theoretical scheme exists by which we understand categories of reward, or make additional assumptions about the rewarding aspects of behaviour, we can predict everything (and nothing) using reward as the key concept. Both Turner and Skidmore make the point that exchange theorists, especially Homans, use concepts in an *ad hoc* manner, when they need them to support arguments. That is, we might see a man foraging in waste paper bins and, to explain his action, suggest that it might have been rewarding to him or else he would not have done it. Whatever he might do, whether it be begging for money, drinking meths or taking abuse from taunting teenagers, the explanation remains the same; there is no way to prove that the theory is either informative or inaccurate. Every activity we engage in is said to have value to us. Why else would we do it? What starts off as an assumption about human nature is turned into a concept for explaining all sorts of human activity.

Skidmore's criticism of exchange theory, and one which is entirely applicable to all those working in the behaviourist strain, is that it 'robs man of his humanity, portraying him as a calculating robot with no regard for anything but his own narrow desires, and, apparently, no conscience either' (1979, p. 109). If the theoretical underpinnings of exchange theory were consistently adhered to, we would be in a stronger position than we are to concur fully with the criticism.

In a nutshell, exchange theory has been considerably more successful in explaining behaviour in 'small group' situations than in analysing the workings of institutions and complex social processes. The theory has not been fully satisfactory when it has attempted actually to explain the origin of norms, that is, why they emerge in the first instance, and to what purpose. But it has been more successful in clarifying the norms' results on people's decisions and actions. Wallace and Wolf pose the question: 'does this imply that exchange theory is intrinsically a "small group" approach?' (1980, p. 213). They argue that Blau himself has come to believe that it does and that exchange theory is, after all, essentially suited only to face-to-face relations and must be complemented, therefore, by other theoretical principles that focus on broader, more complex processes in society. Homans, on the other hand, continues to argue that sociological arguments depend ultimately on psychological propositions.

This is a traditional problem facing social theory, namely, to what extent are processes at micro and macro levels of social organization subject to analysis by the same concepts and to description by the same social 'laws'? As Steven Lukes puts it, methodological individualism is a 'doctrine about explanation which asserts that all attempts to explain social (or individual) phenomena are to be rejected... unless they are couched wholly in terms of facts about individuals' (1973a, p. 110).

Such a doctrine is shared by all those of the behaviourist strain. The utilitarians held a methodological individualist position with, for example, John Stuart Mill maintaining that the laws of the phenomena of society are, and can be, nothing but the actions and passions of human beings; numerous social scientists share the view, most obviously those who have appealed to fixed psychological elements as ultimately explanatory factors – for instance, Malinowski's 'needs' and, of course, the work of Homans.

Methodological Individualism advances a range of different claims in accordance with how much of society is built into the supposedly explanatory 'individuals'. From, for example, 'genetic make-up', through 'aggression' and 'co-operation' or 'power', to 'voting'. Lukes considers that there is a continuum of individual predicates from what one might call the most non-social to the most social. For our present discussion it is pertinent to consider 'co-operation' and 'power', as they are central concepts in exchange theory.

Such concepts have only a limited reference to society in that they presuppose a social context in which certain actions, social relations and mental states are picked out and given a particular significance. They do not, however, involve any propositions about any particular form of group or institution. Lukes concludes that:

> social phenomena have not really been eliminated; they have been swept under the carpet. Methodological Individualism is thus an exclusivist, prescriptive doctrine about what explanations are to look like...[and]...it excludes explanations which appeal to social forces, structural features of society, institutional factors and so on (1973a, pp. 121–122).

Turner discusses the problem in terms of the 'issue of reductionism': 'if it is accepted that sociological propositions are reducible to those about men, then those about men are reducible to physiological propositions, which, in turn, are reducible to biochemical propositions, and so on, in a reductionist sequence ending in the basic laws of physical matter' (1974, p. 253). Importantly, what Homans is concerned with is the nature of the explanation involved in the analysis of social phenomena, not whether or not social phenomena exist.

All those in the behaviourist strain are, by virtue of their theoretical stance, committed to seeing society in terms of the individual's behaviour. True, certain patterns of activity seem to go on century after century and take on a life of their own, like marriage, but such things are ultimately reducible to the behaviour of people and, in the exchange theorists' view, explicable in terms of the reciprocal rewards partners offer and extract.

Societies are of the utmost complexity and are composed of bewildering patterns of exchange that defy analysis in these terms. Yet people like Homans and, before him, Skinner, would insist that, theoretically, every strand of the complicated, multilayered web of relationships can be studied and explained with the concepts of behaviourism, the most basic being those of stimulus and response. Exchange theory is more helpful in accounting for change in that it provides conditions under which strains and imbalances in relationships lead to sanctions or withdrawals of reward, but there is a sense in which all human behaviour is manipulable from the outside – as depicted in the early pre-behaviourist models. People are self-interested and seek pleasure; if conditions outside them can be changed so that they have to behave in various ways to get their way, then we can guarantee they will do so.

So, here we have a model of man as a self-motivated respondent to outside stimuli with no relevant facilities of creativity or spontaneity: he is more or less passive at birth and subject to continual pressures from outside him. It is the accumulation of learned responses to outside stimuli that makes him human. That humanity is programmed into him. He has the illusion of behaving freely and wilfully but reality is not as it seems and, on careful analysis, he is but an organic android – albeit a sophisticated one – ultimately determined and having little or no control over change.

'Society is about individuals', every theorist of the behaviourist strain would argue. Yet there are other strains that would argue forcefully against this. In the next section we will meet theorists who, like the behaviourists, are convinced that study should proceed by looking at actual people in face-to-face situations, but not by leaving it there. Behaviour is not the only subject for the social theorists for, in this model, the actual observable behaviour performed is but one dimension of an appreciably richer, more complex, multifaceted phenomena called social reality.

## Technical Terms

**Axiom:** A basic principle, usually thought to be self-evident and used as the basis for producing more elaborate theoretical knowledge.

**Explanation:** Used in a variety of ways, but generally it is thought to be an account of the occurrence of an event, or events, by reference to either prior events (causes) or conditions (facilitators). Unlike mere descriptions of events, explanation tries to identify factors that are not immediately recognizable in the event itself.

**Hedonism:** A philosophical doctrine originating in the 4th century BC by the Cyrenaics who claimed that human life consists of maximizing pleasure of the senses and avoiding pain. In the 18th century, this doctrine was used by, amongst others, Jeremy Bentham, as the foundation for *Utilitarianism* (see below).

**Individualism:** A social and moral theory favouring the free action and expression of individuals as opposed to constraining them in the interests of the common good of the collectivity (not to be confused with *Methodological Individualism* as used in the text).

**Norm of Reciprocity:** A term coined by Alvin Gouldner in 1960 to capture the idea that human exchanges entail obligations that supersede the interests and motivations of any individuals. The norm is a binding principle of give and take.

**Primary Needs:** These refer to basic human requirements of life, like shelter, food and physical contact. These are necessary for the sustenance of human life.

**Reductionism:** The belief that human collective behaviour can be reduced to, or interpreted in, terms of that of lower animals, and that in the last instance, can be reduced to the physical laws controlling the behaviour of inanimate matters. It also refers more generally to any doctrine that claims to reduce complex events to simple principles.

**Sanction:** Any means of enforcing behaviour – it may be positive in the form of a reward, or negative in the form of a punishment. It is a term usually used with reference to control: to secure conformity to certain standards or, in the case of experimental psychology, the standards imposed by the experimenter. As such, the sanction

may range from long-term imprisonment to electric shocks. Alternatively they may be positive, like social approval or the granting of food.
**Utilitarianism:** 'The greatest happiness of the greatest number' is the organizing theme of this doctrine associated with the classical proponents, Bentham and John Stuart Mill.

## Further Reading

*Exchange and Power in Social Life* (1964) by Peter M. Blau is basic reading.
*Social Behaviour: its elementary forms* (1961) by George C. Homans is similarly essential reading.
*Social Exchange Theory* (1974) by Peter Ekeh is a comprehensive survey of exchange theory, which also emphasizes the 'two traditions' of exchange theory.

## Advanced Reading

*Rational Choice and Social Exchange* (1976) is Anthony Heath's personal, and rather dismissive, account of exchange theory.
'Exchange theory' by Harry C. Bredemeier in *A History of Sociological Analysis* (1979) edited by T. Bottomore and R. Nisbet is an assessment of the significance of the history of exchange theory in social science.
*The Structure of Sociological Theory* (1982) by Jonathan H. Turner, part 3, is a quite difficult but rewarding (!) account of exchange theorizing.

## Theory into action

## Sex, Violence and the Media

H. J. Eysenck and D. K. B. Nias' *Sex, Violence and the Media* is concerned with the view that 'violence, vandalism, cruelty, and undesirable sex practices are encouraged by their representation in the media, and that these representations may in part be responsible for the undesirable changes in our national life which have taken place in recent years' (1980, p. 15).

They begin their account with a discussion of the 'acknowledged facts'. For example, in the UK, crimes of violence against the person have increased ten-fold in the quarter-century since 1951. Similarly, regarding the popularity of TV, in the United States, the average family has a television set in use for about forty hours each week, and, in England, children aged six to eleven years watch an estimated twenty-five hours a week (1980, p. 19).

Sex on TV, the authors argue, has been fairly strictly controlled, with a 'definite relaxation' in recent years; they note that a survey of the years 1967 to 1971 revealed a rate of 7.5 violent episodes per hour during prime time: 'It has been estimated that the average American child will have witnessed more than 11,000 murders on television by the time he is fourteen' (1980, p. 20). Eysenck and Nias point to the difficulty of substantiating the increase in the availability of pornography, but offer some figures to indicate the 'size of the problem'. At the last count, there were 264 'kiddie porn mags' of the Lolita type produced each month in the US, 'where child pornography is one of the fastest growing industries, 300,000 children under sixteen being involved in the commercial sex industry' (1980, p. 21).

There are three arguments usually put forward for believing or disbelieving in the harmful effects of the showing of violence and explicit sex in films in pornographic magazines:

1. The argument from advertising: if ads make people buy things by simply showing models, buying and enjoying these things, why should the same not apply to showing actions of a violent or sexual nature which apparently are satisfying the people portraying them on the screen or in the magazines?
2. The argument from socialization: TV gives a view of society and gives repeated examples of how to behave in different situations.
3. The argument from case studies reported in the newspapers showing how TV violence and pornography may exert their influence on individual cases: 'Thus much was made of the fact that Ian Brady and Myra Hindley, who

were convicted of murdering and torturing a ten year old girl, were found to have sadistic literature at home' (1980, p. 24).

Of course much of the previous discussion assumes a comparability of violence and pornography, but, as Eysenck and Nias point out, people tend not to consider them in such a way: 'Violence is deplored by practically everybody... but... pornography, on the other hand, does not seem to present anything like the same kind of problem, and indeed many people see nothing wrong in the portrayal of perfectly normal and ordinary human intercourse in the great variety of ways in which it can be achieved' (1980, p. 32). But Eysenck and Nias argue that the difference may not be as clear-cut as at first thought: 'there is good evidence to show that physiologically and psychologically there is a close connection between violence and sex; some pornographic films may stimulate violence, and violent films may stimulate sexuality' (1980, p. 33).

The theoretical approaches they consider to be of importance in the area are theories of conditioning, imitation and modelling and 'so-called' cognitive theories. As an illustration of the importance of conditioning they point to the development of sexual preferences. They cite McGuire *et al* who advanced the theory that repeated masturbation accompanied by the memory of an erotic incident is the mechanism by which a deviation is formed and shaped (1965). Eysenck and Nias add that the theory was arrived at after interviewing forty-five sexual deviants who were receiving treatment. The role of imitation is unquestionable, and sometimes this can have tragic consequences: 'a ... direct influence from a film was suggested, in a case concerning *The Omen*, which includes a gory scene in which a child's nurse gets stabbed in the throat. Half an hour after the presentation of this film at a cinema, the manager of a local betting shop lay dead having been stabbed through the throat. A man who had been watching the film had robbed him of the day's takings and knifed him in a very similar way to that shown in the film' (Eysenck and Nias, 1980, p. 67).

Laboratory evidence, they argue, linked with well-developed psychological theory 'provides the best evidence in this field'. Eysenck and Nias offer a few examples of the laboratory method. To begin with, according to the catharsis or 'safety-valve' theory, watching a violent film should act to reduce any tendency to be aggressive. Siegel, however, puts this prediction to the test by showing pairs of nursery school children a Woody Woodpecker cartoon, regarded as violent, and a non-violent cartoon. After each film the children exposed to Woody Woodpecker showed more rather than less aggression – thus contradicting the catharsis theory.

In another experiment to study the effects of witnessing violence, an inflated Bobo doll was weighted so that it returned to an upright position when struck, and for many children it 'invites' attack. These toy dolls have been used in many studies to assess aggression, the usual procedure being for an adult model armed with a mallet to assault Bobo with accompanying cries such as 'Kick him' and 'Pow'. The first study of this type was by Bandura *et al* (1961). Nursery school children, matched for previous aggression, were assigned to one of three groups in which they watched either a violent model, a subdued model, or nothing. A frustrating experience, in which the children started playing with very attractive toys but were then stopped, was introduced at this point to increase the chances of aggression occurring. Each child was then placed in a room with an assortment of ordinary toys including a mallet and a Bobo doll. As expected, those who had seen the violent model tended to imitate the various forms of physical and verbal aggression.

Eysenck and Nias then turn to the notion of 'desensitization': 'people, by constant exposure to violence, will eventually become 'desensitized' and no longer be upset or aroused by witnessing violence' (1980, p. 178). Thomas *et al* (1977) attempted to produce temporary desensitization by showing children a violent TV police drama, and then assessed the effect in terms of their response to a videotape of two pre-school children fighting. Compared with a control group who were shown an exciting volleyball game, the 'desensitized' children responded with fewer galvanic skin responses when shown the videotape of 'real' aggression. This again provides evidence that the viewing of TV violence can make children accustomed and hardened to real-life violence, only this time there is the additional information that after watching TV they feel less emotional when witnessing scenes of real fighting. The study was repeated with students, except that news films of riots were used instead of the fighting scenes, and similar results were obtained, at least for males.

Eysenck and Nias argue that conditioning appears directly relevant to the development of sexual deviations; they cite the example of Rachman, who was interested in the possibility that a boot fetish could be created by classical conditioning (1966). Three male students were selected who responded with some degree of erection when shown slides of sexually provocative women. A picture of a pair of black knee-length female boots, which did not evoke such a response, was then shown to each subject immediately before one of the pin-ups. This procedure was repeated eighteen times during each of several sessions. According to the theory of conditioning, the neutral stimulus of the boots should in time become associated with the reward provided by the pin-ups. This is what happened, since after thirty or so pairings each of the subjects began to respond with erections to the boots. Eysenck and Nias go on to assert that: 'the theory of conditioning, combined with the evidence from... studies... indicates that it might be possible to create a rapist or sadist in the laboratory by presenting scenes of rape or sadism immediately prior to normally arousing scenes' (1980, p. 190).

Individual differences are considered, and Eysenck and Nias point out that it would be 'foolish to disregard genetic factors' or indeed the interplay of such factors together with environmental influences, as 'sets of causal factors' (1980, p. 228). Following on from this comment on the interplay of factors, they assert that there is much evidence to support the view that maleness and femaleness are not just roles which boys and girls are taught in infancy; it would appear, rather, that these roles 'are predetermined by biological factors... and that society emphasizes the direction of the push given us by those hormonal factors, by undertaking to prepare us in our infancy for the roles nature intended us to play' (1980, pp. 231–2).

Eysenck and Nias conclude:

1 'The evidence is fairly unanimous *that aggressive acts new to the subject's repertoire of responses, as well as acts already well established, can be evoked by the viewing of violent scenes portrayed on film, TV or in the theatre*' (1980, p. 252);
2 '*That pornography has effects on viewers and readers can no longer be disputed, but these effects can be quite variable.* It may produce titillation in some, in others it may elicit feelings of guilt or revulsion, while in yet others it may provoke anti-social sexual behaviour, or help condition them into deviancy' (1980, p. 253).

On the basis of these conclusions, they make a number of recommendations, including that film and TV makers etc., and others concerned with the portrayal of violence should show more social responsibility than they have done so far and that 'forms of censorship should apply to the portrayal both of violence and of perverted sexual behaviour' (1980, p. 256); also: '*that the content of a presentation should be judged in relation to the prevailing tone of the presentation*'.

The study contains elements that make it an exemplary piece of behaviourism in practice. They are: a belief in the efficacy of such processes as conditioning; an emphasis on the profound influences of the environment and of genetics (often in interplay); a playing down of individual differences and individual's frame of meaning; an importance attached to scientific methodology; and a belief in the ability of certain forms of knowledge or evidence, on which to base recommendations of policy.

# Part Two: Interactionism

- Action Man
- The Selves
- Society as Process

# 4

# Action Man

### The importance of meaning
'You can take a horse to water, but you can't make it drink.' An old saying which points to the inviolability of will: working the animal to a foaming sweat, so that it thirsts, then dragging it to a trough and thrusting its nose in the water may establish the conditions conducive to the horse's imbibing; but, if the horse decides not to drink, no power on earth can make it.

It sounds perfectly plausible; stating the obvious, one might say. But, social theorists have, in a way, committed themselves to reaching beyond the obvious, asking questions about, and probing into, the reality most of us take for granted. So we don't doubt the legitimacy of the claim that horses cannot be made to drink water if they do not feel so inclined. Skinner would. In fact, for Skinner and theorists of the behaviourist strain, the whole story is nonsense: it is illogical, based on inaccurate and insufficient information and is entirely wrong.

Though it might seem to state the obvious, it only obscures some of the complexities of social reality and conveys a false impression of its nature. Of course, we can make the horse drink, behaviourists would contend: it's simply a matter of arranging external conditions in such a way as to provoke stimuli which will elicit the required behaviour in the animal. The conditions may well be intricate and complex. But, once they are discovered, they can be used time and again to gain the same reaction.

As we have seen, freedom of choice is a somewhat vague, ill-defined and misleading notion for those of the behaviourist strain. It is merely a convenient and comforting way of masking the fact that all living creatures are subject to forces which lie outside their control. For behaviourists, animals and human beings can not only be taken to the water, but also made to drink. To accomplish this, we need not bother ourselves with the wills, wishes and feelings; we need only to establish the precise conditions in the environment which will stimulate the appropriate responses.

For other theorists, however, the behaviourists' account is inadequate and offensive in the extreme. Maybe, under certain conditions, the horse, foaming with sweat and confronted with a trough full of cool liquid, will drink. Even the most stubborn person will drink if the alternative is daunting. There are very wide limits to our behaviour, and under certain circumstances we can and will do strange things, when not doing them has unpleasant consequences. Self-destruction is no exception to this rule, as was illustrated in Michael Cimino's film *The Deerhunter* in which the captured US soldiers in VietNam are set in positions opposite each other and handed a pistol loaded with one bullet. A bizarre game of Russian roulette ensues, with the terrified Americans taking turns at holding the gun to their temples and squeezing the trigger while the amused VietCong soldiers take bets on who will be first to kill himself. Fellow soldiers are cast against each other in a game of survival because conditions stimulate such behavioural responses.

But many other theorists would reserve the right to suggest that, no matter how many times the account works and the horse drinks, or the soldier pulls the trigger, there will be exceptions. And, because of these exceptions, the behaviourist's understanding of events lacks the component which might enable the social analyst to explain fully the behaviour. Explanation comes by attempting to get to grips with the meanings people give to their behaviour. And to rescue humans from being depicted like billiard balls being struck around a table, rebounding off cushions and sunk into pockets, other theorists try to incorporate precisely that component about which the behaviourists have no regard: meaning.

In the last section, we saw how the strain of behaviourism developed a model of human beings in society based on processes that are experienced and analyzable as external to the consciousness of individuals – whether humans or animals. Men firing partially-loaded guns at their heads can be analyzed by using exactly the same techniques as rats opening trap doors or pigeons playing ping pong. Such analyses can clarify a great deal of the mystery of social life, but they miss what is, for many, a crucial dimension, the dimension of subjective consciousness. And many theorists from a variety of intellectual backgrounds believe that a comprehensive understanding of any social reality must include this.

It would be misleading to characterize the variety of thinkers with their copious theories by simplifying their often complicated accounts, but, nevertheless, the recurring theme which unites the theorists to be considered in this section is: that all social reality has the essential component of consciousness, a complex of meanings that allows humans to map out their social worlds and negotiate their ways through the events in their lives and encounters with others. Further, theories about social reality must pay close attention to this dimension – consciousness. Those working in the strain started by people like Watson and Pavlov have neglected this and so have turned up only partial explanations. A businessman who commits suicide after his involvement in large-scale corruption is exposed, may go through exactly the same behavioural motions as the VietNam prisoner in pulling the trigger of a gun held to his head; but the meaning he gives to his act is entirely different. Some appreciation of the meanings behind our behaviour is essential to an adequate account of social life.

Social reality is the product of people encountering each other, interacting with each other, at all times, attaching meanings to their events and relationships. Social life in this light, is a web of meanings which we can call reality definitions. One of the prominent theorists of the tradition emphasizing the significance of meaning was William Isaac Thomas, who made abundantly clear that whatever people experience as real in any situation is the result of such definitions (Thomas and Znaniecki, 1918). People do not simply react in given situations, as behaviourists are prone to suggest: they perceive the situations in which they are involved, take stock of the meaning of it and act upon that basis. They define their reality.

Definitions can alter dramatically from one context to another. Similar experiences can be defined very differently in only slightly different contexts. Let us take as an example a man who experiences a propensity to dress in women's clothes. If he was living in nineteenth century England he would in all likelihood not have defined himself in medical terms, that is, as sick or pathological. If he lived at stages in the twentieth century, he might for example, interpret his experience in other ways. He may well understand himself to be undergoing chromosomal irregularities and take medical advice. On the other hand, changing the context completely, if he lived in a Navaho Indian culture, he would count himself fortunate and be afforded great favouritism by other members of the culture (see King, 1981).

In other words, similar experiences can be defined quite differently and have different consequences. It all depends on the meaning given to those experiences. Although this meaning is subjective, it is generally shared. Elements of our existence are always being shared with others; it is precisely because we are able to agree on the meanings of experiences and objects that we are social creatures. We are constantly assuming that others share our meanings and define situations similarly. Most of us interpret changes in the weather as exactly that: changes in the weather, shifts in cloud formations. It is possible, however, that for some individual or another, they may presage the end of the world as we know it. That we don't live in a state of panic every time it rains attests to the fact that we attach broadly the same meanings to the weather changes.

With these elementary, but important, observations in mind then, we are able to examine the works of theorists to whom this vital element, meaning, was indispensable in any understanding of social life. Their different approaches reflect different concerns, but they are locked together in a theoretical frame of reference which elevates human consciousness to a prime position in the understanding of man.

The attempt to incorporate meaning into the study of the social world was, in large part, a reaction to the intellectual tradition deriving its theoretical models and techniques of study from the natural sciences. Impressed by the advances made in branches such as chemistry and biology, some thinkers decided it was perfectly appropriate to borrow the perspectives of natural science and see how man looked when standing alongside molecules, plants and so on. Though there are specific subdivisions, the tradition took the generic title of positivism. For example, Skinner's attempts to detail precise cause and effect sequences of behaviour by detached observation with no references to inner states, was a venture to place an objective science of man on a firm foundation.

Very profound exceptions to such attempts came from those who saw in man something unique: a capacity to behave purposefully – to attach meaning to his behaviour. Mindful of this, Wilhelm Dilthey, born in 1833, deepened the distinction between the study of nature and the study of humans by suggesting that the kinds of facts, principles and laws to be discovered in natural sciences were inapplicable to human sciences. Explanation of the natural world came through objective study, approaching the objects from the outside (1976).

The social world, however, did not lend itself to this approach, because this world is held together by shared ideas, emotions and ambitions. This is not to be explained but, rather, understood through the process of reliving men's experiences: imaginatively reconstructing thoughts. So the method of study was empathy, and this marked the whole discipline off from natural sciences and aligned it more with humanities, like the study of art or literature.

The counter-current to Dilthey's division came through other German theorists who accepted the basic philosophical dictum of Immanuel Kant. Simply put, Kant, in the eighteenth century, introduced the concepts of 'phenomena' (the objects of the world as we directly experience them) and 'noumena' (the actual objects that exist quite independently of our thought and are therefore unknowable). All science is concerned with phenomena. Nature is not 'natural' in the sense that it lies outside us. Rather it is how we refer to the way we assemble and order the confusion of the noumenal world. This way of knowing is structured by our total life experiences; we have no direct commerce with noumenal reality. Yet we do possess known-before-hand and prior-to-experience categories of knowledge; we have 'slots' into which we fit experiences and Kant called these *a prioris*. Man is therefore not seen simply as a *tabula rasa* on which experience is written.

Born 30 years after Dilthey, Heinrich Rickert accepted Kant's idea that it didn't matter whether the phenomena were parts of the natural or human world; they were all objects of scientific inquiry even if they had to be approached in different ways. Because it was so young, social science had simply not achieved the precision of other branches of science. If there was to be a distinction, Rickert argued, it had to be between history and science, the former analyzing unique events and therefore producing 'idiographic' knowledge, and the latter trying to establish general causal laws, and so bringing forth 'nomothetic' knowledge. Both human and natural worlds can be studied historically and scientifically, each requiring different methods (1962).

Kant's conception of phenomena was approached in a different manner by Georg Simmel, a contemporary of Rickert, who asked the question 'how is society possible?' (1910) Earlier, Kant had posed the problem, 'how is nature possible?' His answer was as we have seen, that nature is a picture created out of our perceptions of the world: it appears in *a priori* categories of mind and these are universal and necessary to all humans. For Simmel, society is made real by a process of consciousness which bestows a structure on an otherwise chaotic array of events and things. John O'Neill notes how the investigation of *a prioris* makes Simmel's original question, ' "How is Society Possible?", not a question about the "idea" of society, but an appeal for the elucidation of the everyday ways in which we know one another and the contours of the situations in which we find ourselves' (1972, p. 176). So society exists because we are able to make sense of it; we give shape and meanings to the people, things and happenings surrounding us. These are synthesized into unities which Simmel called 'forms'.

There is, however, a difference between the unities of society and the unities of nature. Natural objects can exist quite separately from people's apprehensions of them, but social objects have no meaning and therefore no existence apart from in consciousness which is sustained through people linking together, relating to each other and influencing one another. This is the process of 'sociation' in which society comes into being. People with different aims and intentions fuse to produce new links. Sociation was, for Simmel, the focus of social scientific enquiry (for more on Simmel, see Wolff, 1950; Coser, 1965; Frisby, 1981).

Running the risk of distorting the positions of the three figures, we can simplify their approaches. Dilthey's was to understand meanings and meaningful relations via empathy. Rickert's was to produce a system of laws dealing with causal explanations. Simmel's was to investigate the *a priori* categories of sociation, the way in which independent people combine to produce social realities.

Simmel, although a German like the others, was to have more influence in the USA, where his conception of society as a continuous stream of interpersonal relationships was given added relevance by later interactionists, including George Herbert Mead. However, the unresolved problems set by Dilthey and Rickert with their different conceptions of social science were tackled by another German, Max Weber.

### A matter of interpretation: Weber

Born in 1864, the year after Rickert, Weber accepted his contemporary's view on the possibility of mounting a study of man on a scientific basis, yet agreed with Dilthey that the basic 'stuff' of social science should be human meanings. His resolution was to try to establish a discipline in which subjective states, such as intentions and motivations, could be permissible as causes of social behaviour. Yet he was Kantian insofar as he claimed no capacity to discover a complete set of causal laws governing social events: Weber's studies were to produce knowledge which was necessarily incomplete. He agreed with Dilthey that reality was an 'immeasurable manifold.'

Much of Weber's work was devoted, as Hans Gerth and C. Wright Mills put it, to 'rounding out' Karl Marx's materialism by adding a variety of casual factors to the explanation of human behaviour (1961, p. 47). In particular, in *The Protestant Ethic and the Spirit of Capitalism*, he was at pains to demonstrate the independent role of ideas and beliefs in historical change (1930). Whereas Marx asserted, as we will see, that the decisive factor in history was pre-eminently economic, and that consciousness was shaped by what he termed the mode of production, Weber claimed that social, historical changes can be instigated by what goes on in the minds of human beings. His was not an attempt to refute Marx by replacing his theories with a determinism in which human ideas are seen as causes of historical and social changes, but he wanted nonetheless to enrich the understanding of human behaviour by laying emphasis on both internal and external factors as causes. Irving Zeitlin notes the complementary nature of Marx's and Weber's theories, adding: 'The human condition is such that no science truly comes to terms with it that ignores either meaning or causality... meaning itself is a causal component of action' (1973, p. 168).

In other words, in contrast to certain other theorists for whom the purposes and meanings of individuals had no place in social science, Weber insisted that he could provide causal explanations of human behaviour in these terms. Choice, deliberation, calculation: such terms entered Weber's theoretical vocabulary, and here lay his central problem

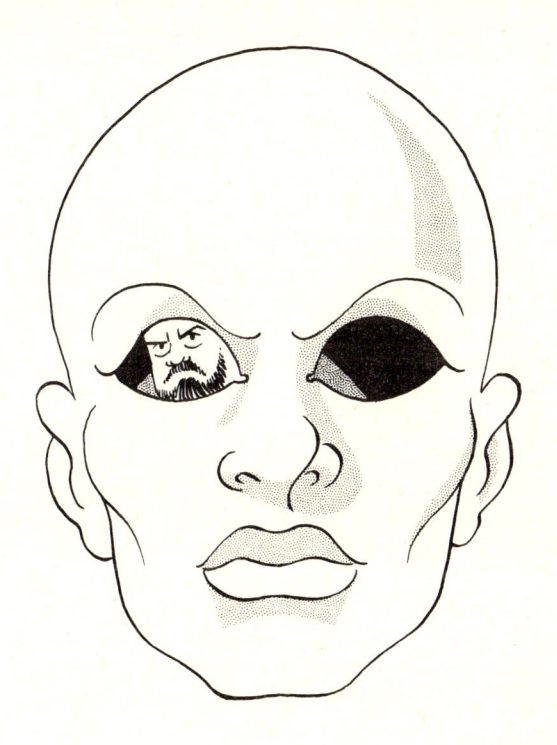

**Max Weber (1864–1920)**

Born in Erfurt, Thuringia on 21 April, 1864. His father was a trained Jurist and municipal councillor. In 1869 he moved with his family to Berlin. His father became a prosperous politician. Educated at the universities of Heidelberg, Berlin and Göttingen, he held teaching positions at Berlin, Freiberg and Heidelberg. His work was both intellectual and practical as he was concerned with the political problems facing Germany at the end of the century and was committed to the establishment of a liberal-democratic system. Many interpret his theories as reactions to Marx's materialism, though others see it as complementing Marx's analysis.

because, unlike the subject matter of the natural science, they were simply not observable.

Whereas followers of the natural science line needed to concentrate on events that could be observed and documented – to keep in alignment with the procedures of natural sciences – Weber thought to examine individuals in their full humanity, which meant tackling the very unique characteristic which separated them from other living matter on this earth. Unlike the behaviourist model, which takes human behaviour to be of a greater complexity but of the same quality as animal's, Weber saw humans as engaging in something distinct, that is, social action. As Weber stated:

> Action is social insofar as by virtue of the subjective meaning attached to it by the acting individual... it takes account of the behaviour of others and is thereby oriented in its course. (1968, vol. I, p. 4).

In contrast to pure behaviour, social action involves endowing one's own moves with meaning and taking stock of others'. Weber's famous example is that of two cyclists who collide accidentally; this is not social action, but something like a natural event. If they sight each other before hand and attempt to avoid the clash, then this is social action, as would be the ensuing insults or fight. This is a rather dubious distinction, for surely the very process of riding a bicycle implicates the rider in social activity, accepting the rules and norms of highway conduct, observing unwritten points of road etiquette, even riding itself means being aware of the possibility of other road users' presence. However, Weber's distinction is clear enough. Behaviour may be mechanical, spontaneous, lack meaning and have nothing to do with others – a blink of an eyelid, say. Social action is meaningful and is produced by an actor with intentions and purposes – a wink at another person, for example.

In the final analysis, many of the institutions we think of as inhuman are very much products of social action, although often the people producing them are not in direct contact with each other. 'Such concepts as "state", "association", "feudalism", and the like designate certain categories of human interaction,' contended Weber. He went on: 'Hence it is the task of sociology to reduce these concepts to "understandable" action, that is, without exception, to the actions of participating individual men' (quoted in Gerth and Mills, 1961, p. 55).

The reduction to 'understable action' was central to Weber's whole enterprise which he called *Verstehende Sociologie*, that is, interpretative sociology. This he saw as a scientific discipline which utilized understanding as a way of interpreting actions with a view to arriving at a causal explanation of its course and effects. This derived from Dilthey's empathetic understanding technique, but went one step further: for

Weber, ideas, beliefs and values – what goes on inside our heads – can have causal efficacy.

Humans can understand, or at least try to understand, their own action through introspection, examining their own thoughts and feelings. They must infer the motives and purposes of others by reference to their professed or apparent intentions. In sum, the interpretative sociologist is interested in the meanings held by actors in specific contexts – their reality definitions.

Interest lies not so much in the actual consequences of a piece of action as the intended consequences; it is important to grasp the goals the actor is chasing, how he thinks he can achieve them; and, of course this raises problems. Imagine trying to interpret the rapid closing and opening of an eyelid. Is it a blink as in the previous example of a purely mechanical piece of behaviour? Or is it a wink? If so, having what significance? Lustful intentions? Innocent good-natured recognition? One disguised as the other?

One might argue that the winker (or blinker) alone knows the meaning of his act, but with Weber's method of *verstehen*, the social scientist is impelled to interpret it with reference to the person's social position and the context in which he performs. We understand the intentions of a boxer winking to his cornermen to assure them he is all right after taking a hard punch; we understand differently the purposes of a dirty raincoat-clad park roamer winking at a young girl. The action is thrust back into its social context to get at its meaning.

## Ironies

Unlike many of his contemporaries, Weber saw his general project as rigorously scientific and so needed to anchor his vision of an interpretative sociology to a seabed of discipline. Like Rickert, an avowed social scientist, he sought causal connections between events. The results of research must be generalizable; this concern is not reflected in the works of his American counterparts, as we shall see later.

In the attempt to establish causal explanations of actions, Weber constructed a typology. Easiest to explain were actions involving a defined end and rationally calculated means to attaining it. *Zweckrational* action has as its prime example economic performances which are geared specifically to prestructured goals; both means and ends are rational for Weber. Not so with *Wertrational* action in which the means are, again, rational and oriented to an objective, but the objective itself is accepted unquestioningly as an absolute end; religious or ethical notions of absolute good are irrational ends, maybe, but the methods adopted in their pursuit are perfectly rational. Action is deemed *affectual* when it is guided by an emotion, for instance anger or lust. Completing the typology is *traditional* action, the conduct here being habitual and unreflective, done as a matter of course rather than as part of a conceived plan of action.

Obviously, a great deal of social action does not operate in such a way as to fit neatly into one or another of these types; often our actions seem to have some elements that fit into one box and other elements that fit into another. The types, in effect, shade into each other. Weber's own work, where the accumulation of capital takes on not purely economic but religious significance for the Calvinist capitalist, illustrates this. But Weber claimed that the subjective interpretation of action would be facilitated and the establishment of causal links permitted by reference to them.

Weber used the categories as what he called ideal types, which were abstractions of patterns of action, or institutions. The ideal typical construction was a methodological device for Weber to analyse segments of society. For example, modern bureaucracy was seen as the embodiment of *Zweckrational* action; so Weber abstracted what he considered to be salient features of bureaucracy purely as a way of bringing certain relationships and events into focus (for further discussion of ideal types, see Fletcher, 1972, pp. 428-39).

Setting actual action against the ideal type brought such focus, for, as Weber claimed: 'By comparison with this it is possible to understand the ways in which actual action is influenced by irrational factors of all sorts, such as effects and errors, is that they deviate from the line of conduct which would be expected on the hypothesis that the action was purely rational' (1947, p. 92).

The imputation of rationality to all sorts of action, then, was for purposes of erecting an ideal typical model of social conduct against which could be contrasted actual performance. Means-end types of action were common and yielded close comparisons with real action; but the categories were not meant to characterize all human action; only to project models to be used in further analysis.

Weber built his theory of social action on the premise that thoughts, ideas, beliefs and values have a part to play in determining the course of human action and therefore history. The scope of his application of the theories demonstrates how precisely he was able to pinpoint the potency of thoughts in shaping broad social changes. This is not to imply that Weber was an undiluted idealist, insisting that what goes on in people's heads is the prime mover in society; but certainly it is a major factor. Hence his insistence that social science, particularly sociology, should take account of the motives, purposes, intentions, in sum, the meanings behind human action.

His *Verstehende Sociologie* was the programme for getting at the meanings people give to their acts. Weber was not interested in so-called true or ultimate meanings, but only in the actor's own definition – and this concern was shared by all the theorists of this strain. Nor was Weber particularly absorbed by whether the intentions and motives were effective: his interest was squarely with how the actor thought it would work. Accordingly, in this context, Weber would have been more concerned with a man's – possibly lustful – intentions in winking, than with the unanticipated smack across the face he received as a result.

Weber shows this with his own more scholarly example of Calvinists with their doctrine of predestination: nowhere does he maintain that they intended to produce the economic patterns of early capitalism; he was aware that their original intentions were quite different. The analysis brings out the provocative irony of much human action, which doesn't mean that ideas are unimportant, but as Peter Berger reminds us: 'It does mean that the outcome of ideas is commonly very different from what those who had the ideas in the first place planned or hoped' (1971, p. 52).

The imputation of meanings to human action via inference and detailed examination of social and historical context is but one step in the analysis, which is not adequately completed until some causal connections are found between the eventual action and the preceding circumstances. The actual actions may be precipitated by certain motivating thoughts and be facilitated by specific, conducive conditions. They have to be precisely stated for the analysis to transcend the purely descriptive stage of imputing meanings.

So far, our depiction of Weber and his theories has revealed a conception of the human being as an active, constructive creature, attaching meanings to his moves, setting himself goals, anticipating consequences and taking into account the thoughts and behaviour of others. But, in finalizing many of his multifaceted analyses, he frequently ended up with the human utterly constrained or overwhelmed by an overarching social order – albeit one of his own construction.

Although his stress is on the socially constructive element of human beings, his analysis brings out the stultifying effects of the social order replete with institutions such as the state and the church, which Weber had been careful to note are only 'categories of human interaction' once they are reduced. Alan Dawe notes how this twist in the analysis is: 'to transform social actors and their subjective meanings, which were Weber's starting point, into mere reflexes of the social order' (1979, p. 393).

Dawe argues that Weber, in his study of how the rise of modern capitalism was facilitated by the Calvinist religious doctrine, showed Protestantism to originate in the actions of thrifty individuals. Over time, it grew in size and impact, at the same time elaborating sets of rules for proper Protestant conduct. 'These rules constitute the accomplishment by its followers of Protestantism as a "self-consciously" formulated doctrine and movement,' contends Dawe (1979, p. 399).

The whole capitalist enterprise was, at its inception, the work of men, but it developed an independence such that it was able to rest on its own 'mechanical foundations' as Weber called them, and eventually developed factory discipline and capitalist business organization which acted as an 'iron cage' inside which men were trapped. Bryan Turner analyses this in terms of 'Weber's tragic sense of fate' and concludes: 'Weber has a clear conception of the structural constraints which determine individual behaviour and of the way in which a system of constraints has a "logic" or "fate" which overrides individual intention and consciousness' (1981, p. 58; see also Mommsen, 1965, p. 30).

The theory of social action turns back on itself to produce an image of a social order structuring human life. This really is a large-scale extension of Weber's irony of social action: producing unintended consequences. But it leaves a rather unsatisfactory tension in the general theory of action, for we are left with no doubts about the potentialities of human beings, but with plenty about their possibilities for developing them.

Humans are autonomous creatures of choice on the one hand, yet they choose their ends in such a way as to subordinate themselves to social orders. This feature of Weber's theory was endorsed by his wife Marianne Weber, who commented: 'in its earthly course, an idea always and everywhere operates in opposition to its original meaning' (1975, p. 337).

It was Weber's ambition that led him to this conclusion: he wanted to paint a picture of man, not in isolation, but in relationship to society and history. In order to achieve this, he needed to organize his concepts in a way that was sensitive to relationships – hence the stress on social action, not behaviour. Social relations are the effects of individuals' wills, but, after they are established, they can generate their own 'logic'.

But, while Weber was writing, other theorists, who were similarly committed to exploring the human's relationships to others and how these effect courses of thought and behaviour, were looking in other directions and finding alternatives to Weber's ironical conclusions.

### The Pragmatists

Along with Weber, the early pioneers of interactionism recoiled at the idea of a science of man adopting and adapting the model of natural science and treating human thoughts and behaviour as caused by external stimuli. They shared with Weber a first principle: that human beings act towards things on the basis of the meanings that the things have for them. Any study that failed to account for the important aspect of meaning and had no place for the role of consciousness in social action was doomed to one-sideness. It was all very well studying objectively the world which lay outside the individual; but that same world as it was experienced by the individual was also of crucial significance. The other main point on which they were agreed was on the status of social phenomena. 'Society,' for John Dewey, was 'but the relations of individuals to one another in this form and that' (quoted in Mills, 1964, p. 436).

These then were the uniting points between predecessors of interactionism and Weber; and, although there were vast differences in ambition, scope and general orientation, the approach each initiated to the study of humans laid great emphasis on the necessity of interpreting the meanings underlying social action. Similarly, both agreed that human action involved anticipating and expecting the reactions of others. Weber's cyclists spring to mind. 'Taking the role of the other' is the phrase popularly used by interactionists to denote the process of anticipating what other people will think and do under certain conditions. We recognize this and try to arrange our own actions accordingly. Our relationships with others are, in a sense, governed by a continuous series of predictions about others. Elementary as it sounds, this simple observation makes clear that any theory of man has necessarily to be of a social nature. It is impossible, or at least misleading, to try to study human behaviour in itself; relationships are always in the process of construction and destruction; humans simply do not operate in isolation but rather with reference to others; even when we are not in another's immediate presence, we are thinking about another or groups of others. All action is social and the extension of this is that the individual and society are not independent units; so they should not be made to seem that way in theories stressing one or the other.

This last point requires some qualification, for in using the concept of society we seem to pose a separation: individual human beings, on the one hand, and society on the other. But, like Weber, interactionists insisted that such a separation is merely a technical convenience and that when we use such concepts as social system, social classes, social organization, or society itself, we are referring to nothing more than human beings relating to each other in stable, often complex, patterns.

It will have become apparent that the name interactionism derives from these basic principles. Society is a process in which people come together to conduct relationships, some fleeting, some permanent, but at all times giving meanings to their actions and trying to anticipate what others will think or do. The action is reciprocal, hence interaction – the action occurs between them. This somewhat simple principle informed much of the theoretical work which was to culminate in symbolic interactionism. To begin with, it is advisable to trace the sometimes unclear development, one might say evolution, of this strain of thought, and, in our view this has its origins in the philosophies of theorists who came to be called pragmatists.

The late nineteenth century was a period which saw the currency of the theories of Charles Darwin rise in Western Society. Men's thinking was changed by the controversial, monumental *Origin of the Species*, first published in 1859, which was seized upon by many theorists and elaborated into a full-blown explanation of not only man's evolution, but also his conduct in society.

Though it is by no means certain that Darwin himself would have agreed with other's versions of his theories, many applied them to the study of human behaviour and progress with the effect that interest became centred on the biological bases of social action. The concept of instinct was integral: human behaviour was visualized as determined by unlearned and unmodifiable traits or characteristics that humans inherited genetically. As such, a broad continuity between animals and humans was suggested; both were, in a sense, governed by the biological equipment with which they were born.

Dissatisfied with this biological conception of human beings or, at least, unconvinced of its adequacy in explaining the intricate patterns of behaviour scored by humans, William James, born in 1842, argued for a consideration of humans as having instincts but with ability to alter and modify them through experiences in society. Unlike animals, humans were not slaves to their instincts: they could learn and change on the basis of that learned experience. In the same way that Weber reacted to studying man as if he were a component of the natural world without unique characteristics, James rejected the continuity implied in social Darwinism and wanted science to recognize the gap in quality between man and the rest of the living world (1948).

James did not dismiss the part played by instinct in human conduct, but

---

**William James (1842–1910)**

Born in New York City, from a wealthy family and the eldest of five children. Moved in intellectual circles. Studied philosophy in Germany, where he suffered a nervous breakdown. He returned to Harvard where he completed a medical degree and eventually taught physiology, psychology and philosophy. In 1878, aged 36, he married and began work on *Principles of Psychology* in which he set out his version of pragmatism, i.e. that all metaphysical disputes could be either resolved or trivialized by examining the practical consequences of alternative answers; scientific theories are instruments to guide further action, and not final answers to questions about nature. 'Ideas must have cash value' – it is true if it has practical consequences.

wanted to temper the outright deterministic, rather rigid, view of man by trying as well to understand how instincts are either modified or inhibited by socially learned habits. The interplay of instinct, a biological concept, and habit, a social one, was crucial to James' analysis. Instinct, for James, meant 'the faculty of acting in such a way as to produce certain ends without foresight of the ends, and without previous education in the performance' (1890, p. 383).

But, like Weber, James recognized that a great deal of human behaviour is directed towards the attainment of pre-set goals and is not propelled by what he coined 'blind instinct.' Humans are born with instinctive impulses to behave in certain ways, but the brain has the facility for retention so that, after the instinctive behaviour has been performed – say drinking water to satisfy the thirst impulse – the end product can be recalled to mind and the behaviour can be repeated as a matter of habit. The whole performance is no longer determined by instinct but guided by habit. It supersedes instincts.

Following James' lead, his contemporary John Dewey added that habit was not merely the repetition or recurrence of specific acts, but an acquired predisposition to respond in a certain way to classes of stimuli. To use one of Dewey's examples, a man's act of standing erect comes: 1) Through standing up 2) Then thinking about what it is like to have the right posture 3) Then developing the habit of doing so that he can evoke the thought at will. 'The act must come before the thought, and a habit before the ability to evoke the thought at will,' wrote Dewey (1922, p. 30).

The influence of behaviourism was therefore evident in both James and Dewey, but this is not to suggest that, for them, humans merely *react* and do not have consciousness of the stimuli. Far from it: James, in particular, wanted to rescue man from such a view; he wanted to perceive human beings as constructive creatures playing a conscious part in running their own lives. For James and Dewey, humans were potentially creative, but this creativity had to be stimulated through associations in the environment.

One of the features of the pragmatism of James and Dewey was the focus

---

### John Dewey (1859–1952)

Began as Hegelian philosopher, and psychologist. Changed to pragmatism after coming into contact with the views of James. Dewey was a close friend of George Herbert Mead. Worked as Professor of Philosophy at Columbia University. Thought that man need not be the passive subject of nature, as he has learned to modify it.

on human adjustment to environmental conditions. Whilst accepting many of the premises of behaviourism, they wished to endow man with the capacity of free will to dictate his own action. Humans, in contrast to animals which would respond to stimuli, apply meaning to and interpret those stimuli. The whole adjustment to the environment from which habit is produced involves a process of thinking: defining objects and others, anticipating possible lines of action and predicting the outcomes of acting in specific ways and their alternatives.

Dewey, in particular, outlined how humans deliberate before acting, trying to formulate alternatives in a kind of dress rehearsal. Neither he nor James denied that there are environmental stimuli to which the human reacts, but they are selectively perceived and responded to by individuals. The human's 'mind' represents man's capacity to react subjectively to objective stimuli through conceptualizing, evaluating, defining and reflecting. Behaviour is not a mechanical reaction to external stimuli but a process involving continual assessment. The mind constructs its environment, so what is represented as a stimulus is, in fact, already predefined by the organism.

This is the theme of Dewey's article, 'The reflex arc concept in psychology' (1896), in which he insisted that the thing we call a stimulus does not so much lie outside the individual but is defined in the context of action. A bus passing before us does not stimulate us to step off the kerb in front of it unless we actually *want* to get knocked over. The crucial feature of our knowledge of the world is its link to practical activity. Here we see why James and Dewey were called pragmatists: in their view, all humans are reality assessors whose behaviour follows on directly from how they define their situations. We learn the consequences of action from experience, structure our behaviour in accordance with those anticipated consequences and organize our conduct in terms of the practical consequences. We wait at the kerbside while a bus passes because we assess the consequences of stepping out into the path of the moving vehicle; in much the same way, the working class do not constantly rise up against the bosses because they cannot predict the consequences on the basis of their immediate past experience and are therefore habitualized to familiar performances.

The grand image is of a society held together by individuals whose understanding is limited to their own environments, each pursuing their objectives on the basis of their anticipations of the consequences of their actions. There is no split between mind and society: mental states can't be disentangled from physical environments. The image converges with that of exchange theory, when the individual needs another's assistance in order to achieve a desired consequence; he has to demonstrate to the other person that he can also achieve desired ends for himself in the process. So social change is hard to come by, as humans cannot conceive of alternative ways or organizing their behaviour if they lie outside their immediate experience.

The assumptions which tie James and Dewey to Weber are that thoughts are efficacious, that the human is deliberating, rational, capable of anticipating consequences and of making conscious decisions that affect subsequent behaviour. Such an assumption would, of course, be about as acceptable to Skinner as a cross would be to a vampire. Following on from this, and equally repulsive to many behaviourists, is the assumption that – and remember it can never be more than that – we base our actions on the belief that others have similar thoughts and that they are aware of us in the same way as we are of them. We all accept this as an article of faith, but for all we know, all other members of society may be sophisticated robots and we may be the only beings on earth who are sentient.

Weber's efforts, as we have outlined, were geared towards the growth of a generalizable explanation, whereas the pragmatists were slightly less ambitious and drew short of causal analyses. They were more concerned with the development of consciousness, its effects on the humans generally and how they might apply their analyses to actual social conditions; Dewey was extremely active in the area of education and wrote widely on the relevance of pragmatism to this area.

We have scarcely done justice to pragmatism, nor, for that matter, have we criticized it; our purpose has been merely to outline how James and Dewey scarred a surface on which the interactionists were to work. We have seen how many of their themes and concepts overlap with Weber's; how these were derived from a humanistic conception of man as a volitional, thinking creature who was not subordinate to, or a respondent of, his environment, but gave meaning to his transactions based on future actions, learned experiences and anticipated consequences. Such a conception involved a rejection of the notion of society as a monolith standing apart from the individual or as possessing characteristics somehow separable from human actions – ideas that will occupy us in the third section of this book.

These then were the themes uniting writers from widely different backgrounds in their search for a theory of man and society. Their differences were many, and can perhaps be summed up by saying that, whilst Weber was interested in using his analyses of man's relationships with others to explain changes and stabilities in society, the pragmatists were concerned with the way in which such relationships affect the individual's development. It might also be said that whereas Weber was interested in getting at the meanings of mens actions, the pragmatists concentrated on the effects of them.

The relevance of all of these conditions to the interactionist strain of thought will become apparent. What needs to be done now is to document another series of related, but different, concerns which were to contribute appreciably to the strain.

## Technical Terms

**Cause:** An event which is said to be a condition for the occurrence of another event. To formulate a causal connection is to posit a strong relationship between two or more events. The existence of A may in itself not be sufficient to B, but it may be a necessary condition. Arguments against this would insist that causes in the social world are unlike chemical reactions and cannot be generalized into 'laws'. Others would suggest that these are causes, but in the form of human motives, intentions and purposes.

**Frame of Reference:** Set of individual or group standards for assessing one's own thoughts and actions and those of others.

**Humanism:** The idea that social theory should be couched in terms of human beings complete with intentions, emotions, expectations and, crucially, potentialities. This is in opposition to social theories stressing only factors external to the human being.

**Instincts:** An innate, unlearned tendency which is fixed and unchanging (see *Invariant*) and shared by all the members of a species.

**Invariant:** Can refer to fixed characteristics of the human mind, but usually refers to unchanging features of societies which persist despite transformations of other aspects. They are constant and fixed. The early *Positivists* were interested in discovering invariant properties of societies, though these were notoriously elusive and many contemporary theorists would argue that the search for them is pointless. The taboo regarding incest is often quoted as an example of an invariant feature of all societies.

**Natural Science:** Often confused with all science, but referring specifically to areas of study concerned with matter *as object*. The techniques employed, experimentation and measurement, are geared to this.

**Phenomenon:** Anything that is capable of being perceived and is, therefore, amenable to analysis.

**Sentient:** Having the capacity of receive stimuli; i.e. the power of sense perception.

**Social Context:** The conditions, human and non-human, surrounding a person's actions. The surrounding conditions are crucial in their affect on the meanings those actions will have.

## Further Reading

'Max Weber and contemporary sociology' (in *The Future of the Sociological Classics*, 1981, edited by B. Rhea). Dennis Wrong reviews, albeit briefly, Weber's influence on modern social theory and research.

*The Making of Symbolic Interactionism* (1979) by Paul Rock, devotes its first three chapters to discussing Kant, Simmel, James, and Dewey, amongst others.

*Sociology and Pragmatism* (1964) by C. Wright Mills, contains a comprehensive overview of the relevance of pragmatism in all its diversity to social thought.

**Advance Reading**
*From Max Weber* (1961) by Hans Gerth and C. Wright Mills, has become accepted as one of the most accessible and well-edited collections of Weber's original writings.
*For Weber* (1981) by Bryan Turner makes a plausible case for seeing Weber as much more deterministic than most see him and presents a scholarly analysis of his thought.
*American Sociology and Pragmatism* (1981) by J. D. Lewis and Richard Smith is an unusual interpretation of the pragmatists which revives the nominalist vs. realist issue i.e. the view that social enquiry describes regularities in behaviour (James and Dewey, according to the authors) vs. the view that enquiry should ask about the nature of things, like the concept of society as an entity in itself.

# 5

# The Selves

**Explorations of consciousness**

From the instant we are born, we are dependent upon others who bring us into the world. In the infant condition, we experience hunger, thirst, physical discomfort and all sorts of unpleasant sensations; their assuagement depends on the attentions of those in our immediate environment. Early development entails interaction between our experience of our own bodies and our experience with other human beings, and the latter can appreciably affect the former. Our early growth and development revolve around our intimate relationships with people on whom we are forced to depend, or, as Peter and Brigitte Berger put it: 'The biography of the individual, from the moment of birth, is the story of his relations with others' (1981, p. 57).

So, in a sense, we are always social creatures because even our most personal experiences are penetrated by others. The Bergers give the example of the infant's craving for food: if he is fed a certain time, and at certain times only, he is forced to adjust to this pattern; and, in making the alteration, his functioning changes so that not only is he fed at those times, but he is also hungry at such times. 'Graphically, society not only imposes its patterns upon the infant's behaviour but reaches inside him to organize the functions of his stomach,' observe the Bergers (1981, p. 57).

The same observation could be made of other seemingly personal, physiological processes such as excreting, sleeping etc. Our habits are structured by the imperatives of others and, if the mother has to go to work at 9.00 a.m. and work a seven hour day, the child's eating and other habits are likely to be organized around this fact. The world of work influences the most basic and early experiences we have.

These are aspects of the process of socialization, that is the imposition of social patterns on human behaviour of even the most personal kind.

Society's interference with our habits is mediated through other people; in early stages, it is our parents whose influence is enhanced by our lack of exposure to alternatives; we are at their mercy and the world as they present it to us invariably becomes the world we experience. Only much later do we become aware of other experiences, other worlds: in the extreme event, our grown-up child might disengage himself from his parents and flee, for example, to 'the moonies' of Reverend Moon's Unification Church.

So far, so good: the basic, obvious point we are starting with is that we develop and expand into a world populated by others who influence our behaviour and experience. At first, we might experience the world as a vast, external, mysterious and confusing reality; but during the course of our interactions with other people and the physical environment, we gain more understanding of it and make it more apprehensible by generating knowledge about it. We learn what behaviour goes rewarded and what goes punished, where we might have freedom and where we are controlled and, crucially, we learn to give things the same meanings as other people. If our parents regard a wooden, four-legged platform with a single upright as a chair and associate that with a utility for sitting on, we are unlikely to regard it as a religious totem to be used for purposes of worship. In other cultures, however, the opposite case may hold.

When theorists write of a world of inter-subjectively shared meanings, they refer to precisely this type of agreement, except on a mass scale. We all agree broadly on what a chair is, as we do on the meaning of poverty, violence, pleasure and so on. Agreements are reached on wooden objects as well as the more abstract categories because of a uniquely human facility: language.

We learn to acquire, convey, retain and, sometimes, change socially recognized meanings about all sorts of things through, at first, being talked to and, then, talking back. The meanings of things are brought home to us by our parents and others talking to us about them. So the complex of meanings we give to things are shaped through language. The most extreme version of this type of view is given expression in the theories of Benjamin Lee Whorf who contended that the languages people learn actually determine the way they perceive the world, so that the words we have in our vocabularies map out for us the world we will experience (1956).

When we pick up the threads of language and begin to use them, we acquire the ability to store meanings, and project into the future on the basis of those meanings. Present experiences can be related to past ones, which can be summoned into consciousness by the use of words. Future experiences can be anticipated and planned for. This is the capacity for reflection, and comes with the acquisition of language; without using words, it would be impossible to think back or ahead. Furthermore, it is through reflection that we become conscious not only of the world about us but of ourselves; we become self conscious – and this is critically important.

Pause to think about yourself. Who are you thinking about? Who is doing the thinking? James had been intrigued by this peculiar duality of human consciousness; we think about ourselves as objects, someone whom we know, yet there is also a subject doing the knowing: 'For shortness we may call one the *Me* and the other the *I*' (1890, p. 176) 'Me' is what is known; 'I' is the knower.

This 'splitting' coincides with what James considered a crucial stage in the development of consciousness, namely when we become sensitive to the opinions of others. Mead was later to call this 'taking the attitude of the other,' meaning that the child recognizes a certain attitude in someone else, understands its meaning and then learns to take it himself. For example, the child might observe his mother taking an attitude of annoyance and frustration every time he throws a plate of jelly on the floor. A behaviourist's interpretation of such a stage would be couched in terms of reinforcement: the mother might have positively reinforced the child by, say, giving him sweets every time he did not throw the jelly on the floor, or, negatively, by slapping him when he did (as we know, the former would be most effective).

But, in the James perspective, the child arrives at the point where he is able to imagine what other people are thinking and feeling. Vicariously, he partakes in their cognitive and affectual activity, placing himself in their position to find out what the world looks like from their standpoint. It is a massive step in the development of the child, for it opens up new realms to explore, new emotions to probe, new perspectives in which to see things. Our private, interior existence dissolves and we gain a public awareness, becoming sensitive to what is going on inside the heads of others.

On this basis, we slot others into categories. Going back to the child's mother, he learns that her entry into the room means that she will have certain anticipations and perceptions of him that will probably differ from those of a stranger entering the room. There are what James Mark Baldwin depicted as three stages:

1 Drawing distinctions between objects and differentiating between others (like mothers and strangers).
2 Initiating others' behaviour and recognizing that behaviour carries with it feelings (like his mother's annoyance when she scolds him).
3 Associating these stages of feeling with conceptions of person and thereby becoming conscious of the feelings of others, what Baldwin called 'ejecting' his own subjective interpretations into others (1906).

To summarize the stages: projective, subjective and ejective. The end result is the formation of consciousness, including a consciousness of one's self. We can perhaps capture this by imagining a child's change in awareness as reflected in his speech. Up to the projective stage he might refer to himself in the third person: 'John is a good boy.' He then develops an awareness of his environment with himself as the 'subject' as central. When he develops self consciousness, this becomes: 'I am a good boy,' and he is able to make this judgement because he is aware that others regard him as good; they to him are 'ejects'.

Baldwin's analysis was, in effect, an attempt to elaborate and improve on ideas floated by James in 1890. James' splitting of the self into 'I' and 'Me' offered possibilities. He defined the self as: 'the sum total of all that the individual can call his' (1890, p. 291). Some elements of the self have empirical sources insofar as they are gleaned from other people. We get to the stage where we can imagine what others think of us and incorporate that view in our own self definitions and so, as James put it, 'we may practically say that he [any individual] has as many different social selves as there are distinct *groups* of person about whose opinion he cares' (1980, p. 294). Our consciousness of our self derives from our many, diverse relationships with others. In gaining introductions to the world as others see it, the child gains introductions to himself as others see him and comes to store aspects of their view until they stabilize into what we call identities. It is almost as if our conceptions of ourselves are reflections of what others think; and this is precisely what Charles Horton Cooley tried to convey with his expression 'the looking glass self.'

## All in the mind: Cooley

By invoking the metaphor of the looking glass, Cooley added imagery to the abstractions of James and Baldwin, though, conceptually, his theories are more or less restatements rather than innovations. He presented the general argument about the development of the self reflectively in terms of the reaction to the attitudes and opinions of other people. It was the way in which he used this idea to promote a broader analysis of society which distinguished Cooley.

Born in 1864 – the same year as Weber – Cooley expanded on the themes of James, Dewey and Baldwin which held that our consciousness and experience are dependent on the particular relationships we share with others, particularly those others to whom we, by necessity, attach significance like our immediate family members or kids in a play group. These Cooley called 'primary groups':

> By primary groups, I mean those characterized by intimate face-to-face association and co-operation. They are primary in several senses, but chiefly in that they are fundamental in forming the social nature of ideals of individuals. (1909, p. 23)

## 80 Interactionism

Through such associations, the maturing child generates a feeling of 'we-ness', meaning that he becomes conscious of his own bodily and emotional feelings and identifies himself as part of a social unit which lies

---

**Charles Horton Cooley (1864–1929)**

Studied under John Dewey, he spent his entire academic career at the University of Michigan although he was considered part of the 'Chicago School'. Son of a Jurist, he did his undergraduate work in engineering and was employed as a surveyor before switching to economics for his doctorate. Not a prolific writer compared to his contemporaries, but his material was written with craft and imagination. Criticized for his conception of society as a 'mental phenomenon' existing only in the minds of individuals. His social theorizing began after his obvervations of his children and most of his theory is based on such impressions rather than systematic research.

outside himself, namely the group. The primary group supplies a link with experiences outside himself, but also structures the experience of himself as a member of a wider unit.

Contacts with group members yield the formation of 'the social nature of ideals' and here Cooley details the group as a source of morality, for it is after sustained involvements that the child learns to subordinate his own individual wants and interests. A sense of social unity is imparted. Principles such as group loyalty and adherence to rules or even laws come through interactions in the group. So what Cooley tried to do was construct an analysis of the child's immersion into groups which could serve as a basis for understanding his consciousness and behaviour; the complex patterns of relationships spreading through all societies derive from early primary group involvements.

The stimulus behind Cooley's theories was his observation of his own children and watching them grow up led him to believe that all social life can be reduced to and be analyzable in terms of group interactions – elaborate, refined, complex, but reducible to interactions. Like the others, he rejected any conception of society or social order which gave it some kind of existence separate from individuals. Society is interaction writ large. And as interactions or reciprocal relationships between group members were, in Cooley's eyes, both the source of the self and dependent on the consciousness individuals have of one another and their material environment, then society would have to be seen as existing only in people's minds. This is a difficult conceptualization and needs expansion. 'The solid facts of society,' was how Cooley (1964) described the imaginations of people. 'Society exists in my mind as the contact and reciprocal influence of certain ideas named "I". Thomas, Henry, Susan, Bridget and so on' (1964).

So, society is 'real' to people: it exists to them. But it is simply this: a mental construction. As such, it exists through the shared expectations and predictable patterns of conduct people build. To see it differently is, as Ronald Fletcher emphasizes, 'an optical illusion' (1972, p. 484). It is equally illusory to see individuals as independent, autonomous beings for, on analysis, their consciousness, including motives, drive and intentions, derive from their membership of groups. Cooley's task was to dissolve such convenient but, in his view, misleading dualities which depicted man in an isolated way, for: 'He has no separate existence; through both the hereditary and the social factors in his life a man is bound into the whole of which he is a member, and to consider him apart from it is quite as artificial as to consider society apart from individuals' (1964, p. 38).

And, as we are incapable of thinking about others or ourselves except with reference to some social group in which we are involved, Cooley argued: 'self and society are twin-born' (1964, p. 38).

We see that Cooley's concepts of the looking glass self and the primary group blend with each other in his coherent images of humans as simultaneously part, and makers, of society. Consciousness comes through interaction in groups and society takes shape in our imaginations. Underlying all this is the distinct human ability to learn through communication; this is the process which makes society possible.

Such was the scope of Cooley's analysis that he was able to offer a view of man and society in unison; thus his theory was both psychological, sociological and, for that matter, philosophical in tone. He sought to extract elements from each discipline and integrate them in such a way as to rescue man from the biological determinism of genetic theories, whilst at the same time stopping short of the stimulus-response plastic man model; but he always stayed within the framework of James and the others, who stressed the centrality of self in social processes.

Cooley accepted that biological heredity produced all the anatomical and physiological characteristics of the organism and the attendant potentialities, behavioural and experiential. But when Cooley wrote of 'human nature' – as he often did – he referred to 'certain primary social sentiments and attitudes, such as consciousness of one's self in relation to others, love of approbation, resentment of censure, emulation, and a sense of social right and wrong formed by the standards of a group' (1964, p. 32).

These sentiments were, it seemed, invariant, and Cooley concluded this was because they were fostered in the contexts of primary groups – in his view, a historical, universal form. All human societies have primary groups through which the individual is shaped. So, although he accepted certain biological endowments, Cooley viewed human nature as a product of group membership. We all exhibit what we regard as human nature but, according to Cooley, 'this is because the intimate groups in which it is formed are somewhat similar.' And crucially: 'if these are changed, human nature will change with them.' (Cooley, 1964, p. 33).

Even something as obvious and supposedly natural as 'all humans have conceptions of good and evil' might be amenable to change. A similar point came across in the Coppolla movie *Apocalypse Now*, with the American ex-officer Kurtz abandoning the war to set up his own commune in the heart of the jungle at the VietNam–Cambodia border. Devastated by continual exposure to, and involvement in, mass atrocities, he dissolves his conceptions of right and wrong and bids his followers – members of the primary group – to do likewise. When his isolated group is eventually penetrated, he tells his unwanted visitor that he will accept any invasion but will not be told that what he is doing is right or wrong; after his many war experiences, his interest is in constructing a community where such conceptions have no relevance. This sentiment was circulated through the group by interaction facilitated by close proximity. Not having right and wrong was a standard of the group.

Standards quite definitely do change; not usually with the vividness of the previous example, but change they do. The changes are not brought about by individuals, nor by what Cooley once called the 'somewhat mystical' society, but by the associations between people – through group processes. New contacts and associations bring fresh experiences, perspectives and consciousness. In this sense, the individual is not the causal factor in social change. But, there again, neither is society, which has no status independent of the people who comprise it. The cause emerges in the relations between individuals; it is an emergent property which has no presence separate from humans, yet resides with no particular individual.

The conception is consistent with Cooley's overall view and this is, as we will see in Part Three, interestingly similar to Durkheim's in this respect. Cooley's total dismissal of individual vs. society divisions forced upon him the need to theorize on the fundamental nature of man and his role in changing himself and his environment. With his predecessors, James and Dewey, he conceived humans as having freedom, but not as having the freedom to exercise it without the co-operation of others. Freedom, in his own words, 'is team work.' He pointed to the basic fact of human nature: it is natural to form groups, and these commission the exercise of freedom.

The primary group, then, is crucial to Cooley's whole model. This is the first and most fundamental unit the individual encounters and it is through his involvements with it that he comes to be aware of who he is, to be cognizant of other people and objects in the environment, to be sensitive to others' thoughts and emotions, to be consistent in his interpretation of experiences and to be appreciative of basic moral values and ideals. Socialization is what we have come to term such a process, though it should be noted that Cooley at no times advocated a passive role for the individual. As a potentially free agent with will, Cooley's individual is a creative force; the will remains untapped until he interacts with others, but he is basically, potentially creative. Creativity could be expressed only within the context of the group and is, in no way, individually-attained, a view contrasting somewhat with that of Freud and others to whom social relationships work as restraint to freedom.

There is no place for biological or social determinism in Cooley's scheme, yet he does point to the invariant quality of human nature in forming the intimate associations of primary groups which are changeable in content but not in form; these 'are found everywhere and everywhere work upon the individual in somewhat the same way' (Cooley, 1964, p. 32). Everyone, everywhere is social and becomes self conscious only because of this.

There are, of course, objections to Cooley's theory, the major one being about his stress on society as a mental phenomenon. This detracts from the ways in which very real, material things impinge on our senses and structure our experiences, possibly to stifle our creativity in ways quite beyond the control of primary or even more complex associations. There is no role for political or economic power as determining influences in forcing so-called human nature into involuntary, restricting associations. However, these are criticisms by no means unique to Cooley's work and we will have to explore them in the wider perspective of all interactionist theories of the relationship between the individual and society. Breadth and range were given to this perspective by the contributions of, first, W. I. Thomas, and, second, George Herbet Mead; to these next.

### The definition of the situation

In an earlier passage, we came across the concept 'definition of the situation', and noted its importance in influencing thought and action. It refers not to the objective features of any given situation, but to how individuals involved in particular situations perceive and experience them; their subjective definitions of reality determine how they respond to them. Whether or not their perceptions are accurate or distorted is not the question, for, as W. I. Thomas, who coined the phrase, noted: 'if men define situations as real, they are real in their consequences' (1928).

This smacks strongly of pragmatism, especially that brand espoused by James who was interested in judging ideas on their consequences and not on their intrinsic merit. If a professional footballer believes a ritual haircut or the wearing of blue socks before a game will bring him good fortune, then pragmatists would not be concerned with the magical power of haircuts or hosiery; only with the player's on-field performance. If the player defines his strange actions as making him play better, then chances are they will.

Thomas' connection with Cooley and the pragmatists may, at this stage, seem tenuous, but all oriented their theories to the effects of ideas on

---

### William Isaac Thomas (1863–1947)

Known principally for his work with Florian Znaniecki which effected a retooling of early pragmatist and interactionist theory in order to equip it for empirical research.

Thomas, the son of a Methodist minister, joined the University of Chicago in 1895 and stayed until 1918, when he was fired on account of a minor infringement of the straight-laced sexual mores of the gentlemen and scholars.

social life. Thomas saw two problems as guiding his work:

1. The problem of the dependence of the individual upon social organization and culture, and
2. the problem of the dependence of social organization and culture upon the individual (1918, p. 20).

Whereas Cooley had dealt with exactly these problems by focussing on the personal growth of children and their involvements in primary groups, Thomas looked at the ways in which adults' consciousness are affected by changing situations.

*The Polish Peasant in Europe and America* (1918), which Thomas wrote with Florian Znaniecki, is probably the most thorough working-through of the concepts and theories of the others. The five volume work was first published in 1918 after a project on the massive Polish emigration to the USA in the early twentieth century (for background on the study, see Madge, 1963, pp. 52–62). The concentration on letters, diaries, notebooks and oral material for evidence reflected the author's desire to get at subjective experiences accompanying the adjustment to changing circumstances. They were interested in how the migrants defined the reality of which they found they were part in the States and how this affected their adjustment to their new context.

The definitions work as a kind of link between objective conditions and action, but they do not spontaneously enter people's heads. Those definitions are accomplished through interactions with others, at first through involvements in the primary groups. As we pointed out earlier, the concept of a chair is, in effect, an accomplishment of more than one human sharing agreed-upon meanings about a particular object; our contrasting example about the same object having meanings as a totem also holds. We have to learn to attach particular meanings to other things and other people for, after all, these are the very material of situations – things in our environment. At first, the family provides us with blueprints on how to define, or give meaning to, our environment and later we innovate on these through communication with others.

The definition of the situation, therefore highlights the paramount importance of consciousness in human behaviour, but also brings into relief the part played by sustained interaction of humans in endowing the environments and each other with significance and, in the process, creating reality. Here the subjectivist bias is still evident enough: the ways in which we register a particular present set of circumstances in which we find ourselves determines how we interpret what has transpired in the past and how we anticipate the future. This principle came to characterize the studies of later interactionists and was known as situational determinism and, as we shall see, the stress was squarely on how people deliberated before opting for a line of action.

Thomas takes the subjectivist stance, but, in developing his position so as to give presence to the definition of the situation, makes sure that social life is more than a mental phenomenon. For Thomas and Znaniecki, it must be seen as: 'a product of continual interaction of individual consciousness and objective social reality' (quoted in Meltzer *et al*, 1975, p. 27).

The subjective meaning we give to the others and to the objects of situations is critical in establishing social reality, but of course, there must be other people and objects to give meaning to. Maybe we can transpose this analysis with a straightforward behaviourist account. Objects in the environment are not stimuli in themselves, but become stimuli when they are defined as such. Skinner might offer a simple example of a man with a thirst drinking from a glass of water, in terms of deprivation of liquid leading to a condition of thirst, followed by the presence of a stimulus – a glass of water in this case – and then a response, drinking. No reference is made to internal states, such as what the individual thinks and experiences about his thirst. But Thomas and the others would say that the glass of water does not constitute a stimulus: it is defined as a stimulus by the drinker only in a specific context. This alternative to behaviourist theory implies, as we have detected, a much freer and more wilful conception of human beings than more deterministic models: people do not automatically react to objects in the environment. Persons deprived of liquid for prolonged periods might not define a glass of water as a stimulus if, for instance, they were Maze prison hunger strikers in 1981. An overarching political ideal supplied relevance to the context and influenced the meaning the prisoners gave to the objects of their environment. Twelve deaths in five months indicates the one-dimensional nature of approaches taking no account of meaning definitions.

Thomas and all the other theorists we have concentrated on in this section issued a challenge to the mechanical conceptions of man. The corpus of their work is a restatement of the problems of human autonomy, violition and innovation; problems that were, in a way, buried beneath the avalanche of scientific reasoning which came at the beginning of the nineteenth century. The guiding themes of thought we have considered surface in the work of all the theorists of this section from Weber to Thomas.

Important ones include: the interpretation of society and the individual; the unique capacity of humans to attach meaning to their environment; the reducibility of all social phenomena to the action of human beings; the apparent plasticity of man in being shaped by others; the importance of involvement with human groups; the formation of consciousness in the development of human relations; and the critical facility of humans to reflect on the past, the environment, each other and themselves, a facility which came with the power to communicate through human language.

Implicit in all these concerns is the question of change: if humans are subject to forces beyond their conscious control, can they be seen to have any say in steering their own futures and implementing changes as they deem appropriate? Or are they merely carried along by other influences? We have seen these concerns shine through the different but related concerns of the writers so far considered, but they were crystallized perhaps most significantly in the theories of George Herbert Mead, most of which were published posthumously from old lecture notes.

## Mead's social theory of mind

Let us begin with the behaviourist riposte to the set of problematical concerns characterizing the interactionist strain. Watson's positivist bent impelled him to deny the importance of conscious awareness: it does not affect the observed behaviour of creatures, animal and human, and so the framework of conditioning is perfectly adequate. As Weber had objected to the omission of meaning in analyses concerned only with observable phenomena, Mead criticized Watson on similar grounds.

For Mead, who was born in 1863, a year before Weber, the internal states of humans should be placed within the scope of scientific enquiry. Yet he accepted the behaviourist framework for such enquiry: he was impressed by the fruitfulness of studying relationships between groups and individuals in their environment, but not by the insistence that only directly observable phenomena be placed in the account. He accused Watson of 'emptying' the human of any social experiences not captured in the observable responses to stimuli. Like Weber, Mead recognized that

---

### George Herbert Mead (1863-1931)

He united a diversity of themes and insights in a theoretical system which later became known as symbolic interactionism. His influences was felt in psychology and, perhaps more profoundly in sociology, but he spent the important years of his academic career in the University of Chicago's department of philosophy under the headship of Dewey. He drew heavily on the pragmatists, but also on his contemporary Cooley and less visibly on the behaviourist Watson and Wundt, the German idealist. Published only isolated articles during his life and had his important contributions published posthumously after students had compiled his lecture notes.

what behaviourists called responses were impelled not automatically, but by intentions, motives purposes, in short, by meanings.

Mead would also have differed significantly from behaviourists in the establishment of focus for study: not stimuli in the environment as things which might elicit cognitive states, but those cognitive states themselves. Mead tied in with Thomas and the rest in studying the individual's subjective states, his definitions of situations, that is the meanings he gave to reality. As those meanings were thought to be not so much internal mental states but processes formed in human associations, Mead's analysis preceded with examinations of those processes: 'Social psychology is behaviouristic in the sense of starting off with an observable activity – the ongoing dynamic social process, and the social acts which are its component elements – to be studied and analyzed scientifically' (1934, p. 7).

Let us begin our interpretation of Mead with an example: a dog bares its teeth to another dog and the other responds to this as a sign that an attack is about to begin. This, for Mead, is nonhuman, social action; social because the actions of the second dog are based on the baring of teeth of the first; this is a gesture for the course of action which follows – a fight. The gesture has meaning: it signals the fight in the same way as a human might crack his knuckles or poke an index finger in another's chest.

Gestures are commonplace in human as well as animal conduct, but humans possess the capacity to talk, so we do not need to use gestures continually. 'I'm going to smash your skull' conveys the message without the unnecessary knuckle cracking or finger poking. Also, gestures are converted into language when a common sign is established by both utterer and hearer as meaning precisely the same thing. The meaning of 'bollocks', for example, means to the hearer that the speaker tends to dismiss something as implausible or of limited utility; which is what the utterer would intend. Language, in its more complex forms, operating within grammatical rules and common frameworks, makes possible a high amount of precise, integrated social behaviour unavailable to creatures without the facility. Note how Mead stays near a behaviourist terminology when he delineates how: 'Gestures become significant symbols when they implicitly arouse in an individual making them the same responses which they explicitly arouse...in other individuals...to whom they are addressed' (1934, p. 47).

Humans have the special capability to use significant symbols and this, according to Mead, 'makes the existence of mind or intelligence possible.' Mind, for Mead, was not a property of the individual, but a process emergent from human communicative transactions. 'Mind develops and has its being in and by virtue of the social process of experience and activity', Mead premissed his 'social theory of mind' (1964, p. 243).

Mead, like Cooley, believed the ability to reflect was an essential condition for the growth of mind. The individual, as we have noted, becomes conscious of others in childhood; he learns to place himself in their positions, simulate their attitudes and, crucially, to see himself as he feels they see him; he gains self consciousness. When this occurs, for Mead, the child has a mind, for it is through reflecting, turning back experiences with others to himself, that he takes on an image of himself. Language is a vital element in the process because it is through talking that we acquire the power to reflect, backwards and forward, inward and outward. This is always a fundamentally social process for as Mead insisted: 'Mind arises through communication by a conversation of gestures in a social process or context of experience – not communication through mind' (1934, p. 50).

In other words, we are not born with minds, as suggested by some philosophies, but we gain them through interaction with other human beings. Conditioning can account for some of the behaviour of early years, but, according to Mead's analysis, it cannot adequately explain the highly elaborate processes of learning connected with human communication. Of course, animals exhibit sometimes quite sophisticated learning abilities in the performance of behaviour that is not related to instincts or imitation, but is related to adapting to the environment. In certain situations, dogs run away from man not because they imitate other dogs, but because they link the scent of man with danger. The scent operates as a stimulus in much the same way as an assailant's swing acts as a stimulus to a defensive posture response.

But, whereas a human can tell another 'watch out for his left hook', a dog cannot communicate the odour he picks up to another dog. Without the capacity to speak, animals cannot think in the same terms as humans: they cannot use abstract categories to summon the past, analyze the present or project into the future (despite evidence about 'talking chimpanzees'). In a nutshell, humans can think imaginatively while animals think in the here-and-now.

By wanting to consider this crucially significant ability to imagine rather than stick with only directly observable phenomena, Mead broke with the behaviourists and sided with his American predecessors and, of course, Weber, whose concept of social action was predicted on the human ability to take into consideration and anticipate the possible outcomes of other action to imagine what they would do. This is a most anti-deterministic stance and it characterizes the whole of the interactionist strain of thought. Men's thoughts and, therefore, actions are not based on instinct, imitation or habit any more than they are based purely on past events. So, they are not predictable in any perfect sense. Their unpredictability is a product of the creative element of the human being. Even allowing for a perfect knowledge of biography and all contingencies, we could still not predict men's thought and actions, according to Mead. This creative element in man lies at the base of Mead's analysis which builds on James' distinction between the 'I' and the 'Me'. The property of mind and the capacity for intelligent action is possible because man can become an object to himself, as we have noted, by taking up the attitudes of other people towards him.

Mead integrated James' concepts into his overall theory by making the 'I' represent the spontaneous element of consciousness and the 'Me' that part of consciousness moulded and shaped by other people in society. Further, conversations between the two are carried on in Mead's analysis. The impulsive 'I' might register extreme anger with reference to the referee of a soccer match and we might want to attack him violently. The 'Me' has, in the course of interactions, appropriated the norm that such things aren't done – well, not usually, anyway. In Mead's view the conversation would go something like: 'I' – 'Go on, run on the field and hit him!' 'Me' – don't do it, it isn't appropriate behaviour.' But – and it is a big 'but' – the 'Me' is never totally regulating: 'The structure of the 'Me' does not therefore determine the expression of the 'I' (1934, p. 210). There are always those occasions when the 'I' eclipses all social rules and conventions and the individual spontaneously and uncontrollably follows his impulses. A few battered referees can attest to that.

The 'I' has a certain ungraspable quality: it is always in process and cannot be thought about. Once we do think about 'I' it is already 'Me'; the 'I' is the actual process of thinking. It appears only in our memories and the act of remembering converts it to a 'Me', an object of thought. The 'Me' as a social concept can be thought of as the organized attitudes of others as we assume them to exist and, as such, it acts as restraint on the innovative, impulsive 'I'. Superficially, then, there is a resemblance to Freud's theory of the id, ego and superego, as we shall see later, though this theory is highly deterministic in claiming that nothing happens without a cause – in this case stemming from psychic energies. However, with both parties, there is an everlasting tension between the impulsive and the constraining elements, the former biologically endowed, the latter socially bestowed.

The 'I' responds to the tension by adapting, thus shaping the person's total self and, in turn, shaping the social environment of which he is part. This is an important point in Mead's formulation and one which tends to be glossed over by those accusing him of one-sided subjectivism. Mead acknowledged both that the human is subject to pressures, influences and controls from outside him, his environment, and that he is able to implement changes in that environment. The 'I' is always an implicit resistance to conformity and this gives the individual the potential for creativity and free expression. With the pragmatists, Mead stressed the very active role that men play in shaping their environments and their destinations.

This is a dialectical view of the individual and society because although, as Mead put it, 'the community exercises control over the conduct of its individual members' and 'community enters as a determining factor into the individual's thinking,' he always retains the capacity to change that community and is never wholly determined (1934, p. 154).

The community to which the individual belongs is the 'generalized other,' which Mead contrasts with 'significant others,' such as family members and personal friends of early childhood. As a way of bringing out the determining influences on the individual, Mead saw the child developing through a nondetermined 'play' stage in which spontaneous thought and conduct evolve, then through a 'game' stage when the child becomes aware of and internalizes the attitudes and roles of other people in his environment. At this game stage, outside, determining influences bear heavily and Mead illustrated this with an individual involved in a game of baseball: 'Each one of his acts is determined by his assumption of the action of the others who are playing the game. What he does is controlled by his being everyone else on that team, at least insofar as those attitudes effect his own particular response' (1934, p. 153).

In game, the individual learns not only to recognize the existence of others, but to abstract himself from his own situation and become others, 'being everyone else.' He learns to take the role of the generalized other and, in an almost paradoxical way, gains new perspectives and consciousness of himself – who he is – whilst surrendering himself to a regime of control. Self consciousness and self control are concomitant developments and they are both made possible by the human capacity to communicate symbolically with language. Without this faculty, no meaningful interaction can occur.

In Mead's terms, the self as an object is something we can consciously think about and it arises out of such interactions between people and groups. Simultaneously, the individual is a product of group processes and a creator of those very groups. He is both controlled and controller.

In formulating his social theory of mind, Mead also developed what he felt to be an improvement on Cooley's theory and an alternative to behaviourism. Substantially, he was in agreement with Cooley, but wanted to give more emphasis to the objective dimensions of the physical and social environments with which individuals interacted, rather than examining them as they appear in the subjective imaginations of people. We have seen how he went about trying to restore the humanity of which he believed behaviourists had emptied the individual and, before assessing how successful he was in uniting this with a social theory of mind, we might briefly recapitulate on the ingredients of Mead's mixture.

Mind is not regarded as some property of the individual existing separately from society, but it is more a process emerging from the interactions of people in groups, communicating symbolically through the medium of language. To achieve this, the child passes through the play stage and, more critically, the game stage where he becomes aware of the consciousness of others and thus subjects himself to a degree of control. He becomes conscious of himself as a self, an object, and this for Mead has two phases: the impulsive 'I' and the social, constraining 'Me'. These two are in constant tension and adaptation, the 'Me' setting limits, though not always completely and successfully for Mead, for the expression of the 'I'. The total 'Self' is seen as a social process going on with these 'two distinguishable phases.' The separation of the two enables the individual to step outside himself, take the attitudes and roles of others, to see himself as others would. It also gives him the power to reflect: to look back to the past or look into the future and relate these to immediate circumstances, to interpret past and future by locating them in the present situation, a theme explored by Thomas and Znaniecki, of course,

We see then that the splitting of the 'I' and the 'Me' is absolutely central to Mead's model. Without the separation, the whole edifice crumbles because we have no conceptual way of seeing how and why reflection can take place; therefore no possibility of meaningful transactions or interactions using symbols. Also the human's proclivity to innovate, create and, generally, operate in novel ways, is ultimately reducible to the 'I-Me' split and the tension which ensues. However, this is the source of problems which were inherited by later interactionists.

Mead's avowed intention was to produce a social theory of mind: he wanted to remove any taint of the metaphysical, in order to make the mind unmasked and unmysterious. He wanted to depict human beings as nothing if not social creatures. Theories which held that human nature existed independently of society were of no use to Mead. Equally as useless were speculations about the human soul or psyche. Mead wanted no distinction between the individual and society. They were not two elements but bound together in one whole: they were, in effect, part of each other. And this contribution alone was appreciable in its impact on subsequent social theory.

Although he made Watson's behaviourism the subject of attacks, Mead seems to have been influenced by it on two levels. First, and most obvious, is the way in which behaviourism was vehement in its disregard for exactly the same kinds of intangibles to which Mead objected; it took a hard, scientific, empirical approach to the study of man and Mead wanted to follow this. Also, Mead was obviously impressed by the basic tenets of behaviourism in the sense that it located the critical factors governing social life as not in the individual, but in his relations with the environment. Behaviourism at least attempted a social theory of man as opposed to an individualistic one and Mead, though taking issue with its relentless dismissal of subjective states, sympathized with this.

We can see his debt to behaviourism reflected in his terminology: 'Stimuli,' 'responses,' 'function,' 'conditioning' crop up in Mead's writing time and again when modifying the conceptual apparatus of behaviourism. For example, symbols, 'instead of being a mere conditioning of reflexes, are ways of picking out the stimuli so that the various responses can organize themselves into a form of action' (1964, p. 185).

There is a basic acceptance of behaviourism in Mead's formulations. But he insisted on adding important dimensions to gain a further appreciation of human action:

> For the conditioned reflex – the response to a mere substitute stimulus – does or need not involve consciousness; whereas the response to a symbol does and must involve consciousness. Conditioned reflexes plus consciousness of the attitudes and meanings they involve are what constitute language, and hence lay the basis or comprise the mechanism for thought and intelligent conduct (1964, p. 184n).

'Conditioned reflexes plus consciousness,' then, are Mead's most basic requirements. But the addition of consciousness in itself effects no decisively significant diminution of the behaviourists' explanatory power. The processes underlying consciousness, such as the taking of the role of the generalized other, the appropriation of others' attitudes, the internalization of others' awareness, we learn through communicating with other people and, at the same time establish bases for forms of action. Our selves and actions are taken ultimately from our internalization of others' attitudes, roles and awareness; and the behaviourist, as we have seen in the book's first section, would have no trouble in explaining this within his analytical framework.

But Mead wanted not only to add to the behaviourist model, but to go beyond it. Whereas Watson and the others had emptied man of vitality, ingenuity and creativity, Mead wanted to refill him with precisely those properties. The pragmatists had also borrowed heavily from behaviourism, but favoured seeing men as having the intangible property of free will. Following this example, Mead took from James the concepts of 'I' and 'Me' and with these prised open a gap between himself and the behaviourists. In doing so, however, he diluted what he intended to be a social theory and left it, rather inadequately we feel, as partially social.

When Mead's theory is broken into its component parts, the creative force in human beings has to stem from the 'I': this impulsive phase of our self is the only element that somehow resists the socialization processes brought about through our social transactions. As William Kolb detects: 'the "I" becomes accountable for everything that cannot be explained by the organized set of roles which the individual takes over in the process of social interaction' (1967, p. 242). Mead himself acknowledged: 'The "I" gives the sense of freedom, of initiative' (1967, p. 177).

The 'I' seems to be Mead's bulwark against accusations that he depicted man as only the recipient of social forces, though some commentators, like Charles Gillin, crititicize Mead for his apparent determinism in regarding society as temporally prior to mind and the cause of the development of mind; so action is purely mechanical in the manner suggested by behaviourists (1975). In a different perspective, G. Gonos blames Mead and later interactionists for being too voluntaristic and neglecting social determining influences (1977). Both critiques have only partial validity, and we believe Mead's attempt to preempt them to be unsatisfactory too. It seems Mead's attempt to produce a fully-social theory is successful only if we ignore the presence of the 'I', which is not a social concept but has some other indeterminate status. Indeed, at stages, Mead terms it the 'biologic I,' and writers such as Irving Zeitlin have stuck to an organic interpretation of it: 'it is the impulsive tendency to act or react to a certain stimulus "under certain organic conditions. Hunger and anger are illustrations of such impulses" ' (1973, p. 228).

But also, according to Jeff Coulter: 'there are several metaphysical aspects to it.' The 'I' is 'the inviolable determinant of creative conduct' (1979, p. 112). It is the concept Mead uses to prevent man becoming a predictable recipient of social processes. It is not a segment of the social character of man, but it is always, to a degree, in tension with this character. As such, it is a pre-social concept; it exists prior to, and independent of, social experience and, if it is to play such a pivotal part in energizing Mead's whole theory, then it rather detracts from the social nature of that theory. If it is not a social concept, then it has some other status, biological or, as Coulter emphasizes, metaphysical. For all Mead's efforts to make what had been for centuries a vague, psychological or philosophical concept called mind into a fully transparent social phenomenon, he backslides with the introduction of the 'I'. It is equally as vague and sheds no explanatory light on the creative element of man for which it is deemed to be responsible.

Mead's theory, then, sits awkwardly on the fence dividing determinism and voluntarism. His general analysis broadens the framework of behaviourism without substantially undermining the premises of the approach. The modifications he affected were aimed at depicting man as a creative, constructive innovative being who realized his potential through interactions with others. But in doing this, he did damage to what he considered a social theory of mind and left it as a less-than-social theory with limited explanatory power in the field of human thought and action.

Later interactionists like Herbert Blumer and Manford Kuhn were to express misgiving about Mead's nebulous construct of 'I' but nevertheless accepted his overall contribution to social theory and methods. They were but two of many different thinkers who were to fashion their own versions of Mead's seminal account and, in the process, form the modern school of symbolic interactionism. This school will be the subject of the next chapter.

## Technical Terms

**Autonomy:** The right of self-determination. The possession of freedom of will and, therefore, of cognition.

**Creativity:** The human ability to be inventive and imaginative as well as exercising routine skill. The anti-determinist model of man holds that all humans have this essential ability

**Culture:** A configuration of ideas, beliefs, values, norms, standards, customs etc. shared by a particular population or sector of a population. Crucially, this is not static, but can be transmitted from one generation to the next via learning.

**Definition of the Situation:** A term originally coined by W. I. Thomas in the 1920s, it refers to the way in which people perceive and experience the situation in which they are involved. The importance of subjective experiences is summarized in Thomas's classic line: 'If people define a situation as real, it is real in its consequences'.

**Dynamic:** Not, as in popular usage, meaning sensational or marvellous, but referring to the energizing or motive forces of social phenomena; the elements or processes which give things vitality or movement. Theories about living matter, mind and society must include a dynamic element unless they are to be useful only as descriptive accounts of how things are as opposed to how they move and change.

**Dialectical:** In Mead's model, this is taken to refer to the process whereby the child gains perspectives of himself as reflected off others, but always contributes to the process himself by creatively interpreting the views of others, i.e. it is never a one-way process.

**Metaphysical:** This refers to the attempt to explore the realm not in any way at all accessible to human sense experience. The metaphysical lies beyond human comprehension.

**Volition:** An act of will preceding movement. An automatic knee jerk is not volitional, whereas lifting a foot to kick an object is intended – it is willed by the kicker and is volitional.

## Further Reading

*The Making of Symbolic Interactionism* (1979) by Paul Rock discusses many of the issues raised by Thomas, Cooley and Mead, particularly the concept of self, in chapters 4 and 5.

*An Invitation to Sociology* (1971) by Peter Berger uses many interactionist insights, particularly in chapter 5, to present 'a humanistic perspective'.

*20th century Social Thought* (1980), 3rd edition, by Ray Cuzzort and Edith King contains a chapter summarizing Mead's task as establishing the 'foundations of humanity.'

## Advanced Reading

*On Social psychology* (1964) by G. H. Mead is neatly edited by Anselm Strauss so as to provide a thematic account of Mead's theories.

*Human Nature and the Social Order* (1964) by C. H. Cooley stands as a classic text, written flowingly with the authority of a theoretical prophet, who states: 'Society, then, in its immediate aspect, *is a relation among personal ideas.*'

*Social Interaction and Consciousness* (1979) by P. D. Ashworth is a critical evaluation of the contribution of Mead and the others to the understanding of the consciousness-social interaction link.

# 6

# Society as Process

**Disembodied society**
There is an automobile accident on a west-bound freeway: an articulated truck jack-knifes, shedding its load and wrecking four other nearby vehicles; traffic comes to a standstill. Travel on the east-bound lane begins to slow as drivers take time to view and examine the wrecks; eventually, a tail-back forms and traffic congeals, thus bringing a halt in both lanes. In one light, the vehicles' immobilization is a direct response to the stimulus of a crash on the opposite side of the freeway. In another, it is symbolic interaction.

'Anything of which a human being is conscious is something which he is indicating to himself – the ticking of a clock, a knock at the door, the appearance of a friend, the remark made by a companion, a recognition that he has a task to perform, or the realization that he has a cold', wrote Herbert Blumer. 'The conscious life of the human being, from the time that he awakes until he falls asleep, is a continual flow of self-indications – notations of the things with which he deals and takes into account' (1962, p. 181).

Following Mead, Blumer took 'the ability to act toward himself as central mechanism with which the human being faces and deals with his world.' It is 'a mechanism for making indications to oneself' (1962). In the above example, the object, that is what the passing driver indicates to himself, is the accident, and, in Blumer's perspective, this is different from

---

**Herbert G. Blumer (1900–    )**
He began doctoral work in 1925 at the University of Chicago, where he was influenced by Mead. He coined the term 'symbolic interaction'. In 1952, he moved to Berkeley.

a stimulus. It doesn't have an intrinisic character that impresses itself on the individual and that can be identified apart from the individual. Rather, the character and meaning of a road accident is something conferred on it by people. The end result of a total traffic standstill, therefore, involves a complex social process quite independent of the actual crash: tens, even hundreds of drivers designate the event, in Blumer's (and Mead's) terms, the object to themselves, interpreting it, giving it meaning, judging what relevance it has for their future actions and making decisions on the basis of that judgement. Deceleration results, leading to a progressive slowing so that, eventually, drivers some miles back who are not even remotely aware of the original object, the crash, are significantly affected to the point where they are forced to stop: traffic jam.

Throughout our lives, we are involved in similar, if small scale, processes of designating objects to ourselves: using a hairbrush to groom our hair, right through to planning our occupational lives. We are surrounded by material things in our environment, by people and events; yet these are not stimuli to us, but objects which we recognize, interpret and act upon. They have meaning for us, they are symbolic.

This is the first and most basic principle of Blumer's social theory, the first parts of which he developed in his article 'Social psychology', first published in 1937, in which he first used the term 'symbolic interaction'. Later, in 1962, he was to extend what is perhaps the most idealistic interpretation of Mead's concepts by describing 'society as symbolic interaction'.

In this latter, seminal article, Blumer brought out the implication of the 'mechanism' of making indications to the self: 'action is constructed or built up step by step through a process of such self-indication' (1962, p. 182).

We see, then, that self-indication is the central process in Blumer's account and it is, in his words, 'a moving communicative process in which the individual notes things, assesses them, gives them a meaning, and decides to act on the basis of meaning' (1962, p. 182). So although his main debt, he acknowledges, is to Mead, the continuities with Cooley and Thomas are also very obvious. And it is James' splitting the self into subject and object so that we are able to detach ourselves and think about ourselves, which forms a navigating principle for Blumer, for: 'The process of self-indication exists in its own right and must be accepted and studied as such. It is through this process that the human being constructs his own action' (1962, p. 183). In other words, all our conscious action derives from being able to think to ourselves in an instant: what does this mean to me?

Blumer added that the process always takes place in a social context. The attribution of meaning is never a solitary affair, as we have seen, for we learn what meanings to attach in the socialization phases. So we line our meanings and our actions up with those of others, thus anticipating their meanings and actions, a theme which has ran throughout this section. The way in which we do this is through what Mead called taking the role of the other, either a specific person or the 'generalized other'. Alignment of actions brings stability and, often, predictability to human interaction.

These three premisses underlie symbolic interaction:

1 Human society is composed of individuals who have selves (that is, make indications to themselves).
2 Action is not, as envisaged by more deterministic theories, a release or reaction, but is built up piece by piece.
3 Collective action is brought about by the process of aligning one's own intentions and actions with others'.

Much of this is repetition, albeit in a distilled way, of other concerns; but Blumer, in his time of writing, was trying to fly in the face of mainstream sociological and psychological theory, which he regarded as either too deterministic, insofar as humans were mere expressions of 'social forces', 'systems', 'institutions', 'norms', etc., or too artificial, insofar as humans were isolated, individualistic creatures strangely removed from real life day-to-day encounters with each other. He felt prevalent theories had denuded man to the bone and so wanted to restore 'selves' to them, which he believed are formed by the process of self-indication. Of course, humans are the recipients of many types of pressures or influences, but they also have selves, in Blumer's sense. They actively interpret the world rather than respond to it. Such a view is in very sharp opposition to the kinds of theories to be discussed in Part Three, in which, according to Blumer: 'The individuals composing the society or the group become "carriers", or media for the expression of such (transcending) forces; and the interpretative behaviour by means of which people form their actions is merely a coerced link in the play of such forces' (1962, p. 186).

Blumer insisted that human behaviour is never determined through the situations of which it is part. Not that he dismissed the notion that action is shaped: the situations to which people act have limits defined by 'social organization', or the framework inside which situations take place. Also, the extent of the social organization's influence is variable: in small, isolated primitive communites it is profound, but in modern societies influence decreases and, where new situations arise, it is nil.

Blumer has a consistent, coherent, logical view of man and one which permits him to make certain programmatic statements about research. Briefly, he advocated trying 'to catch the interpretative process' as it occurs in the experience of the human actor. This involves 'sensitizing concepts', ones which would alert us to and gain us insight into how the participants to situations define their reality. Gone were the grander analytical concepts of structure, class, culture and others. In this light, Blumer's following of Thomas' lead is expected; diaries, autobiographies, letters and interviews were to be the basic stuff of sociology and psychology and they were to be studied through a process of sympathetic introspection, a method not unlike Weber's *verstehen*.

Blumer, like many of the other theorists in this section, wanted to dismantle concepts such as social systems and institutions and make them intelligible as man-made, and nothing more. He is also perhaps more vehement than most in his repudiation of the role of 'psychological factors' such as drives, motives, attitudes, in producing social action. His emphasis on situations as the shapers of actions was also consistent with the others, though one is never quite certain about the part of social organization in influencing thought and action. In Blumer's words: 'Social organization enters into action only to the extent to which it supplies fixed sets of symbols which people use in interpreting their situations' (1962, p. 190). And, as we pointed out, it often 'does not shape the situations'. This has led some critics, like Zeitlin, to conclude that Blumer's image of: ' "Society" is thus nothing more than a plurality of disembodied selves interacting in structureless situations' (1973, p. 217).

In fact, Blumer was not quite as 'over the top' as this but nonetheless stressed that: 'Structural features, such as "culture", "social systems", "social stratification", or "social roles", set conditions for their [humans'] action but do not determine their action' (1962, pp. 189–190). So, whilst acknowledging the boundaries imposed by phenomena lying outside the individual, Blumer is at pains to retain the fundamental indeterminacy, unpredictability and novelty of humans for his analysis. Mead's influence is very apparent here though Blumer, like his mentor, never adequately spelled out whether the uncertainty that characterizes human conduct derives from the somewhat unsatisfactory concept of 'I', the impulsive tendency, or from an interplay between the 'I' and the 'Me'. Blumer inherited exactly the same tension besetting Mead's theory.

Whatever the source of creativity and novelty, Blumer asserted that these are vital properties and must take a central place in social analysis; the experience of the process of interpretation is what the research must 'catch'. So the tendency is towards what is called a 'naturalistic' perspective, stressing the necessity for studies of actual situations rather than either detached analysis or the artificial construction of survey studies or social experiments. This very pronounced subjectivist bias, of course, adds more fuel to the critics' fire. Richard Lichtman, for example, takes issue with this bias, insisting that: 'Human action can neither be understood apart from or solely in terms of an actor ... the channelling of interpreted meanings is class-structured and is formed through lived engagements in the dominant institutions of society which are class-dominated and bear a specific class structure' (1970, pp. 77–83). This Marxian critique dovetails with Zeitlin's and those of others to whom the subjectivist bias in tantamount to idealism and a neglect of the massive and urgent outside influences on human action.

The overall thrust of the attack is that Blumer's theory and, by implication, his method, by emphasizing the voluntaristic or undetermined nature of human action and concentrating on subjective aspects of experience, omits some of the more substantial influences affecting that action and restricting those experiences. 'If some men control property and other resources while other men do not, and the latter are able to earn their livelihood only by working for the former, would Blumer deny that the relationship is a determinant of action?' asks Zeitlin. 'Is prison a mere framework? School? family?' (1973, p. 217).

The question is whether Blumer's soft approach in delineating frameworks as limits to action does injustice to the ways in which such 'structural features' (his term) severely determine how we might think and behave. A similar criticism might be levelled at the whole theoretical strain, but it is perhaps most aptly directed at Blumer's extreme subjectivist stance. If, given Blumer's naturalist strictures, it is not acceptable for the observer to stand objectively and make inferences about his subjects using analytical concepts imposed on, as opposed to derived from, the actors, then, Zeitlin contends, 'it becomes crude positivism or empiricism for which the only reality is the immediately observable' (1973, p. 216).

The fundamental question remains and the argument still rages: as we shall see, there is no straightforward answer to the question of whether the social scientist should concentrate on the people he studies and try to produce statements about reality as his subjects interpret it. Alternatively he might attempt to distance himself and develop a more comprehensive, encompassing picture of reality which details the features of society unknown to the subject, but still massive in their influences on his thought, action and relationships.

Blumer quite obviously opted for the former approach. Later theorists, whilst working within the interactionist strain as we have outlined it, moved in both directions, either accepting Blumer's approach but elaborating on it in such a way as to accentuate his subjectivism, or to modify his position in order to incorporate those 'structural features' Blumer left out.

To close the last chapter, we indicated that Mead's theory contained a tension arising out of his pragmatist stress on human creativity and his behaviourist framework for the analysis of human development. Blumer was concerned primarily with exposing and refining the elements of

Mead's work, emphasizing the voluntaristic nature of man and, therefore, his creativity. The more deterministic strains in Mead were developed though the work of Manford Kuhn, who worked in the same period as Blumer.

Whilst beginning from the, by now, familiar conception of human capability to respond to themselves as objects through their capacity to create and manipulate symbols, Kuhn sought to embellish Mead's model by adding a more firmly contoured social terrain in which man could operate. Sheldon Stryker summarizes Kuhn's harder approach thus: 'Accepting the view that social structure is created, maintained and altered through symbolic interaction, he also regards social structure – once created – as constraining interaction' (1980, p. 100).

In practice, Kuhn tried to extract from Mead's theories the concepts he considered clear and defined enough to be used in research, and operationalize them. 'Self', 'social act', 'social object' became transposed onto a research setting and experimental conditions were established for tests using such questions as: 'Who are you?' or 'what kind of person are you?' (Kuhn's questionnaire quoted by Meltzer *et al*, 1975, p. 60). These were precisely the nomothetic, or generalizing, methods to which Blumer took exception and we presume Mead himself would have found them unsatisfactory (see also Kuhn and McPartland, 1954).

The difference in methodological outlooks has its root in a deeper philosophical layer, for Kuhn's vision of man was much nearer the behaviourists than Mead's. There was no consideration of the interplay between 'I' and 'Me' in the process of self formation. InABhn's model, the social 'Me' is the determining influence: the actor's definition of situations and of self were internalized in the process of interaction, but it is as if the human's creative role in the process is nonexistent, for the important, decisive influences come from others outside him. By banishing the impulsive and, as we have seen, puzzling concept of 'I' from the scene, Kuhn is able to remove an intangible that is not amenable to empirical research – certainly not in the form Mead intended it.

The upshot of this is that human thought and action is, in principle at least, predictable. They are determined by exterior factors, which, once known, can be analysed by their effect on the individual. Bernard Meltzer *et al*. put it this way: 'If we know the actor's reference groups, according to Kuhn, we can predict his/her self-attitudes; and, if we know these, we can predict his/her behaviour' (1975, p. 62).

Kuhn's was the first and, in our view, crudest attempt to link Mead's conceptual apparatus to a fixed positivistic structure and analyse human properties, individual and collective, by examining observable phenomena without recourse to the kinds of introspection advocated by Blumer. True, Kuhn did add a considerable social structure and gave it causal power in determining action, but the human's relationship to it was very mechanical. More sophisticated attempts to provide interactionism with more indentifiable referents outside the individual's consciousness – thus making it more sociologically viable – came through various other theorists, many of whom made capital out of the concept of role.

## Roles and Identities

Uniting all those in the interactionist tradition is the unremitting effort to dispense with reified social concepts, those that seem to have a status separated from man. If there is an essence of interactionism it is that the social world is a human production and nothing else. Ralph Turner took what he considered 'an ideal conception which constrains people' and showed how a role is not a position or category into which people slot, but a creation of human beings in interaction with each other (1962).

In Mead's theory, taking the role of other was a pivotal developmental process in the expansion of consciousness for it enabled the child vicariously to participate in another's realities, most particularly at the game stage. Turner objected to the notion of 'role-taking' as it implied 'taking the existence of distinct and indentifiable roles as the starting point' and offered instead the process of 'role-making'. This, he felt, moved the emphasis away 'from the simple process of enacting a prescribed role to devising a performance on the basis of an imputed other-role' (1962, pp. 21–23).

This is an extension of Mead's ideas about our being able to imagine ourselves in another's shoes and adjust and modify our actions accordingly during the interaction, trying to consider what he is thinking. Turner's argument stays with Mead's, stressing that symbols like particular words, dress, mannerisms and so on, act as clues to the other's thought and future behaviour. These are part of the 'imputed other-role': we act as if others in the interaction are playing roles in a similar, though much more fluid, way to actors with a script. This is only an assumption, but the others in the situation make similar assumptions about roles and this provides a platform for stable communication. In this way, people, whether acquaintances or strangers, are able to form basic expectations about each other and tailor their own actions to these requirements.

We might speak in terms of mothers, brothers, or salesmen, strippers, etc. and we certainly organize our actions in terms of what we expect from those roles. But, under the interactionist spotlight, no one is the incumbent of a position for which there is a fixed set of rules defined by culture. We infer the roles of each other, then test the inferences. I might be a strip club patron who makes certain inferences about the role of the performing stripper in much the same way as, if I entered a car showroom, I would make inferences about the salesman. The stripper and the salesman regard me in similar lights: as a club member or as a customer. Then we both tentatively test our expectations. I don't expect the stripper to emerge fully clothed and approach me extolling the virtues of Fords, anymore than I expect the salesman to start peeling his clothes off. But that doesn't mean they won't, so interaction is always more or less a tentative process, as Turner put it: 'a process of continuously testing the conception one has of the role of the other' (1962, p. 23).

Roles, then, undergo 'cumulative revision' providing a stable framework for interaction only for short periods. They are never fixed so that they ensure conformity from the actor and the nearest they get to this is in formal organizations where certain, specific demands are made of behaviour.

Turner's conception remains true to the interactionist line in depicting role as having no existence independent of the people involved in the interaction. We act as if roles were real and objective entities and have this view validated by the actions of others, but they exist in our imaginations. Sometimes we have the opportunity to test our imagined roles in face-to-face contacts; other times we have not, such as in the case of the murderer role — few of us have chance to relate to someone in the role of the murderer, fortunately. Nevertheless, we do group behaviour into consistent units which correspond to generalizable types of people, whether strippers, salesmen or murderers. Shaping roles in our minds enables us both to interact more smoothly with people we meet and make sense of those we don't.

During the course of the interaction, the individual tries to convey basic data about himself which will not necessarily be the same as data about the role he is creating. The car salesman may, in the particular interactional sequence, inform his customer of his role through appearances, gestures and expressions, but might at the same time harbour a conception of his true self which is at variance with the role. Turner developed this in two articles in the late 1970s, in which he merged the concept of role with that of self conception or identity and tried to link his insights with a broader vision of social structure (1976, 1978).

'The real self', according to Turner is a subjectively held sense which people have of who they really are, or, to put it in contexts covered earlier, the self as the object. 'The relationship between self and social order is put in more comprehensive terms when we distinguish between self as anchored in *institutions* and self as anchored in *impulse*,' suggested Turner (1976, p. 991). A person might feel his is 'really' himself when acting in an institutional setting such as at work or in a religious organization. Another might regard his true self as coming to the surface in more impulsive moments. American society has witnessed a shift in locus, 'from institution to impulse', as the subtitle of his article indicates. More and more people believe they can find their true selves in circumstances of lowered inhibitions and openness. It becomes evident that for the 'institutionals', as Turner called them, the making of a role in a formal organization would provide the opportunity for a synchronization of self and role, whereas for the 'impulsive', the process would be suppression.

We see that the interactionist conception of role allows that the individual has the awareness and ability to modify and control his actions in accordance with his anticipations of others' roles. Taking up this point, George McCall and Jerry Simmons, in 1966, published an ambitious attempt to unite symbolic interactionist conceptions of role with the process of identification, a process which they considered absolutely central to social life. *Identities and Interactions* was, in a way, an elaboration on some themes of Anselm Strauss' essay *Mirrors and Masks* (first published 1959; in UK, 1977), in which the act of naming or placing or categorizing others and one's self was stressed. 'Identification, in the generic sense', according to McCall and Simmons, 'consists of placing things in terms of systematically related categories... Identification in terms of broad social categories like military rank yields a person's social identity, as opposed to his *personal identity*, which is derived by identifying in terms of categories referring to unique individuals: categories like Sam Friedson of Pine Buff, Arkansas; Henry Jones of Pitman, New Jersey; and the like' (1966, p. 64–5).

Earlier, Strauss had attempted to pull out some of the implications of the interactionist approach to the study of identities, beginning by emphasizing the crucial importance of language for human action and identity: 'naming' meant implicitly making evaluations of persons and their acts and, of course, one's self and one's own acts (1977). He developed this into a discussion of the indeterminancy or uncertainty of identities in constantly changing contexts due to the open-ended, partially unpredictable nature of social life: 'interaction is guided by rules, norms, mandates; but its outcomes are assumed to be not always, or entirely, determinable in advance' (1977, p. 10).

Strauss was concerned with how we interact not so much as persons but as members of particular groups. The way in which we address each other hinges on how we classify each other in particular encounters and how we think of ourselves in particular contexts. Classification enters into everything we do, in the view of McCall and Simmons: 'For every plan of action, there is a classification of things in terms of their relevance to that plan. For the plan of "eating", for example, there is at the crudest level a classification of things into the broad dichotomous category set of "edible" and "inedible" (1966, p. 65).

When we identify people, we do so in terms of their social positions and so conjure up sets of expectations of them; these expectations constitute the social role and they are not adequate guides for future action, serving only as 'very broad limits' on the sort of behaviour that will be approved of in given settings. 'Wedding guest' is far too vague a definition to predict in any detail the behaviour of a particular guest at a wedding. What actually happens in the performance McCall and Simmons term the 'interactive role' and this is 'not specified by the culture but is *improvised* in some variable fashion with the broad demands of one's social position and one's character' (1966, p. 67). 'Character' refers to the conception we hold of our self, which acts as a filter through which the demands of social position pass. These elements and processes come together in what McCall and Simmons call 'The role-identity model.' They define role-identity as: 'the character and the role that an individual devises for himself as an occupant of a particular social position. More intuitively, such a role-identity is his imaginative view of himself *as he likes to think of himself being and acting* as an occupant of that position' (1966, p. 67).

This is how we envisage ourselves in social positions, and it is an idealized view insofar as it incorporates actions and abilities we would like to achieve but never consistently manage in day-to-day performances. Put badly, it is how we fancy ourselves; there are elements of Walter Mitty about us all, but it is on the more mundane level that our imaginings influence social experiences. We do not only imagine ourselves as the stud or the rock singer, but as the guy who summons up enough courage to ask the office girl for a date or who plays the piano at the club on Saturday night.

Role-identities may be idle daydreams but, alternatively, they might function as the primary source of daily plans of action. Inevitably, they take into account the reactions of others to one's hypothetical performance, such as the expression of envy on a colleague's face when he hears of the date with the office girl. The colleague might even be imaginary. For that matter, so might be the office girl. People and events, real and unreal, are built into our role-identities.

Into the role-identity of Sarah Woodruff, *The French Lieutenant's Woman* of John Fowles' novel, were built fragments of a past affair which was never consummated. Community members believed her to have had sexual liaisons, thus breaching the mores of the period, and she incorporated this fiction into her view of herself, at one stage proclaiming to her eventual lover Charles Smithson: 'I am the French Lieutenant's whore.'

This was no titillating fantasy, but an intricate, imaginary event that loomed prominently in the substance of her role-identity and had enormous impact on how she conducted her social life. Generally, role-identities form frames of reference for appraising the thoughts and actions Mead would have called the 'Me'. Role identities give meanings to our daily lives because they determine our interpretations of situations, events and other people we encounter: 'By providing us with plans of actions and systems of classification, our role identities go far to determine the objects of our environment, their identity and meaning' (McCall and Simmons, 1966, p. 70).

The role-identity forms a sort of bridge between society and the individual in the sense that it resides firmly in the imagination of the individual yet is derived, partially at least, from social sources and, then, acts backs on society through determining our plans of action. What McCall and Simmons call the 'conventional contents' of role identities are acquired in the socialization process, so are learned from interactions with others. But, the image is not of a passive human accepting totally the conventions, norms, values, rules and so on, of others, for, according to McCall and Simmons: 'The conventional expectations provide the structural framework of a role-identity, whereas the individual embellishments put some human meat on these arid bones' (1966, p. 70).

So there are inevitable, idiosyncratic variations in role-identities. Not too much however: we modify and elaborate the culturally defined roles but, if we over-elaborate, the roles may become unrecognizable to others and we may be regarded as eccentric or even insane. But the tolerable limits of elaboration allow us to adjust our role-identities in accordance with what we perceive appropriate to the role of the audience: I imagine myself differently in the presence of friends in a bar than I do when having tea with the vicar; we classify the two sets of persons in terms of their social positions and structure our own role-identity accordingly. Role-identities change as persons and situations come and go.

Often, the fit isn't perfect and role performances in actual situations jar with our role-identities, and difficulties and embarrassments result. So we always have to devise perspectives that allow us to maintain idealized views of ourselves even though, at some deeper level, there are contradictions. McCall and Simmons say we 'legitimate' our role-identities in this way and it is accomplished in role performances, conducting ourselves in manners consistent with the contents of our imaginative view of our self. The reactions of others, of course, affect appreciably the role-identity, for they might confirm one's own view, thus providing 'role support.' Also, these supports are not merely perceived but are inferred and interpreted in a way consistent with the imagined self. More attention will be paid to the reactions from an 'important audience', such as the family, teachers or lovers. Because our role-identities are precarious, we need continual support. 'Like radio-active elements, role-support is unstable and decays as a function of time', reckon McCall and Simmons (1966, p. 74). So we must prove ourselves to our audiences day in, day out, demonstrating that our past performances can be replicated and also performing in front of new audiences which we feel the need to impress.

The model of man presented by McCall and Simmons is a complex one and it is given further depth by the fact that man is seen to have many role-identities, all influencing each other and ordered in tiers so that McCall and Simmons are able to talk of hierarchies of prominence. If we are particularly committed to a certain role-identity, then it ranks highly in the order of prominence and our performances will be constructed with care. We are seen to have vested interests in some role-identities more than others because we gain satisfaction, both intrinsic and extrinsic, from them. Here the authors bring in elements of Blau's exchange theory to highlight how we develop relationships in such a way as to derive gratifications from the performance of roles and the fulfilment of corresponding role-identities (see McCall and Simmons, 1966, pp. 76–82).

We have scarcely done justice to the intricacies of the McCall-Simmons theory, but, in this context, merely wish to abstract pertinent themes which keep them in harness with other interactionists. Their use of the concept of role-identity is ingenious and flexible in attempting to tie the individual, replete with creative imagination and self-interests, to the social structure which contains conventions, rules, norms etc. Many of the terms used by McCall and Simmons evoke a theatrical atmosphere: role, performance, audience, supports. Theirs is a systematic attempt to locate man and society in a dramaturgical perspective, meaning to see people as resembling actors in mammoth, elaborate, often unrehearsed, so frequently spontaneous, dramatic production – society as the ultimate complex play. But, whereas the work of McCall and Simmons is highly theoretical and lacking in detailed empirical study, the contributions of Erving Goffman to this perspective are based on the microscopic observations of human behaviour in everyday settings. We will now concentrate on his early writing which seems to enrich the interactionist strain.

**Back-stage with Goffman**

In one of his most famous examples, Goffman describes how a head waiter, when in the kitchen, might curse and remonstrate with the chef seconds before slipping smoothly into the restaurant where he is cool, dignified and deferential in the presence of his customers. The theatrical metaphor is employed to highlight how the waiter engages in 'impression management', creating a deliberate dignified air when 'on-stage' in front of his audience and relaxing this when 'back-stage' in the kitchen. Social life can be seen as this type of stage show writ large, with individuals conducting their lives in a sequence of performances, each designed to suit the particular situation as they define it. In attempting to avoid embarrassment or public humiliation, the individuals project images of themselves, a theme brought out in the title of one of Goffman's influential books, *The Presentation of the Self in Everyday Life* (originally published 1959).

It should be stated before continuing that, while Goffman's work exhibits many of the tendencies of the dramaturgical approach, it also shares themes with Georg Simmel's theories. Simmel, whom we considered briefly in Chapter Four, tried to build a 'formal sociology', by which he meant an attempt to capture certain shaped or patterned aspects of social life present in a variety of situations, possibly having no resemblance in content. He explored the influence of numbers on social relationships with 'dyad' representing groups of two and 'tryad' groups of three people. Simmel analysed in minute detail the differences between such groups in all sorts of contexts and relationships, always stressing their fluidity. A particular shape or form develops out of interactions and Simmel suggested that we can take groups with very different contents and see how they share similarities in the structure or form of relationships. Conflict might occur in religious groups, football clubs and economic institutions and, despite the different settings, they may show properties which provide the basis for a formal generalization. Breakdown of the structures of interaction in such groups might reveal opposition, association and cooperation.

Simmel's search for the invariant forms led his critics to conclude that he placed severe limitations on his analyses which tended to abstract from contexts and cut sociology from, as Pitirim Sorokin put it, 'it's other more vital parts' (1928, p. 313). Many years later, Alvin Gouldner was to make a similar criticism of Goffman's approach to the study of society which: 'dwells upon the episodic and see life only as it is lived in a narrow interpersonal circumference, ahistorical and noninstitutional, an existence beyond history and society' (1971, p. 379).

---

**Erving Goffman (1922–1982)**

Gained two graduate degrees from the University of Chicago, gaining a Ph.D. under Blumer's supervision in 1953. Worked at the University of California at Berkeley and the University of Pennsylvania. Adopted a dramaturgical approach to the study of social life staying in an interactionist tradition but drawing on the ideas of such people as Simmel, Burke and Sartre. In his later work, he turned his attentions to such things as the relations between men and women as implied in modern advertising (*Gender Advertisements*) and on language as a way of making gestures (*Forms of Talk*).

The reason for this criticism – and it is one frequently made of interactionists – is that Goffman studies society not by theorizing on power, structures and institutional patterns as they might influence life, but by focussing on interpersonal relationships as they actually happen. His sphere of operation is narrow, yet, within the narrow confines of the areas he studies, he attempts to find revealing themes which inform us about the operation of society generally. Whilst not denying the influence of certain functions and processes, he seeks to show how these are reflected in our behaviour.

Let us return to the head waiter: Goffman considers his behaviour as akin to theatrical performance. He has to communicate to others, whether they are kitchen staff or customers, who he is; he does this through his dress, his way of moving and talking, and through his props like trays or napkins. He convinces, or fails to convince, his audiences in much the same way as an actor does on stage. Our working day involves us in similar performances of theatrical proportions, in that we are continually communicating to others images or impressions of how we would like, and expect, them to perceive us. We organize our appearance, speech and mannerisms in such a way as to convey ourselves.

Like an actor, the individual leans on the support of others and they collectively operate as 'teams', all cooperating in sustaining mutually satisfactory images of each other, thus producing an orderly gloss to social life. In this way, Goffman depicts life as a sort of constant and continuous information feed, with all parties attempting to control the flow while simultaneously trying to process the information coming in from others. This general orientation takes Goffman to the face-to-face level of study, where he divides his analyses up into performances or, to use one of his terms, 'encounters' (1972).

In a way, then, Goffman goes behind what Thomas and Znaniecki called the definition of the situation, trying to pull out the parts played by each participant in producing a situation which is acceptable to all. When this doesn't happen and a failure to agree upon a certain definition threatens the interaction, embarrassment ensues and the actors must spontaneously evolve strategies for saving 'face', another concept used with effect by Goffman (1967).

There is the possibility of deceit in many of the encounters, for actors give the impression they find most gratifying a kind of idealized version, much like Turner's 'real self' or the 'role-identity' of McCall and Simmons. The individual is careful to edit the information he transmits in a way designed to elicit the image of what he would like others to see as his essential self. But, at the same time, he must show a different self in every different situation. The playboy of the nightclub situation presents a different self to the store assistant of the warehouse, even though they might be the same person.

Notice how Goffman depicts people not as respondents to stimuli nor derivatives of social orders, but as creative individuals always engaged in ingenious, spontaneous performances, working from ill-defined scripts about the rules, norms and values they are expected to observe, but continually innovating and constructing anew in each situation they encounter. In this, Goffman allows for the presence of Mead's 'I', though, in other moods, he seems to vacillate. On the one hand, he etches in great detail the manœuvres of creative people in their attempts to control their self conceptions in changing situations and, on the other, he alludes to a social order, lying outside the individual, which constrains and represses their actions.

This second strain comes out in a more defined way in *Asylums* (1961) when the previously unanchored, relatively unstructured presentations of the earlier book are transposed to the context of a total institution in which formally-administered rules regulate the daily lives of large numbers of inmates. They are constantly under the surveillance and control of a single authority, the focus of power. Goffman's actor is no longer a free-floater drawing on an extensive repertoire of roles and identities, but is forced into accepting relationships and associations with others. The script is supplied for him and there are no off-stage areas.

The beauty of Goffman's work is the way in which he teases out of this rigidly structured, debilitating institution, seams of an underworld in which the inmates create existences nearly, but not quite, independent of the dominant institution. A form of resistance takes place with inmates establishing 'free places' to construct relationships or hide the types of possessions they are supposed not to have. Ordinary items like mirrors and matches take on new significance. Personal territories are staked out. Property and places are structured in this underlife and raw coercion rather than formal authority is the cutting edge which slices them up unequally, thus creating a hierarchy. The inmates not only devise strategies for conducting a resistance to authority, but they also exploit their fellow patients to maintain an authority in the underlife.

What Goffman is putting across here is not simply an observation about an asylum, but about human beings' efforts to resist incorporation into a readymade structure. Alan Dawe considers Goffman's view a glimpse beneath the social system revealing 'the spectacle of actual people desperately trying to manage themselves according to its massively conformist demands, while at the same time attempting to preserve something of their individuality against its crushing weight' (1973, p. 250).

Those inhabiting Goffman's world always seem in control of themselves and their situations in the face of dominating and often stifling structures.

Their efforts are always directed at, to use another Goffman phrase, 'working the system' rather than being mere components of it. But, Dawe reckons, 'the pressure of that system is so great that their attempts can amount to nothing more than public performance and personal concealment' (1973, p. 250).

In Lamont Johnson's 1975 film *Lipstick*, we find the central character, Chris McCormack, a successful, celebrated photographic model whose life is a sequence of public performances in front of camera lenses and behind layers of cosmetics. Her public presentation of self as 'the woman every woman would like to be', as she puts it, seems to congeal with her private conception as she demonstrates a continuity of role performances. Then the public image is devastated after she is raped and is persuaded to press charges against her offender. The court case is made a media spectacle of a different order and she finds herself involved in a drama in which she has a new part: a raped woman seeking recompense – and unsuccessfully. Eventually, on an impulse, she discards her established roles to take revenge, gunning down her attacker with a hunting rifle.

The point about Goffman is that he allows for Mead's 'I' and uses this as a lever between overarching social orders like institutions or bureaucracies and the self. He demonstrates how, as 'creatures of variable impulse', humans are never just products of socialization, but always retain some essential part of their individuality. But, and this is crucial, it is '*against something*' that the self can emerge'. If the structure of the asylum is a condition for the emergence of an innovative self, then, Goffman asks, why can't this be true of society at large? The types of things social theorists conventionally think of as suppressing or even extinguishing creativity, like formal organizations and institutional areas, are, for Goffman, necessary for the development of the self, for it is in opposition to these that the self emerges.

This important issue of the autonomy the individual holds in the roles he plays forms a theme in Goffman's early work. His concept of 'role distance', for example, explores how people like surgeons and policemen manage to 'embrace' their roles yet confirm their individuality, perhaps not consciously, by revealing a detachment from those roles. The role becomes an object to the individual as he stakes out distance between his self and it, a theme explored in a different manner by Simmel. The chief surgeon jokes ironically in the midst of serious, and delicate operations. But his deviant inclinations are always to be seen in relation to the dominating surgeon role. As Goffman points out, his actions are to be seen as part of the process of 'unbecoming a surgeon', so the structured role with its expectations and obligations is still present even in the innovative acts.

Goffman's art – and many would argue that it is more art than science – is in extracting from endless everyday situations the seemingly insignificant features which help maintain order yet allow us to remain human. Stylized rituals, stage-managed impressions, role distances are invariant properties of social encounters regardless of the content or purpose of our motives behind them. 'Humanity as the big con' is how Ray Cuzzort and Edith King describe Goffman's view: 'To be human is to perform, like an actor, before audiences whom we con into accepting us as being what we are trying to appear to be' (1980, p. 288).

These rituals of everyday interactions express an orderliness at one level yet a resistance to order at another. By preserving their humanity in the face of what are perceived as externally imposed structures, actors create their own stylized social orders. These are novel, but always in adaptation to the overarching structure. In short, Goffman's man has freedom and the capacity to create, but realizes these only when confronted with what seems a massively dominating structure. Through his resistance to it, he develops his self and, in so doing constructs a micro-order complete with roles with his partners in the interactions.

Goffman's analysis, like Simmel's, concerns polarities of social life and men's attempts to reconcile them: the individual and the group, the need for individuality and conformity, for flexibility and stability. Individuals, whether in large, rigid institutions or in street meetings, form his focus and his method is pure observation and intuition.

Stratification enters his study of human conduct only when behaviour is interpreted as one-upmanship, or keeping a strategic edge in interaction. Power becomes a string of successful impression coups; class becomes a question of appearances. Life for Goffman is a rich and complex drama, but he avoids what many critics would contend is the important question: who owns the stage? Like other interactionists, Goffman reduces such phenomena as class, power, wealth and status to the everyday level and neglects the crucial ways in which these things set limits to our thought and behaviour in ways we may not immediately apprehend. Social reality is negotiated, as he insists, but this is not to imply that everyone has equal negotiating rights. Different individuals and groups bring unequal amounts of social power to their interactions and Goffman's treatment rather masks this. It is also masked in the work of a related group of theorists called ethnomethodologists.

## Society as a house of cards

The thread connecting the groups of theorists we will now consider with interactionists is that both regard everyday face-to-face relationships as the centre of interest in that it consists of meaningful communicative activity and involves mutual interpretative work. For them, this is the very stuff of social enquiry and it through its examination we uncover how social reality is accomplished.

The term ethnomethodology was coined by the American Harold Garfinkel to mean quite literally members' methods: the methods members of society use for making sense of familiar events and commonplace sences. His enormously influential work is a sociological development of the philosophy of, amongst others, Edmund Husserl, Maurice Merleau-Ponty and Alfred Schutz. Their approach became known as phenomenology, defined simply as an attempt to unravel human experience by studying the obvious. This involves trying to remove our assumptions, and making problematic those things we might normally take for granted, like, for example, seeing an elephant as a large grey animal with a trunk, tusks and big ears and assuming others see it as that; or saying something and assuming the hearer receives the message that you give.

Schutz began by agreeing with Weber that human beings attach meanings to their acts and experience the world with reference to others. But he thought Weber's scheme somewhat linear in its suggestion that an action holds a single meaning for the actor, whilst ignoring the way that meanings generally seem to be agreed-upon by more than one individual (1927). In other words, Schutz believed Weber had missed an important dimension of social intercourse, namely, the way in which everybody's understanding of the world seems to overlap in such a way as to make social interaction possible. Schutz wanted to open up for investigation this world of intersubjectively shared meanings and try to expose the ways in which obvious things we take for granted are the product of our agreement about the meanings of those things.

In the late '60s, Garfinkel tried to put some of these ideas into action in a series of 'breaching experiments'. Everyday situations based on unproblematic, taken-for-granted assumptions were disrupted by the intrusion of one of the experimenters who would pretend to suspend his

---

### Harold Garfinkel (1917-    )

Born Newark, New Jersey. Graduated from Newark 1939, received a M.A. from North Carolina 1942 and a Ph.D. from Harvard in 1952. He saw military service in the USAAF from 1942-46. Has taught at the Universities of Princeton, Ohio State, and at California at the Los Angeles campus where he has held a chair in sociology since 1966. His *Studies in Ethnomethodology* appeared in 1967. Garfinkel began a movement which rejected comparisons with other micro-sociological perspectives, and saw itself as challenging most of 'conventional sociology'.

shared meanings. A common greeting like 'how is your girlfriend?' would be responded to with further questions probing: 'What do you mean, "How is she feeling?" Do you mean physical or mental?' (Garfinkel, 1967, p. 42-3).

In another, students were asked to act like lodgers in their homes thus provoking confused reactions from others in the family with whom they pretended not to share assumptions. So Garfinkel took Schutz's notion of intersubjective meaning on which social order is said to rest and tried to uncover the methods by which it is accomplished or not accomplished.

Meaning, in the sense that interests interactionists, is not Garfinkel's concern, for he is preoccupied with *how* individuals make sense of each new situation by using shared meanings. The methods used in interaction form the focus of ethnomethodology: what actors actually do and say to keep the appearance of order. This is a public order: it is produced by people, is recognizable to them and is made to seem obvious. But Garfinkel's task is to spell out the activities through which this sense or orderliness is accomplished. Selecting psychiatric patients for treatment or discharge, handling juvenile delinquency, sustaining sets of informal rules at a prisoners' halfway house, identifying places in conversation when taking turns to speak – these are some of the activities occupying the research interests of Garfinkel (1967) and others of his persuasion such as Aaron Cicourel (1968), Lawrence Wieder (1974), Emmanuel Schegloff (1974) and the late Harvey Sacks (1974).

In all these studies, the methods used by 'members' of society to make sense of their situations and produce shared meanings are the topic of enquiry. In much social research, they are used implicitly as a resource and not regarded as problematic. This is one prong of the ethnomethodological critique of other forms of theory and research: other research rests on assumptions about the 'givenness' of phenomena from 'shared meanings' to 'social structures'. Ethnomethodologists, following Schutz, seek to uncover the procedures through which people achieve the meanings or gain a 'sense of social structure'. So, whereas the 'conventional sociologist' – as some are prone to call this straw man – might use statistics as a resource, an ethnomethodologist will examine the manner in which members of bureaucracies draw on background assumptions and various identifiable categories, and relate to each other so as to elicit an agreement as to what is recognized as a 'fact' which can then be used as a statistic.

Also, these activities, once researched, are not meant to provide the basis for a general grand theory on the accomplishment of social order, for the sense produced is done so by particular people in specific situations on certain occasions. As such, we have always to consider the practical reasoning work done *in situ*, in its original place, and not in an abstract way. Each piece of enquiry has to stand on its own. Whereas an interactionist talks in general terms of the definition of the situation, an ethnomethodologist continually asks about the actual process by which the defining gets done in each new situation. The meanings are accomplished anew by actors as they move through episodes and they have no relevance outside those episodes; they are indexed to the situation in which they were produced.

Social theories' neglect of indexicality in the pursuit of generalizable statements had led to the construction of what Thomas Wilson calls 'the normative paradigm', which he contrasts with 'the interpretive (*sic*) paradigm', in which 'definitions of situation and actions are not explicitly or implicitly assumed to be settled once and for all by a literal application of a pre-existing culturally established system of symbols' (1971, p. 69).

The relevance of this criticism will become apparent in the sections which follow, but let us follow through the ethnomethodological alternative. Everything is 'doing'. We 'do' bureaucracies, roles, identities; society itself is an act of doing. So research must be directed towards these activities as they happen in actual contexts, through communications in physical settings in which meanings are formulated and made 'accountable' – that is to say made intelligible to the participants creating the context (which is itself defined and described by them during the interactions, what Garfinkel calls 'reflexivity'). In doing this, Garfinkel contends, we try to 'remedy the indexical properties of members' talk and conduct' (1967, p. 11). We 'gloss' ambiguities and problematic features as they crop up and experience the social world as having a facticity or substance that is beyond and independent of us. Crucially, we are able to experience this precisely because we do not bother to investigate the methods we employ and assumptions we make in establishing sense. If we did, it would prove most disruptive, as Garfinkel's early experiments were meant to indicate.

Social theorists are members of society in the same way as everyone else. They do not have privileged positions, but operate at the same everyday levels, sharing the same assumptions, experiencing the same experiences and doing the same social practices as other people, with other people. The very doing of social theorizing could well be a topic of enquiry for ethnomethodology, for every social accomplishment, however seemingly mundane and trivial, is fair game.

It shares with interactionism and preoccupation with the minute, microscopical details of face-to-face encounters in actual settings (not hypothetical ones), an imperative to reduce constructs such as institution and class to social processes and a view of man as recognizably thoughtful and creative – not what Garfinkel calls a 'judgemental dope'.

Ethnomethodology is more unremitting in its insistence not to impose what Schutz called 'second degree constructs' and would therefore find the employment of such things as Goffman's dramaturgical metaphor unacceptable. But, as Stephen Mennell suggests: 'Schutz, on the other hand, I believe, to have intended his remarks in the contrary sense... he accepted such concepts as roles and goals... He admitted that a great part of social science can be performed "at a level which legitimately abstracts from all that happens in the individual actor" ' (1980, pp. 139–40).

There is a second divergent strand picked up by Anthony Giddens: 'Garfinkel has no interest in developing the kind of motive-analysis favoured by the former author [Schutz], but is concerned with how the "natural attitude" is realized as a phenomenon by actors in day-to-day life' (1976, p. 36).

This is, in our view, what distinguishes ethnomethodology from all other social theories and, in a way, prevents it from being a theory at all. Its concern is not with meanings, consciousness, identity or many of the other central concepts of interactionism, but with the process of doing social action. The question it asks of the social world is: How?

Predictably, it has been savaged by critics for its indulgence, its tunnel-vision, its general eschewing of the influential properties of social life – the 'Why?' aspects. There is a sort of impasse, however, because, if critics argue for the inclusion of such phenomena as structure, power, organization and so on, then they have to assume that the status of these is unproblematic. Ethnomethodologists would reply that these elements may indeed be important features of social life, but the production of them is identical to the assignment of sense or intelligibility to them, and to understand how they are produced, we have to identify the procedures used by people in making sense of them. This constitutes a considerable reorientation in social thought, and ethnomethodology has move phenomenology in new directions. What nags, however, is that people often have their lives affected by things they do not find 'accountable' and of which they cannot make any sense; and these, it could be argued, have more profound consequences than anything that might emerge out of everyday interactions.

Society is a prison with a difference: its prisoners busily keep its walls intact. So wrote Peter Berger: 'The walls of our imprisonment were there before we appeared on the scene, but they are ever rebuilt by ourselves' (1971, p. 141). The arrangement is possible because the prisoners do not apprehend the walls as products of their own activity; they apprehend them as if they were something else. They dehumanize their own construction. This is a key process in what Berger and his co-author, Thomas Luckmann, called *The Social Construction of Reality*, a synthetical work which blended the insights of Schutz with those of Mead, Cooley and others. 'Reification implies that man is capable of forgetting his own authorship of the human world, and, further, that the dialectic between man, the producer, and his products is lost to consciousness' (1971, p. 106).

The dialectic is summed up by the authors: '*Society is a human product. Society is an objective reality. Man is a social product*' (1971, p. 79). In 1966, McCall and Simmons wrote in an interactionist vein: 'Reality then in this distinctly human world, is not a hard, immutable thing but is fragile and adjudicated – a thing to be debated, compromised and legislated' (1966, p. 42). By a coincidence, the Berger and Luckmann treatise was published in the same year and began from exactly this foundation, that all reality, defined as things we cannot 'wish away', is precarious. It is created through the interaction of humans sharing intersubjective meanings. Yet, it becomes opaque to them and they experience it as something obdurate, standing apart from them and over which they have no control; it becomes an objective reality with firm, solid structures. We are brought up to accept its objectivity, and the rules, norms, values, beliefs and so on which are thought to be part of its structures enter our consciousness. This is how we become social beings: by inhabiting a world that is 'real' to us.

Mead's analysis of socialization provides the framework for the Berger-Luckmann theory. The human is born into a world that is preinterpreted; in other words, all people, objects and events have meanings and it is up to the child to apprehend them using those or similar meanings. He is taught to do so through interactions with significant others, adopting their attitudes and roles and making them his own. Eventually, he is able to divide his self and reflect. The significant others collectively function as Cooley's 'looking glass' and the child acquires a coherent and plausible identity from the attitudes first taken by others.

He simultaneously appropriates an identity and a world, the world as significant others see it. An identity is, for Berger and Luckmann, 'a location in a certain world', so, in finding his location, the child also discovers his world. These are two aspects of the one process of internalization, meaning the retrojection of the social world into the subjective consciousness. The choice of the word retrojection is telling, because Berger and Luckmann mean to convey that the world of things and meanings created by humans and transmitted through generations is turned back into the mind of the human and appears to confront him as an objective reality: 'The product acts back upon the producer', summarize Berger and Luckmann (1971, p. 78).

In their model, this amounts to a necessary paradox but to some critics, like Peter Hamilton, it is an unacceptable contradiction:

> For to posit that man is free to reproduce his social and natural conditions in limitless fashion and then to limit that reproduction in terms of a system of

external and internal constraints – institutionalization, legitimation and socialization – presents a contradiction that can only fatuously be called 'dialectical' (1974, p. 139).

Well, there are three moments in the Berger–Luckmann dialectical process. One is externalization, meaning that social order is not part of the nature of things, but is derived from man's inherent instability and the imperative that he, with others, provides a stable environment for conduct; he is biologically equipped to manipulate the external environment and, in the act, externalizes himself so that the way he experiences the world is reflected in the environment he creates. (This observation, as we will see, forms the basis of Marx's analysis; but Mead also used the interesting concept of a continuum between man and his environment as part of his critique of dualistic philosophies which made them appear as two distinct entities.)

Objectification denotes the human capability to express subjective experiences, principally through language, and make available to others inner feelings; man's ability to produce symbols with his language makes it possible to devise highly elaborate, abstract systems of meanings often far removed from face-to-face interactions: religion, art, philosophy and social theory (!) are examples of these.

The third moment is internalization and this refers to the re-entry of the elements of the social world into the subjective experience; this occurs during the socialization process which, for Berger and Luckmann – as with other interactionists – is a continuing process which lasts throughout the individual's life. Through the process, 'the reality of the social world gains in massivity'. (1971, p. 79). We rarely question its nature or its power. Institutions, or habituated patterns of activity, seem legitimate to us and this legitimacy is transmitted from one generation to the next.

These three processes happen simultaneously in socialization, which the authors divide into 'primary', that is, taking place in childhood, and 'secondary', in subsequent periods (resocialization is any induction to new realities such as those encountered in radical religious movements). Mead's analysis in this respect is vital to Berger and Luckmann, for, without it, the minute attention to the consciousness, the whole model of social structure is precipitated into a conceptual void. The continuing dialectical interplay between consciousness and society is the motor of the model. One cannot exist without the other, for we acquire consciousness through our membership of society and society does not exist without our being conscious of it (in the next section we will see how Marx used a slightly different type of dialectic to fashion his theory of society).

There is not a single reality, but rather versions of it, and Berger and Luckmann escape many of the criticisms levelled at others of the interactionist strain by incorporating the power dimension into their model.

Realities are legitimated: life must be made meaningful for individuals and groups, so there must be some sort of explanation, and justification, of why things work the way they do. People's acceptance of such explanations function as a means of social control or restraint.

There is an ever-present heretical tendency to develop deviant versions in contrast to the 'official' version. If it comes to a confrontation, when the deviant makes a challenge to the legitimate, there may be little in it in terms of intrinsic plausibility: 'Which of the two will win, however, will depend more on the power than on the theoretical ingenuity of the respective legitimators' (Berger and Luckmann, 1971, pp. 126–7). Put bluntly: 'He who has the bigger stick has the better chance of imposing his definitions of reality' (1971, p. 127).

The imposition is, of course, never complete and neither is socialization; otherwise there would be no social change and men would be little more than conditioned automata of their own manufacture. History suggests the opposite. To return to Berger's prisoners. Occasionally they 'de-reify' their environment and become aware of objectionable features of their existence which impel them to stop building and begin demolishing the walls of their prisons. And this possibility makes sure that: '*All* social reality is precarious. *All* societies are constructions in the face of chaos' (1971, p. 121).

But, some critics, such as Ian Jarvie, believe that reality is not so precarious and feel that it does have an existence separate from the consciousness of individuals. This view makes the prison analogy inadequate, for: 'The social world, like the natural world, is much as it seems. It is not a house of cards that will collapse if we blow on it' (1972, p. 146).

In a way, we could infer from this point a criticism of every theory considered in this section, even that of Weber who argued for the efficacy of ideas of changing social conditions. If we want a common denominator of all interactionists it is a commitment to the interdependence and interpenetration of consciousness and society, thus making the existence of society hinge on men's perceptions, apprehensions, beliefs, emotions and generally, their subjective states. This is not closeness, it is exactitude: society and man are one, not separate entities. The Berger and Luckmann account demonstrates a possible way in which man produces his society over and over again yet sees it as an independent object; yet it is never more than a continuing series of symbolic interactions. Men are biologically equipped with language and this enables them to to be meaningful, imaginative and creative in their constructions. The phenomenon of social order is their ultimate production. But it is a production based on a fundamental biological tendency. Berger, in one of his works on religion, makes the judgement: 'Men are congenitally compelled to impose a meaningful order of reality' (1969, p. 22).

Reality is socially constructed, but biologically compelled. This isn't entirely satisfactory in a social theory and it does tend to make the creation of order and stability into a subsocial or even suprasocial imperative, beneath, or unrelated to, social processes. Nicholas Abercrombie argues that: 'Berger and Luckmann are therefore obsessed with the necessity of certainty and they believe the basic mode of human cognition is the drive for certainty' (1980, p. 157).

Both sets of criticism arise out of the attempt of Berger and Luckmann to stay within the Meadian framework, build in elements of Schutz and yet make their model fully social without being deterministic. In delineating the process through which men create a social structure they upset those who wish to see such a structure as more powerful and constraining, and wielding influences on the shaping of human thought and behaviour. Yet, while they continually stress the creative nature of man, they never locate a social source for it and have to reduce this capacity to a biological cognitive drive for order and certainty.

In a way, these define two extreme positions through which Berger and Luckmann try to steer a middle course. There are theorists who would want to argue against their voluntaristic approach and give a lot more weight to factors lying beyond the human grasp in influencing, maybe moulding, thought and action.

Factors like this might be said to reside in areas external to the individual in the social structure, or internal in the biological or even psychological constitution. In both cases, the human's volition is diminished by the existence of structure. In the next section we will give such views close attention.

## Technical Terms

**Indeterminancy:** A quality referring to the unpredictable, perhaps unknown, parts of human relationships.

**Interpretive Paradigm:** A term of Thomas Wilson, who contrasts it with the *Normative Paradigm* of 'conventional sociology' which starts from the assumption that there is a social order 'out there' with values, norms etc. that are agreed upon. His alternative is to make problematic the status of the social order and try to investigate the ways in which people 'accomplish' reality through interpretative procedures.

**Nomothetic:** The mode of study seeking to generate or 'discover' general laws about all aspects of human behaviour, as distinct from the *Idiographic* mode that attempts individual, nongeneralizable descriptions of only certain aspects.

**Norms:** Rules, standards, procedures that people internalize and which act as guidelines for their everyday thought and actions.

**Phenomenology:** The study of man which begins from the inspection of one's own conscious experience. In this inspection, all assumptions about the external influences are suspended or 'bracketed'. More socially oriented phenomenology has attempted to study the more 'obvious' or taken-for-granted areas of everyday life in an effort to dig out the intersubjective assumptions beneath reality.

**Social Organization:** The way in which people in groups (or societies) assemble their activities in such a way as to make life orderly and, to a degree, predictable. The arrangement has an enduring quality.

**Reification:** For Berger and Luckmann, this is the process by which human beings forget or lose sight of the fact that it is they who construct society and begin to perceive the social world as lying beyond their reach. They see the products of human activity as facts of nature, or the results of cosmic laws or manifestations of divine will.

**Dialectical:** In the Berger–Luckman model, this refers to the 3 simultaneous moments in the creation of social reality: objectification, internalization and externalization.

**Indexicality:** An index is a pointer or a guide to something; an expression also points to something – its meaning. Ethnomethodologists claim the meaning of an expression is linked, or indexed, to the particular situation in which it is used (and they object to theorists who abstract from unique situations to make generalized statements).

For the ethno, each feature of a social scene is indexed to the actual context in which it is produced. Take the word 'racket': it can point to sports equipment, noise, a scheme for making money etc. The only way we know what it points to is by examining the context in which it is used. And this is one of the reasons why ethnos concentrate exclusively on particular situations rather than general analyses.

## Further Reading

*Sociological Theory: Uses and Unities*, 2nd edition (1980), by Stephen Mennell has an interesting chapter called 'The Mind and Sociology', in which ethno-methodologists are discussed along with Levi-Strauss, to whom we will be moving in the next chapter.

*The View from Goffman* (1980) edited by Jason Ditton is a collection of essays mostly in appreciation of Goffman, but with some relevant criticisms.

*Class, Structure and Knowledge*, (1980) by Nicholas Abercrombie is about the sociology of knowledge but contains chapters on Schutz and Berger and Luckmann which summarize competently both their works.

## Advanced Reading

*Studies in Ethnomethodology* (1967) by Harold Garfinkel is a very difficult, technical work and hardly for apostles seeking first principles. It does, however, contain accounts of Garfinkel's early experiments and so gives some idea of the early ethnomethodological thrust; very much a 'bible' for ethnomethodologists.

'Exchange as symbolic interaction' (in *American Sociological Review*, 47, 1972) by Peter Singleman explores the convergences between interactionism and exchange theory noting that many of the concepts explicitly used by interactionists are implied in the work of Homans, Blau and others.

*Role Theory* (1979) by Bruce Biddle is one of the most up-to-date and comprehensive accounts of the use of the concept of role in social theory.

## Theory into action

# Sexual deviance

Kenneth Plummer's study, *Sexual Stigma* (1975), is an account of sexual deviance in an interactionist perspective. By taking an area traditionally reserved for psychologists, physiologists or clinicians and treating it as a viable area for interactionist interpretation, Plummer tries to show how even the most personal, private, often secret, aspects of our lives are massively affected by social influences not only at the lofty levels of laws, norms and standards but also at the interpersonal levels.

He prefaces his analysis with quotations from Blumer and McCall and Simmons, the latter indicating the fragility of social reality and the persuasiveness of particular groups in having their interpretations ratified as 'true reality': 'Those who do not [succeed] are relegated to the fringes of the human world, are executed as heretics or traitors, ridiculed as crackpots, or locked up as lunatics' (1966, p. 42).

Though not executed nowadays, sexual deviants are often locked up and frequently ridiculed. People labelled fetishists, pedophiles or homosexuals are popularly regarded as having a pathological or, in some way, abnormal, 'condition'.

True to the interactionist strain, Plummer abandons the notion of an overarching natural order and contends that what appear to be 'natural' are man-made productions. Sexual experiences and objects fit into this category. Whilst not denying the reality of such biological 'facts' as orgasms and genitalia, Plummer insists that the meaning we attach to them is a product of learning through symbolic interaction. He quotes Manford Kuhn thus: 'Sex acts, sexual objects, sexual partners (human or otherwise) like all objects to which humans behave are *social objects*... The meanings of these social objects are mediated to the individual by means of language' (Kuhn, 1954, p. 123).

Plummer summarizes: '*Sexuality is a social construction learnt in interaction with others*' (1975, p. 30). It follows that there is no absolute, invariant series of sexual norms that holds throughout time and space. In modern western societies, the norm may be heterosexual, coital sex in a missionary position performed in the bedroom at night, preferably in wedlock. Deviation from this standard is tolerated, but once the limits of tolerance are crossed, the issue becomes problematic and may be designated as undesirable, even dangerous. Adult sexual attraction to young children, for example, brought pedophiles into the public eye in the late 1970s and they became the recipients of stigmata.

But, whereas pedophilia is stigmatized in contemporary Britain, man-boy sex play is openly accepted in Melanesian society – as R. C. Suggs (1966) points out. In different historical periods and in different cultural contexts, similar behaviours may be given entirely different meanings. The ancient Greeks' experience of all-male relationships had an entirely different meaning to homosexuality in Britain in the '80s; and the Eskimos' form of wife-exchange cannot meaningfully be likened to the urban wife-swapping scene.

Not only do sexual meanings vary across cultures, but within cultures: a man placing his fingers in a woman's vagina may be sexual in one context, but completely asexual if the man is a gynaecologist and the setting a clinic. The participants to this scene would, we presume, define the situation in terms of a medical internal examination rather than sexual foreplay, so the interaction would be structured accordingly.

Plummer draws on the work of Berger and Luckmann to highlight how humans are born into a 'pre-existing sexual world with its own laws, norms, values, meanings on the cultural level ... [it] exists independently of any specific actor, confronts him as massively real, and exerts a tacit power over him' (1975, p. 40). In other words, the standards of sexuality we observe and break are not our own inventions, though in learning to accept them, we give them sanction and support, and add more weight to the feeling that they are 'right'.

'Deviance', according to Howard Becker 'is not a quality of the act a person commits but rather a consequence of the application by others of rules and sanctions to an offender. The deviant is one to whom that label has successfully been applied; deviant behaviour is behaviour that people so label' (1963, p. 9). This is the central insight in the interactionist interpretation of deviance and it guides Plummer's account, which concentrates on homosexuality. He is not interested in the ultimate causes of sexually deviant behaviour for these are of little concern to an account which focusses on the reaction to acts rather than on the motives behind the acts themselves. Plummer's emphasis is on: the general process of becoming sexually different; the process of how sexual 'problems' become defined; and the interplay between subjective experiences and reactions towards them as deviant (1975, p. 45). This approach avoids divorcing the deviant from the social context, a practice which makes him appear psychologically pathological or just plain sinful.

One implicit ambition of Plummer's analysis is to shake us into recognizing that what we unreflectively regard as normality is a lot more problematic and precarious than we might at first think. He does this by studying the meanings certain experiences have in society and how those meanings get transformed. Homosexuality is a case in point and, although not entirely adequate, laws at first against and then permitting this 'abberant' practice indicate changes in the meaning attached to it.

Also, he looks at the critical variable of reaction, asking: 'Who is reacting – self, significant others, control agents, media etc.?' A particularly volatile reaction against a form of sexual behaviour can force it underground, thus stigmatizing those practicing it. In a different volume, Plummer looks at the sometimes hysterical reactions to pedophiles (1981, pp. 221–50). He is also particularly concerned with the way in which such reactions affect the deviant: he might adjust conceptions of himself to bring them into alignment with others', or possibly neutralize reactions by insisting they are inaccurate or misplaced. 'Self-labelling,' is the term Plummer chooses to express the way in which the deviant reconceptualizes his experiences and identity and he locates phases or 'turning points' in the process of stabilizing an identity. The ability of the human to become an object to himself, and to indicate objects and actions to himself, of course enables him to reformulate his identity at these turning poings: a sort of 'perhaps I'm not really what I thought I was before' mechanism.

Plummer's treatment of sexual deviance is not deterministic in the sense of suggesting that homosexuals actually have to be reacted against by members of society or that, when so labelled, they will automatically acquiesce: 'I suspect that most homosexuals are never publicly labelled and that self-labelling is much more important an area for analysis. Likewise some individuals who are publicly labelled as homosexuals may spend considerable time neutralizing or disavowing such labels' (1975, p. 202).

The title of Plummer's later book, *The Making of the Modern Homosexual* (1981), reflects his approach to the subject: underlying human action is a ongoing process of interaction between selves and others 'in which life is constantly built, altered but never completed'. The homosexual is not a type of person who has always been with us. But ways of experiencing sexual attraction and gender behaviour are products of historically specific cultural milieux. In short: they are not born, but made socially. Plummer presents a model of sexual deviance which contains many interactionist elements. It is underscored by the assumption that man has freedom of action and that he is constantly negotiating an emergent social reality through negotiations with others. 'He is only marginally restrained in his daily life by the tyranny of biological processes, and then sets about analysing the ways in which sexual meanings are constructed, modified, negotiated, negated and constrained in conjoint action with others' (1975, p. 29).

An appreciation of the social context is necessary for comprehending sexuality as it is commonly experienced, because man does not just act on the basis of biological forces or instincts; 'rather he constantly sets about interpreting inner feelings and making sense of the world around him' (1975, p. 37).

Plummer sums up his own interactionist position by stating: nothing is sexual but naming it makes it so. It is symbolized by humans in their interactions and is transmitted through generations via language; we learn about sex and impute to it meanings in a way of which animals are not capable.

The rejection of determinism in favour of 'marginally restrained' freewill; the pliability of human feelings and behaviour; the unremitting emphasis on subjective meanings attached to acts and objects; the importance of language in communicating those meanings and endowing objects with symbolic status; the capacity of man to reflect on himself and view himself as he perceives others might see him ('the looking glass self'); and the critical influence of significant others in the identification process: these matters are all of importance to Plummer and serve to make his work part of the interactionist strain.

# Part Three:

# Structuralism

- Social Wholes
- Psycho-structures
- Mistrust of Consciousness

# 7

# Social Wholes

**Greater than the sum of the parts**
Think of a departmental store. It is a building made of bricks, concrete, glass and various other materials; inside are store assistants, delivery men and assorted personnel along with customers moving from department to department, and in and out of the building. These are its basic component parts and we are asked to analyse it but without moving more than three feet away from its outer wall. We can knock out bricks for examination, we can scrape the concrete for samples, we can even talk to the people inside the building. We gain a lot of information from our close-up investigation. What we cannot adequately grasp are the relations between the component parts, the patterns or shapes formed by the process of people relating to each other and their physical environment. These constitute what we may call the structure of the departmental store. We cannot apprehend it directly through our senses like we can bricks and glass, but we are aware of its presence.

The word 'structure' itself has its origin in the Latin word *structura* from the verb *struere*, to construct, and, although Berger and other interactionists talk of the 'construction' of reality and the man-made nature of society, the meaning it has for another group of theorists is quite different. For, while the interactionists are interested in the investigation of the process through which people build up their relationships, these others are interested in the product of those relationships, the total structure. For the structuralists, relationships between the parts has priority over the parts themselves. This totality is the focus of enquiry.

One of the tasks of the structuralist, then, is to abstract from the directly observable: he cannot see, grasp or understand patterns through direct observation and experience. He has to distance himself and analyse on a level far above that of the interactionist whose view of people and societies is always from ground level – where the action happens. The structuralist's interest is in defining recurrences, regularities and stabilities in patterns of relationships, so he must extricate from data gleaned from specific studies and weld this into a coherent whole. Scattered information is to be ordered and made sense of in terms of an underlying coherence that cannot be revealed even through the most detailed empirical studies. Adam Podgórecki and Maria Los use a musical analogy: 'As in a sonata, one tune may persistently repeat itself in a scale of tones, so, in a similar manner, structuralism tries to find its way (and recognition) through various already established products of human activities' (1979, p. 32).

Relationships between components are seen to fall into patterns and the researcher's task is to search for precisely those patterns. The relationships may refer to social or mental phenomena; the ways in which people act or the ways in which they think; they may refer to the arrangement of words in speech or the organization of the written word in literature. And the pursuit of such patterns in men's behaviour and thought is by no means new, as Tom Bottomore and Robert Nisbet point out: 'To discover the fundamental, constitutive, *structures* into which the sensory data of human observation and experience fall: this was a cardinal objective of the ancient Greeks to go back no farther in time' (1979, p. 557). Plato and his student, Aristotle, were interested in configuration of ideas as they registered in the consciousness. The attempt here would seem to have been to uncover a structure of mind and, if so, Plato began the tradition of intellectual enquiry we will consider in the next chapter. For now, we want to look at the origins of social structuralism.

Genealogically, we can trace lines of development back to the Italian Giambattista Vico whose work *Scienza Nuova* ('New Science') was first published in 1725. Generally ignored at the time of publication, the work contains a progress theory of history, meaning, to quote Robert Nisbet, 'that mankind has advanced in the past, is now advancing and will inevitably advance in the foreseeable future' towards some indeterminate end-state (1980). Implicit in the theory was that there were continuities in societies throughout the progression.

Like many later structuralists, Vico posited a law of historical development comprising precise cycles, or *corsi*. Nisbet summarizes the stages as: the 'age of the gods', in which all acts and thought are considered to be dictated by gods of myths; the 'age of heroes', when tensions and conflicts develop; then 'feudalism', when powerful monarchs emerge and the culmination comes with the 'reliance on rationalism' and technique; and this eventually collapses, giving rise to a renewal of the *corsi* (1980, pp. 160–7).

'Vico's determinism' is not 'iron in nature', according to Nisbet (1980,

p. 160). But the idea of historical inevitability would certainly seem to rule out much possibility of humans being able to carve out their own destiny in a voluntaristic way. The theme of an historical progression is a recurring one in structuralist theory and almost forms a cycle of its own through the thought of Comte, Durkheim, Marx and others.

Throughout Vico's stages there endures a distinct, irreducible pattern that, according to Nisbet, following Isaiah Berlin, 'characterizes all the activities of any given society; a common style reflected in the thought, the arts, the social institutions, the language, the ways of life and action of an entire society' (1980, p. 166).

What Vico tried to do was find recurrent patterns or structures of events as they might be inferred from the study of history. Leon Pompa argues that Vico disputed the claim that similarities and persistences in belief and action were inexplicable in terms of a single origin of mankind: they had to be understood as arising from embedded capacities in the human mind (1975, ch. 1). In this context, Edmund Leach points out the parallels between his work and the later theories of Claude Lévi-Strauss, whom we will review in the next chapter (1969).

The attempt was to make general sense of man's history by fitting together pieces into a whole which would be the basis of the 'new science' of man. He looked for continuities and recurrences in history and, according to Bottomore and Nisbet, tried to blend them: 'The essential point here is simply Vico's effort to combine the intramental and the extramental in patterns, the recurrence of which in human history should be the starting point for the science of mankind' (1979, p. 564).

It's a matter of some conjecture whether Vico can meaningfully be spoken of in the same breath as the other structural theorists we will be considering. But, the diversity in range and concern of those expressing interest in structuralist analysis is very pronounced. In Vico, however, we find certain themes which resurface in later works. The interest in the nature of the human mind characterizes the theorists of the next chapter, but Vico shares with the thinkers in this chapter a preoccupation with the course of human history and the persisting shapes of society as it moves through the phases of that course. Fragments of history, eras or epochs, have to be integrated into a total pattern, a whole structure. And, crucially, this totality is not only a combination of parts but has a status over and above its constituent parts.

The theories of Auguste Comte share certain imperatives with Vico's. The first and most basic one is the effort to establish a 'new science' of men and society. For Comte, this was to be achieved through 'positivism', the intellectual tradition seeking to apply the theories and methods of natural sciences to the study of human beings; observation, experiment and comparison were to be the techniques allied to pre-formulated theories.

Flowing from this is Comte's belief that societies are subject to influences akin to 'natural laws'; like Vico, he saw certain tendencies in history which made it possible to abstract patterns and predict the future. Thirdly, he recognized that, although men could accelerate or retard the tendencies, they could never arrest or control them: their actions were largely inconsequential against the historical evolution. His science, therefore, would focus not on individuals but on social wholes, or as he put it: 'A society therefore can no more be decomposed into *individuals* than a geometric surface can be resolved into lines, or a line into points' (quoted by Bottomore and Nisbet, 1979, p. 559).

His remarkable – some would say bizarre – synthesis of these three themes brought Comte recognition as the founder of sociology, though Robert Bierstedt argues for Vico: 'If, by some fluke of circumstance, he had happened to coin the word "sociology" as the label for his enterprise, he and not Comte would today be regarded as the founding father' (1979, p. 22).

Comte, like Vico, argued for information to be gained through systematic observation and actual experience rather than speculative theorizing. Monumental achievements had resulted from the scientific revolution in Europe and Comte, from France, was obviously impressed enough to think similar progress could be made in human sciences. Anything that was not observable or accessible through experience was not to be considered as rightful subject matter for scientific investigation. What isn't certain is whether Comte was directly influenced by Vico's formulations. Bierstedt reckons Comte did not read his work until 1844, two years after the completion of *The Positive Polity*, Comte's major statement of his theories. Indeed, Comte, in his effort to remain unaffected by other theories, read only poetry whilst working on his own – in the interests of what he called 'cerebral hygiene'.

With positivist sociology, Comte thought he could analyze history and society in exactly the same way as a botanist studies plants or a physicist studies matter. At times, he even used the term 'social physics' to describe his enterprise. His principal 'discovery' was the law of three stages

---

### Auguste Comte (1798–1857)

Conventionally recognized as the founder of 'scientific' sociology, he worked with the philosopher Saint Simon from 1817–23, before developing his own positivist approach to history and society. He rejected social philosophies, offering instead a study of society based on observation, experiment and comparison, in short the techniques of natural sciences.

through which all societies passed. In the theological stage, religious or supernatural explanations of the human life proliferate. This concedes to a metaphysical stage in which a necessary, but only provisional, phase occurs when people criticize past ideas, but continue to seek understanding through transcendental explanations. The eighteenth century Enlightenment, for Comte, exemplified this stage. During the former stages, men's apprehensions of the world were imperfect. But, with the coming of the positive stage, knowledge of the world would be truly scientific. Speculative philosophies would be made redundant as our understandings would be hewn out of observations, experiences and scientific procedures. Doubts would disappear as we became positive about our knowledge of the world.

As with Vico, there is very deterministic tinge in this scheme of history, which follows directly from an earlier conception of Saint Simon, writing at the turn of the eighteenth century, for whom there were necessary stages in history over which man had no control. So why study man? Comte's alternative was to study 'facts' that were quite independent of any individuals, and were the proper subject matter of sociology. To this end, Comte recommended two main areas of enquiry, statics and dynamics. Statics referred to the studies of total societies and, as Cohen notes: 'Underlying this was the notion that all of the institutions, beliefs and morals of a society are interrelated as a whole, so that the method of explaining the existence of any one item in the whole is to discover the law which prescribes how this item coexists with all of the others.' (1968, p. 34).

Dynamics was also about discovering social laws, this time about how whole societies changed, an approach Cohen calls 'holistic', the study of wholes. The main practical implication of Comte's programme is that we can pitch our investigations of the social world only at the level of social wholes. 'Thus the growth of social conflict between workers and managers is explained by the fact that modern society is passing through a "critical" stage before the re-establishment of the new "organic" stage, which will be positivistic', state Russell Keat and John Urry (1975, p. 75).

There is a contradiction here, for Comte, as a positivist, insisted on studying observables. Societies as wholes, however, would not seem to be apprehensible to the human senses: they are abstractions of Comte's theory rather than palpable realities. Theories, therefore, serve to guide research and make intelligible the results, as Comte stressed: 'No real observation of any kind of phenomena is possible except in as far at it is first directed, and finally interpreted by some theory' (1853, vol. 2, p. 97).

## The organic model
Through the middle period of the nineteenth century, there occurred in

Europe what Nisbet calls 'the revolt against individualism': 'the dominant ideas of past centuries about the natural individual, his innate character and self-sustaining ability' were replaced by a fresh set of perspectives constituting an intellectual reorientation (1979, p. 7). Comte contributed to this reorientation in stressing the primacy of society over the individual and, in a radically different way, Karl Marx also did. They shared, along with others, the aim to provide an analysis of society by showing how each of the component parts related to the whole. Comte's ideas were instrumental in prompting later theorists to bring in models which were seen as analogous to societies.

The organic model, that is the use of the arrangement of organs in a living body as a blueprint for understanding social phenomena, was used in the 1800s by both Herbert Spencer, an English contemporary and follower of Charles Darwin, and Emile Durkheim, a French sociologist.

Spencer took many of Darwin's concepts and theories about the evolution of organisms and applied them to the study of society. For Spencer, the anatomical organization of organs was similar to society in a number of respects: both grow and develop; increases in size in both creates greater complexity and differentiation, leading to differentiation in the functions fulfilled by organs, or parts; in organisms and societies the individual parts can live on, even when the whole is dead; and crucially, parts of the whole in both are interdependent, so that changes in one will necessarily affect the functioning of others and, therefore, change the whole.

The organs of the body, for Spencer, were not separable from the biological whole of which they were part, in exactly the same way as parts of society could not function except in relation to the total society. Both exhibited a structure which was the pattern connecting the parts. Over generations this changed so, as Darwin argued for a theory of biological evolution, Spencer put forward the theory of societies gradually, but continuously, evolving towards states of complexity. Definite changes in structure were inevitable (Spencer, 1969).

One important distinction noted by Spencer was between structure and function. Simply stated, structure refers to the complex whole, the way in which it holds together, whereas function means what each indiual part or organ does in relation to the others. Changes in the functions of parts have effects on the whole complex leading to an eventual modification of structure.

Here the influence of Darwin is very obvious, for Spencer believed all human societies to be in a process of evolution with structures changing, giving rise to new forms and going out of existence. The similarity with Comte and Vico is clear, though there were several others espousing evolutionary ideas about societies in a continuous process of natural and directional change.

In Spencer's scheme, societies evolved from simple to complex structures with differentiated functions: 'Societies, like living bodies, begin as germs, originate from masses which are extremely minute... out of small wandering hordes have arisen the largest societies' (1966, p, 451).

Underpinning the change, for Spencer, was the idea of equilibrium, a natural state of balance. Organs have a way of accommodating change without severe disruption. For example, if a human kidney is irreparably damaged, the other kidney will take over full functions and keep the whole body working smoothly. Changes in society were effected in the same manner. So, societies are thought to be complexes of parts, or institutions like the economy, religion, or politics, working together and yielding a healthy functioning whole, which would adapt to internal changes and to external ones, such as natural catastrophes. Like a creature in Darwin's model, it adapts to survive.

Spencer detailed three vital functions important to the survival of any society: regulation – they have to be governed; distribution – goods have to be produced and circulated; sustenance – populations have to be reproduced in orderly sequence. Institutions such as governments, economies and families serve to fulfil the functions. This type of analysis later became known as structural-functionalism, though it was through the theories of Durkheim that it first grew to prominence.

Durkheim, like his predecessor Comte, used a positivistic approach to the study of society, and this is evident in his first major work in which he suggested that simple societies are characterized by 'mechanical solidarity' where each part resembles other parts; each segment of society is a micro-version of the total society. People are bound together by shared values and similar experiences; they lead similar lives (1964).

The transition to modern industrial societies brings bigger populations and more specialization in work roles – the division of labour – and, like an organic whole, the parts differentiate so that people's experiences and values are diffused. People are connected with each by interdependencies: the worker has to have transport to his work, so depends on the bus driver, who, in turn, has to get up early and so depends on an alarm clock sold by a jewellery retailer who buys from a wholesaler, who depends on a foreign manufacturer who employs workers, who depend on multiple others, and so on. The various people may never see each other, they may have different attitudes and interests, but they depend on each other and are parts of the same structure which holds together – it has 'organic solidarity'. And this solidarity, like an organ, splits, differentiates, subdivides, and continues to grow without disruption.

Like the German theorist Ferdinand Tönnies, Durkheim traced social evolution through two forms: in Tönnies' case, *Gemeinschaft* and

*Gesellschaft*; in Durkheim's, mechanical and organic. Like Comte and Spencer, he saw the transformation as akin to organic growth, the total structure seeming to have a self-perpetuating dynamic which kept stability and order, thus preventing the structure from collapsing.

The concept of solidarity, therefore, is important in Durkheim's early work and he conceived this as a collection of beliefs, sentiments, and practices common to individuals in society, but existing apart from any one of them. As such, it has a constraining effect on them. Durkheim, therefore, felt no compulsion to study the people themselves, only the social facts. These were the influential features of society and they could be analyzed precisely and scientifically to produce what he felt to be an 'objective sociology' 1965).

The suicide rate is Durkheim's most notable example of a social fact. It exists quite separately from the individuals who commit suicide, yet is evident in all societies. This indicates that the suicide rate is a social property and cannot be reduced to the people who contribute towards it. Perhaps we can use the example of a youth culture like punk of the 1970s or new romanticism of the early '80s: both were collective phenomena involving musical styles, external appearances, gatherings at particular discos and concerts, yet individuals who were involved in the cultures could not be said to *be* them. The cultures came into existence because of the ideas and actions of many people and they took on a status over and above them and, in many ways, imposed themselves so that the styles and music influenced what youths thought and did.

Societies, in Durkheim's view, were composed of multiple social facts all fitting together into an integrated whole like segments of an orange – you can take away the pieces for analysis (or eating) but a full comprehension must take into account the way each fits in with the others. The whole was to be seen as quite distinct from its parts; in Durkheim's terms, it was *sui generis*, it was a separate, independent entity.

It follows that, when we are trying to explain the existence of a certain social fact, we should look to other social facts for causes. So, for instance, Durkheim, in his classic study of suicide, did not limit his search for causes to the level of psychological dispositions or climatic conditions, but concentrated on other social facts (1952). He specified three types of suicide occurring in, and caused by, particular social circumstances. 'Altruistic' suicide is the outcome of conditions promoting self-sacrifice for the benefit of the group or collectivity – wars are an obvious example of this; 'egoistic' suicide is caused by isolation or lack of group cohesion; the 'anomic' type is the result of upheavals in society, such as economic disasters, which leave a sort of vacuum in which the norms or guidelines for thought and conduct are removed – confusion leads to a general state of disintegration. Thus, 'anomie' is Durkheim's opposite to high social cohesion or tight integration. Interestingly, and in total contrast to the theorists of the last section, Durkheim was not at all concerned with the motives or meanings behind the suicide acts, but only with uncovering the patterns of observable behaviour in relation to general social laws (see Douglas, 1967, part 3, for criticism).

Durkheim upheld this logic in his analysis of crime which was in total opposition to the prevalent studies of his day. In contrast to criminologists of the early part of the nineteenth century who searched for the chimera of the 'born criminal', Durkheim dismantled the individual-oriented theories and proposed a theory in which crime is treated not as an individual act, but as a social fact (1964).

Definitions of the content of criminal acts differ from one society to another and from one period to another; the thing they share is that they are universally disapproved of by members of the particular society. A crime is an act which offends the collective conscience, which transcends the conscience of any individual. Punishment is a mechanism of vengeance, but it operates at another level in reaffirming rightness. The process of punishing a criminal offender reminds members of a society that the offender is wrong in committing certain acts and they are right in not committing them. In this, it restores values by bringing together what Durkheim called the 'upright consciences'.

Seen in this light, crime is quite 'normal': it is present in all societies; only when its rate drops way below or rises high above a certain level does a 'pathological' state occur. Also, crime is functional for the continuance of society; it reaffirms commonly held values and reinforces social solidarity amongst members. All societies have crime and it performs vital functions. Thus we have two important insights, one about the independent character of crime in all societies over and above individuals, the other about its functional character. It fits into the total structure of society as a component part and it functions effectively along with the other parts: this was Durkheim's structural-functionalist interpretation.

His last study, of religion, originally published in 1912, demonstrates the structural-functionalist approach once more. Religious beliefs, rituals and ceremonies had the effect of uniting people morally and so fostered social solidarity. Australian aboriginal tribes, for example, were geographically scattered but came together in religious activities and so demonstrated to each other that they were parts of a single society with moral rules, expectations and obligations which existed over and above any of them.

The totem has special significance for them as a sacred symbol and the fact that they worshipped it, expressed, for Durkheim (1964b), their belief that the society of which they were part was superior to any member of it. So, by worshipping, they abided by certain constraining principles, and simultaneously maintained the religion which served the vital function of promoting cohesion and togetherness. Religion was intertwined in the general structure of aboriginal life and it functioned effectively.

Durkheim's use of structural-functional analysis is not separable from his conception of social science, for he believed that, for the study of society to be fully scientific, society itself must be assumed to have a nature of its own that is quite separable from that of the individual members. Society as an entity is to be seen as the source of all social phenomena.

We should recognize that Durkheim was as opposed to individualistic accounts of human behaviour, but, in a totally different way to the

### Emile Durkheim (1855–1917)

Born in France, the son of a Jewish rabbi; entered Ecole Normale Supérieure of Paris in 1879 and after three years study began to teach philosophy. Between 1885–86, he studied in Germany and, on his return, inaugurated the first social science course to be offered in France at the university of Bordeaux. His doctoral dissertation *The Division of Labour in Society* was published in 1893 and in this he formulated his theory of the change from mechanical to organic solidarity.

theorists of the last section, who also rejected ideas about invariant properties of mind as causal factors.

So, when we attempt to explain social phenomena, whether it be racial conflict or family disintegration, we never resort to individuals but only to other social facts. And, of course, the imperative need to dispense with psychological, biological and related explanations is straight from Comte: societies must be analysed in terms of entities which are themselves social. Of course, Durkheim inherited a similar set of problems to Comte's, for, if he was to maintain a tough positivist approach and leave nothing to impression or intuition, then he should have based his analyses on the observable, visible aspects of social life. But the structuralist is forever making generalizations and abstractions in his effort to see persistencies and relationships. Further, to use a functionalist mode means imposing a scheme of interpretation on phenomena. We cannot observe the functions people perform when going to church every Sunday and going through elaborate rituals; we can document what they do – that is visible – but we have to theorize how their behaviour fits into the wider social whole and how it functions to reinforce social solidarity in communities. The social fact of this phenomenon is independent of the subjective inclinations of the performers.

Now, this might be regarded as deterministic in the extreme: not allowing people any part in constructing realities which only the social scientist can discern. But Durkheim did not disallow the possibility of basic human creativity in the same way as he disallowed instincts or 'human nature' in his analyses. We could see the Durkheimian enterprise as an attempt to reconcile the view that social facts do have a severe constraining effect on individuals with the acceptance that those individuals have reasoning, deliberating capacities and can reflect on their own thoughts and actions. Mennell stresses how Durkheim used the term 'relative indetermination' to show that men do not automatically respond to the coercive powers of society: 'Nevertheless, Durkheim did not find it easy to define exactly the balance between society's undoubted influence in shaping the individual's actions and the individual's scope for autonomous and innovative behaviour' (1980, p. 26).

With his contemporaries, the pragmatists and Cooley, Durkheim tried to remove from the study of man frozen notions in which invariant properties of the human mind were to account for complex patterns of conduct. As the reader might anticipate, the 'all in the mind' subjectivism of these theories did not suit Durkheim's palate.

If we take the work as a whole – and Durkheim would insist we did so – it presents a programme for the future study of society based on a vision developed in part by Comte and Spencer. The prime importance of social, in contrast to individual, factors is a crucial theme retained by all social structuralists. The evolutionary scheme suggests a determinism in perhaps a softer form than his predecessors. These two themes are united in the structural-functionalist mode of analysis. As we will see, Durkheim was immensely influential in the development of sociology, but perhaps his most immediate impact came in the realms of social anthropology, and we will now enter this realm.

## The anthropologists

It was part of Durkheim's programme that societies could not be adequately understood by reference to the everyday meanings, motives and actions of the man-in-the-street, whereas these were precisely the points of reference for interactionists. For Durkheim, it was necessary to go beyond the actor's definitions of reality and discover the fundamental components of society.

Durkheim's nephew and student, Marcel Mauss, used this approach when analysing *The Gift* (originally published in 1925; 1954). The title describes Mauss's version of a social fact: an elaborate, ritualistic exchange of possessions practised by Trobriand islanders and Kwakiutl Indians. The material things themselves which pass between individuals express a certain type of relationship, one bounded by reciprocity. Mauss believed the exchange process rested on a three-fold obligation: to give, to receive and to repay. As we have already seen, to those exchanging armshells and necklaces, it may be a voluntary, even spontaneous activity, but to a structural-functionalist, it is a deeply-embedded obligatory transaction which contributes to social solidarity.

In the study, Mauss drew on a variety of different patterns of gift exchange, ancient and modern, to demonstrate that what appears to be a straightforward transfer of objects is symbolically important in defining and maintaining roles and status, thus strengthening social bonds. In other words, the gift exchange could not be appreciated as an isolated piece of behaviour in which articles were transferred, but had to be set in the general context of which it was part. Only by seeing it as an element of a social structure would its function become apparent, so the researcher links one aspect of social life with others to reveal what Mauss called *faits sociaux totaux*.

Although his approach is Durkheimian, Mauss showed no interest in establishing invariant laws of society, nor in charting evolutionary courses by using biological analogies. Nor was he so set against the admission of psychological data into analyses. His work tended to soften the determinism of Durkheim's and, interestingly, it was an Englishman who took Durkheim's first principles to apostolic extremes when he applied them to the study of other cultures.

A. R. Radcliffe-Brown's first significant work was published in 1922, ten years after Durkheim's final major study of religion. Radcliffe-Brown was a thorough-going positivist, believing that the social sciences were part of the natural sciences, the logic running something like 'humans are part of the natural world and their behaviour is observable, so study them as such...' The similarities with the behaviourist approach are most pronounced.

It was his desire to be scientific, or positivistic, in his studies that made him look to Durkheim rather than Spencer for his inspiration, as he explained:

> The concept of function applied to human societies is based on an analogy between social life and organic life. The recognition of the analogy and of some of its implications is not new. In the nineteenth century the analogy, the concept of function, and the world itself appear frequently in social philosophy and sociology. So far as I know the first systematic formulation of the concept as applying to the strictly scientific study of society was that of Emile Durkheim in 1895. (1948a, p. 178).

The elements of the total structure, institutions like marriage, gift exchange, religion, have functions in that they satisfy the 'needs' of the social organism. A central assumption then is that there are, in Radcliffe-Brown's words, 'necessary conditions for existence' for all societies and these can be discovered through scientific study. There is, in his work, an unremitting insistence on studying social structures, which he saw in the same light as most of the theorists of this chapter: 'the sum total of all social relationships of all individuals at a given moment in time'. This doesn't involve a problem because: 'Although it cannot, naturally, be seen in its entirety at any one moment, we can observe it; all of the phenomenal reality is there' (1948b, p. 55). Social structure, for Radcliffe-Brown, is an observable reality: it comprises sets of relations which link people together. (As we shall see, this approach to structure contrasts with the more abstract notions of later theorists.)

Radcliffe-Brown, unlike Mauss, was interested in excavating what he thought were natural laws in society and was hostile to psychological and historical data, as Miriam Glucksmann points out: 'Social structure in Radcliffe-Brown's sense is not reducible to psyche, and the lack of historical data is not a hindrance since natural laws apply at all times and can be discovered at any time' (1974, p. 18).

A good deal of Radcliffe-Brown's research was spent showing how an institution meets social 'needs'. When discussing the ceremonies of the Andaman islanders, for example, he analyses how dancing enables people to engage in the same action and perform 'as one body'; painting the body 'serves to keep alive in the mind of the individual a certain system of sentiments necessary for the regulation of conformity to the needs of society' (1948a. pp. 238–9).

Nowhere in Radcliffe-Brown's work does he resort to human motives or purposive behaviour. What people do is observed as part of a larger sequence of activity, an institution which connects organically with the larger structure. The structure itself is real and tangible and it is this which is the central focus of study, oblivious to social change and the existence of man. 'But direct observation does reveal to us that these human beings are connected by a complex network of social relations. I use the term "social structure" to denote this network of actually existing social relations' (1948a, p. 190).

In agreement with Durkheim, Radcliffe-Brown insisted that all explanations of social life can be cast strictly in terms of social facts with no resort to psychological or even biological concepts. Not so with Bronislaw Malinowski, the other major anthropologist of the period who formulated his own distinct functionalist approach in which human biological needs were accommodated: 'man has, first and foremost, to satisfy all the needs of his organism' (1944, p. 116). Nor did he deny the importance of historical analysis: 'such a scientific approach does not by any means override or deny the validity of evolutionary or historical pursuits. It simply supplies them with a scientific basis' (1944, p. 42).

Both he and Radcliffe-Brown sought to have the conceptual tools of the science of man by using functionalism. Don Martindale summarizes Malinowski's 'foundations' (1970, p. 458):

1 It is accepted, first of all, as an axiom that human beings have need for food, reproduction, shelter, etc.
2 It is assumed that human drives are physiological but restructured by acquired habit.
3 Culture is conceived as a conditioning apparatus which through training in skills and norms amalgamates nature with nurture.
4 It is taken as fundamental that man never deals with his difficulties alone; he organizes into families, communities, tribes, with authority and leadership culturally defined.
5 The symbolism of language is a component in all technology and social organization.

### Bronislaw Kasper Malinowski (1884–1942)

Born in Poland, he gained a Ph.D. in physics and mathematics before moving to England where he studied social science. His famous study of the Trobriand islanders was conducted 1915–18. An early influential advocate of functional analysis, though not a *structuralist* functionalist in the manner of, say, Durkheim or Radcliffe-Brown. Known to be a commanding, dogmatic exhibitionist and often abrasive with his students.

6   Cultural satisfaction of primary biological needs imposes secondary imperatives on man.
7   The functional theory postulates that the system of production, distribution, and consumption must be carried on even in the most primitive of communities'.

Building on these foundations, Malinowski produced a model of society as an integrated, coordinated structure, the dynamics of which was the nature of man. Every aspect of society, however complex, is, in the last instance, a derivative of human needs; institutions are fulfilments of needs though, as Jonathan Turner and Alexandra Maryanski detect, new needs can emerge: 'Thus, once humans create social structures, or institutions, these emergent structures have imperatives or needs, as vital and real as those of the individual organism, that must be met if the "social organism" is to survive' (1979, p. 50).

So a society needs the institution of, say, education for the transmission of knowledge necessary for its continuance, as another might need magic as a way of bringing its members to order (through, for example, supplying alternatives to natural explanations of floods or other calamities: members might believe they can avoid such events through the practice of magic, and this promotes order).

Although Malinowski differs from the others in regarding human biological needs as determinants, his overall scheme displays marked similarities: the stress on social totalities as the units of analysis; the shunning of history in the furtherance of the scientific study of the present – 'synchronic' study, for Radcliffe-Brown; the explanation of events and process in terms of their functions; the attention paid to the cooperative and harmonious workings of elements of the structure; the vision of societies as well-integrated and smoothly-functioning wholes – like clockwork oranges.

There are, of course, criticisms of this model and Cohen lists them under three headings. First, logical: it explains the existence of things by showing that they have beneficial consequences for another. This is teleological reasoning, like showing that religion is caused by the need to sustain the moral foundations of society, when it might be argued that religion is as much a consequence of the moral foundations as a cause. Other logical complaints are that structural-functionalism throws up hypotheses that can't be tested and that, if every element of a social structure has to be analysed only in the context of the structure of which it is part, then we can never make comparisons between one structure and another – such as comparing English and French family units.

The second criticism is substantive: it minimizes the importance of social conflict by concentrating too much on solidarity and the harmonious nature of societies, so that the analysis leaves little or no room for accounting for why social change occurs.

Thirdly, ideological criticism: functionalism tends to paint a very rosy picture of reality, with the whole structure working nicely and harmoniously and with little friction – 'as though it were the best of all possible worlds' (1968, pp. 47–64). In another way, Martindale calls the organic conceptions of society 'almost foolproof'; 'Why should one add to a living whole? What organism needs two heads or a spare lung? What should one cut out of a living whole – its liver, or lungs, or stomach?' (1970, p. 127).

These last two criticisms are the most recurrent, for societies manifestly don't function smoothly and effectively at all times. Civil unrest, riots, revolutions and assorted other less visible clashes of interest show us that there is often conflict, restrained or unrestrained, that structural-functionalism either disguises, or out of which it makes a function. We might argue that class inequalities promote conflict, whereas the functionalist account of Kingsley Davis and Wilbert E. Moore asserts that inequalities are extremely necessary for the continuity of society (1945). This view contrasts sharply with one we are going to consider next: that of Karl Marx and Friedrich Engels.

### Building Sight: Marx and Engels

What matters in the Marx-Engels model of society is production. Humans distinguish themselves from other living creatures by *producing*. They fashion their natural environments for their own needs and uses and, in the process, fuse their conception of the task with its practical execution. That is, in shaping their environments to suit their own purposes, they bring intellectual capacity to bear in practical activities. Animals do not produce as such: they act instinctively. People, in contrast, produce consciously and creatively.

So production is the ultimate determining process in history and society. The human relationship to the material world has to be seen as prior to everything else, for as Engels put it: 'mankind must first of all eat, drink, have shelter and clothing, before it can pursue politics, science, art, religion etc.' (1973, p. 429). This approach is termed historical materialism and its first and most fundamental tenet is that the way in which humans work to support life has a most crucial influence, *the* most crucial influence, on their whole existence. (It may be interesting to compare Malinowski's theory of 'needs', considered earlier.)

Historical materialism was, in many senses, a reaction to the absolute idealism of thinkers such as Georg Hegel, who wrote in the early seventeenth century. Simply stated, Hegel's view was that the mind was the critical aspect of reality and had to be seen to logically precede all other aspects. Distinct human thought was an ever-changing sequence of opposites, a dialectic. For every idea we conceive in thought there has to be an opposite, such as light and darkness, old and new, creation and destruction. This first idea is the thesis and its opposite the antithesis, or negation. An interplay between the two generates a new synthesis, which in turn, is opposed by its contradiction. In this way, thought develops; it is continuous and stays in constant flux.

The dynamic, or 'motor', of the process was what Hegel called *Geist*, which equates to pure intelligence. It follows from this extremely voluntaristic conception of man, that he can be, and do, anything he has a mind to be or do; this conception proved influential with some of the theorists of

### Karl Marx (1818–1883)
Born in the Rhineland and educated at the Universities of Bonn and Berlin. He was influenced as a student by, amongst others, Hegel and Feuerbach, but added to their philosophical materialism. A journalist and editor of a radical publication, he blended his theoretical writings with political activism around Europe, eventually settling in London in 1850 where he wrote *Das Kapital* in the British Museum. His 'scientific study of society' paved the way to many later theorists and revolutionaries and made him arguably the most influential social thinker of the nineteenth century.

the previous section, and particularly one, as Paul Rock notes: 'Indeed, in the embryonic interactionism of Charles Cooley, little of Idealism has been rejected. To Cooley, society constituted an organism which derived its life from the collective existence of its members' (1979, p. 65). Objects of the social world are constructions of our thought; we grasp them through our ideas and can change them in the same way. We can freely will changes by changing our consciousness of things. And change, for Hegel, proceeds through the dialectical sequence. The way we apprehend the world is always challenged by opposites and the negation leads to a new synthesis, and a new conception, of reality. History progresses in this conflicting rhythm, with the mind always dictating.

Whilst accepting the dialectical logic in the abstract as the sequence of change, Marx and Engels counterposed a dialectical materialism in which the mode of production, that is, the way people collectively support their lives, does the dictating (1968). To elaborate: in order that they will survive, men enter into relationships with each other, make and use tools and hunting weapons, organize divisions of labour. What materials they have available and what they make, and gain, out of them, whether a carved bone or a computer, a basic hunting skill or a knowledge of microprocessing techniques, are the 'forces of production'. The organized relationships between men designed to maintain subsistence or improve the quality of life are the 'relations of production'. Factors used by men to create necessities, or wealth, such as raw materials, instruments, factories, or whole industries, are the 'means of production'. These are three key concepts in Marxian theory; the manner in which they combine is the mode of production and this exercises the decisive influence in the dialectic.

For Marx and Engels, Hegel's scheme stood on the metaphysical and, therefore, non-social premise, that of the existence of the intangible *Geist*. In contrast to this, Marx and Engels argued that what goes on in the human mind is a reflection of what people do in the material world. Ideas are not independent of production at all; quite the opposite. So the scientific investigation of man in society must start not with an examination of subjective states, but an analysis of the ways in which men produce: how they modify nature and the relationships they piece together in order to accomplish the modification.

Two contentious points must be stressed. First, although Marx and Engels were attempting to place the study of man on a scientific footing by developing a fresh approach for empirical work, they were not hard-line positivists. Keat and Urry call their method 'realism' in which: 'To explain phenomena is not merely to show there are instances of well-established regularities. Instead we must discover the necessary connections between phenomena, by acquiring knowledge of the underlying structures and mechanisms at work' (1975, p. 5).

Zeitlin reckons: 'This approach is directly opposed to that of positivism which treats facts *in their immediately given form*, as truth' (1981, p. 96). It is necessary to study human beings, taking account of what they actually do through observation and documentation. But, it is insufficient to let the analysis rest there: men must be seen as enmeshed in networks of relations of production which are themselves tied to specific modes of production. Like the other structuralists, Marx and Engels wish to theorize at levels quite beyond the reach of the people they study. They distance themselves so as to catch sight of the patterns of relationships, the interconnections, the total shape of man's productive activity; they see the social structure.

Also, while Marx and Engels referred to the material world of natural objects and events, they stressed that it is always a humanly created world. Men work on their environment, shaping it to their own designs as far as possible. Nature is pliable and can be moulded in many ways to suit multiple purposes; yet there are always limits, even if very wide ones. Man can make metal fly if it suits his purpose to set foot on the moon, or elsewhere; yet he cannot stop storms even though they might threaten his interests and endanger his chances of flying. Man, in the Marxian vision, is a resourceful, creative and, of course, productive creature allying the objects of nature to his own needs: *homo faber*. But he is always restricted by nature and can never be seen as independent of it. So, within the natural limits of the forces of production, materials, level of skill, knowledge and expertise, men relate to each other and join in the enterprise of production; and out of this interaction of men with nature and with other men comes the mode of production.

Creative and deliberating creatures we may be, but our perceptions and apprehensions of the world are not determined by consciousness, but *vice versa* as Marx insisted: 'The mode of production in material life determines the general character of the social, political and spiritual processes of life. It is not the consciousness of men that determines their existence, but on the contrary, their social existence determines their consciousness' (1904, pp. 11–12).

The essential features of man, for Marx and Engels, are his capacity to create with other men and his proclivity to produce and reproduce his means of subsistence in an imaginative way. There is no natural state of man: he has to be seen in the context of which he is both part and producer. There is certainly a determinism in the theory, but it is a sort of self-determination.

Man attempts to shape his environment and, in the process, creates working conditions which provide parameters or limits for subsequent generations. Thus, the decisive factor is the mode of production which is ultimately a part-human, part-natural creation – a fusion of both.

Like the structural-functionalists, Marx and Engels emphasize the importance of the whole society and the one-sidedness of studying man in isolation or in particular contexts: structure is of primary importance. All elements have to be analyzed as they fit into the structure and, therefore, as they relate to each other. So, there are obvious resemblances to the organic model. Marx, like Durkheim, deflated religion by suggesting it was a mechanism for maintaining social order: it had to be viewed in relation to other institutions such as private property and wage labour and the total structure of capitalism, in which men constructed explanations and justifications of life's inequalities by locating their salvation in the afterlife – 'the meek shall inherit the earth' principle. This linked in with the exploitation of the believers because, by holding such views, they tended to accept their positions in society and do nothing to change them. Religion fitted in nicely with the interests of capitalism, but worked to sedate and give comfort to its believers, as Marx and Engels stressed: 'It is the opium of the people' (1959, p. 263).

There is partial agreement with Comte and the evolutionary theorists when it comes to historical stages of progress: the Marxian model sets up definite phases of history culminating in communism. There is a large measure of disagreement as to whether these stages are reached independently of human consciousness and action or whether they are brought about by conscious action, and we will discuss later this split in contemporary Marxian interpretations. But, regardless of the mechanisms underlying historical transitions, there appears to be an inexorable movement at the heart of Marx' theory.

Despite the general theoretical leaning towards structuralism, however, there are profound departures from the functionalists' version. Whereas Durkheim or Radcliffe-Brown would see each institution in society as performing a function and so contributing to the support of the structure, Marx and Engels would see the whole structure as racked with contradictions and therefore in a process of continuous, dialectical change. All societies are in motion because they contain opposing forces; they consist of opposites and are in a state of struggle. The resolution of the struggle gives rise to a new synthesis and this, eventually, is opposed.

Let's use one of their examples to illustrate this. The downfall of feudal society came through opposition between a new, rising group of mercantile urban dwellers and the traditional group of landed aristocrats. There was a basic conflict in the interests of the two groups. As the mercantilists gained more resources, they were able to seize power from the feudal lords and clear away obstacles to their own enterprises. For example, old laws relating to land which were tailored to suit feudalists' interests were changed in order to meet the new mercantilists' need to create more wealth.

In the abstract, we could see the contradiction as being between the relations of production, i.e. the way in which people were tied to land by a set of relationships with land owners, and the changing forces of production, incorporating new forms of monetary exchange, industrial growth, increased scientific and technical knowledge. The changing forces demanded a flexible, mobile labour force, which was denied by the old system of villeinage. So an opposition developed because the forces were inhibited by the relations. Together, the forces and relations of production comprise the 'economic base' of society and social change, for Marx and Engels, comes about through contradictions within that base.

Now, there are various interpretations of Marx and Engels on this point, for many argue that their theory is one of 'economic determinism': changes in society are caused by men's economic interests and as these change, so do societies. Others would argue that this interpretation tends to blunt the sharpness of Marxian analysis, that, in fact, changes come about when contradictions become visible to people, who then take action to remove obstacles to their economic well-being. In the first version, there seems no place for men's consciousness, for changes occur in the social structure quite independently of their actions. In the second, men must become aware of their positions and do something about the contradictions before changes happen.

Unlike the functionalist model, then, the Marxian society is riven with oppositional tendencies. Hence it is sometimes called the 'conflict model' and is used to counter the functionalist theory in which all the parts of society fit harmoniously together. For Marx and Engels, there are contradictions everywhere, but the decisive ones in shaping society are in the economy. In capitalist society, the ownership of the means of production produces an opposition between the owners and those who are made to work for them. There is a fundamental conflict of interests between the owners, the bourgeoisie, and the working class, the proletariat. Because they have no control over what they produce and what eventually happens to the products, the workers are detached from their production and, given the importance Marx attached to the production process, they are said to be 'alienated' or set apart from their products – and, indeed from their fellow workers – because of the way industrial work is fragmented. The materialist argument dictates that the way in which men earn their 'bread and butter' has the most profound effects on their whole lives; even in intellectual and emotional areas, workers are alienated from society. Remember here Marx's stress on production, a creative, intellectual and practical enterprise through which the worker expresses himself. The division of labour flushes the creative element out of work and renders it rather meaningless and unfulfilling for the workers, who sell themselves virtually as commodities to the capitalist bosses. The link with work is purely the earning of money, 'the cash nexus'.

The fundamental conflict, Marx and Engels theorized, would surface in a revolution when workers would 'throw off their shackles' and seize power, in the process breaking up the capitalist mode of production and replacing it with a communist alternative. There is an irony here because the analysis sees all history in a motion of contradictions, the dialectic, yet the consummation comes with the movement to communism, when human creativity can be developed unhindered by countervailing tendencies. Society seems perfectible; and this almost Comtian vision has prompted many actual social revolutions.

The emancipatory pay-off comes when the evolutionary path widens and the revolutionary transformation reveals to the working class the manner in which its members have been constrained. They aspire to a new genuine consciousness and rid themselves of the 'false consciousness', or distorted form of thought, with which they have laboured under capitalism. The breaking of the capitalist mode of production leads to a new clearer perception of the world in which the worker understands how previous structures have stifled his creative potential. The perception doesn't just arrive. It is produced, built by actual people. This new sight comes not through speculating or philosophizing but by acting, the conjoinment of theory and practice – in Marxian terms, *praxis*.

Yet Marx's model is often used as the diametrical opposite of the Comtian and functionalist versions of social reality and it is easy to see the dissimilarities: the sanguine vision of a harmoniously functioning society is replaced with an everchanging sequence of oppositions in a continuous state of tension. Marx made no effort to explain the origins or presence of elements of society by reference to their being functionally necessary to the structure as a whole. 'However', as Keat and Urry detect, 'his analysis of modes of production does depend on the establishment of functional interrelationships between its elements. Thus he claims that there are certain functional needs that must be satisfied for a particular mode to exist' (1975, p. 114).

But, we could not, for example, explain the existence of a bourgeois ideology by showing that it performs functions for a capitalist structure. For Marx and Engels, this lacks the depth which comes with detailed historical documentation of the contradictory tendencies underlying the development of specific types of structures. Functionalist analysis proceeds with the analysis of social structures at a particular moment in time rather than their developments through history, what Radcliffe-Brown called synchronic, as opposed to diachronic, analysis. This caught only one dimension, as far as Marx was concerned: social analysis must include accounts of historical processes, otherwise it is not dialectical. Economic activity is seen as pivotal in these developmental processes and is not just one of a number of enterprises.

The debate about whether Marx and Engels were determinists in seeing history as moving inexorably towards an end-state with little or no human intercession continues. Certainly, the theme of historical inevitability keeps Marxian theory together like a string holds pearls, and the model's attraction in this century has been due as much to the vision it evokes as to the style of analysis it offers in historical materialism. Marx charts the course of history in a way which suggests there are laws in which men can have no part, and here there are similarities with Comte, Spencer and the other evolutionists, for as Engels reflected: 'Just as Darwin discovered the law of development of organic nature, so Marx discovered the law of development of human history' (1973, p. 429).

But, as Tony Bilton *et al.* insist: 'this "law" is only a general principle and we should not assume all historical change can be reduced simply and directly, to economic factors' (1981, p. 722).

Well, the issue is by no means settled: do men have a role to play in shaping history through their conscious intentions and purposive action, or are they subjects to 'laws' emanating from economic forces? Some interpreters of the model, like Wladislaw Bienkowski, insist that 'creative human inventiveness' allows the 'dynamic to function' (1982, p. 12). Zeitlin argues similarly of the 'rational kernel' that lies at the heart of the whole model: 'It was the critical insight that humans are active, creative beings who constitute their world, and thereby themselves by means of their practical activity' (1981, p. 1).

So, society is, in the first instance, a human production, but it comes to exert force on the human being, so much so that other interpreters, such as Alan Sheridan, would suggest 'that all man's activities, even his cherished beliefs, are in the final analysis determined outside the consciousness of the individual subject' (1980, p. 92). If the latter is the case, consciousness is less a creative impulse, more a reflection or 'superstructure' of the economic base of society (including what we believe through the media or religion, education, culture, etc.). Marx's own writings provide no unambiguous statement on this though his later writings are markedly more economic in emphasis and have encouraged many contemporary theorists to view the mature Marx as the 'scientist' rather than the pre-1846 philosopher. We will return to this issue.

Despite all the arguments, Marx and Engels certainly warrant inclusion in the same section as Comte and Durkheim if only because of the way their analysis depicts a society's structure as independent of human will. Man is seen as a creative engineer, producing his environment, but he is always – some would say ultimately – constrained by economic relations in ways which he cannot understand and so cannot control. The capitalist bourgeoisie, whose interests the economy favours, are controlled as much as the proletariat; they're not engaged in a secret conspiracy to feather their own nests, but operate under the same structural conditions as everyone else, and so are as alienated as the workers. The economic structure of society is a product of human endeavour, yet it has an existence quite separate from any single human being and cannot be reduced ontologically. Its status is beyond individuals and has to be studied as such – as a whole. Marx's approach is holistic and his eventual analysis structuralist.

But, whilst retaining the deterministic strain, other theorists have contested the efficacy of social influences on humans and argued that the initial factors lie not outside but inside the individual. Structures exist, but they exist in people's heads. The next chapter deals with this psycho-structuralism.

## Technical Terms

**Dialectical:** Originally, a method used by Socrates and others to attain the truth by discussing different points of view, but built into social theory by Hegel and Marx, who argued that social reality is in a constant state of change, with inter-relationships between, and contradictions in, the elements of reality. Therefore, an aspect of human reality cannot validly be examined in itself without relating it to the process of change; nothing is static. Thus, history is seen as following a dialectical logic, in which aspects are in a state of tension with opposing aspects, giving rise to a different form of reality which itself contains contradictions.

**Teleology:** Explaining the existence of a phenomenon by asserting that it is necessary to bring about another phenomenon. Structural-functionalists were often criticised for theorizing in this way, e.g. that institutions existed because they had beneficial consequences for the continuance of whole societies.

**Historical Materialism:** For Marx and Engels, the scientific method of analysing history from the viewpoint that the ultimate determining element of social life is production. Man has to eat, drink, clothe and shelter before he can pursue politics, religion, science or art. His first consideration must be material existence, he must produce. So historical development must always be explained by reference to material circumstances, rather than, say, through changes in men's thoughts.

**Function:** Usually refers to the objective consequence of a social phenomenon has on the rest of society. Robert Merton contended that phenomena can have either manifest functions which are intended and recognized, or latent, which are neither. So religion has the manifest function of giving people spiritual support and communal gratification, but latently functions to maintain group solidarity.

**Absolute Idealism:** From Hegel the belief that the objects of our perception as known to us consist of our ideas about them; the objects have an existence outside our ideas, but we can only grasp them as filtered through our ideas of them. It follows that social changes can come about through changes in our ideas, as our grasp of objects changes, our action towards them changes. *Note:* in social theory, the term is not usually meant to refer to the principle of acting on impractical ambitions, as it is in popular usage.

**Mode of Production:** Arguably, the

key concept in Marxian theory, it refers in general terms to the entire way a society produces and reproduces itself. Human beings, unlike animals, produce consciously and deliberately not from instinct but from imagination. They feed and shelter themselves in particular ways and create methods of subsistence. The manner in which they organize these, expresses their lives and influences their whole existence, material, intellectual, cultural. 'What they are, therefore, coincides with their production', wrote Marx and Engels. So the mode of production is effectively the mode of living.

**Means of Production:** Factors that labour uses to produce necessities and wealth. Marx said that the means consisted of raw materials and ancillary products, like machines and tools. The main split in capitalist society is between the owners of the means by which people produce and those who do not and are, therefore, dependent on others for their subsistence.

**Synchronic:** A type of analysis that treats social reality as a 'snapshot' rather than studying its development in history, an analysis called *Diachronic*.

## Further Reading

*Functionalism* (1979) by Jonathan Turner and Alexandra Maryanski examines the works of Radcliffe-Brown and Malinowski in its second chapter.
*Social Theory Revisited* (1975) by Clinton Jesser is an edited collection with evaluations and has sections on Comte, Spencer, Durkheim and Marx.
*Karl Marx* (1963) edited by T. Bottomore and M. Rubel is a selection of readings that serves as a most adequate introduction to Marxian theory.

## Advanced Reading

*Emile Durkheim: his life and work* (1973) by Steven Lukes is acknowledged as one of the most authoritative, scholarly and comprehensive studies of the classical social theorist.
*Selected Works* (1973) of Marx and Engels is a distillation of the important themes developed during their collaboration.
*The Nature and Types of Sociological Theory* (1970) by Don Martindale still stands as an almost encyclopaedic volume on the older schools of social thought, tracing social theory back to the ancient Greeks and bringing it up to the 1950s, with all the theorists of this section evaluated.

# 8

# Psycho-Structures

**Of madness and majesty**
Despite the almost bewildering variety of human types and cultures across the world and throughout history, there is an impressive unity. We all display features that tend to link us together: we all use language, we all perceive, have habits and beliefs, and have certain similarities when analyzed carefully. It's very provoking to think that two people brought up in totally different environments to talk in different languages, believe different things, see things differently, even conceptualize the world in totally dissimilar ways can come to communicate with each other and adapt to each other's ways of thinking. The encounters of Carlos Castaneda with another culture of people immersed in what he called 'a separate reality' tells us a great deal about the human capacity to communicate and, in particular, the mind's seeming uniformity (1973).

Is it something in the nature of man which gives him the ability to build conceptual bridges and adjust his perception of reality to fit those of others? Well, certainly many theorists would argue that there is a central unity, indeed uniformity in the human being. The theorists of the last section were interested in the ways in which people are bound together by overarching structures of society and carried along by the unstoppable flow of history. But other theorists saw the unity as not outside the individual in society, but inside him – in his mind. There idea was that there are permanent structures of the human mind into which experiences, thoughts, perceptions and memories fit and, despite differences in the actual contents of the mind, the frameworks, or the structures into which they slot are all ultimately the same.

The imperative of this group of theorists is, as Frederic Jameson puts it, the 'explicit search for the permanent structures of the mind itself, the organizational categories and forms through which the mind is able to experience the world' (quoted in Hawkes, 1977, p. 18).

## Sigmund Freud (1856–1939)

Born in Moravia, a part of the Austro-Hungarian Empire, in May 1856. Three years later his father, a Jewish wool merchant, decided to move to Vienna. He studied physiology, biology and anatomy at the University of Vienna, and in 1881 he decided to pursue a medical degree. In 1885, at the age of 29, he went to Paris to study with Charcot, who was at that time interested in hysteria and hypnotism. He returned in 1886 to set up private practice as a consultant on nervous diseases. 1900 saw the publication of *The Interpretation of Dreams,* the first full piece of psychoanalytic work to be published. Freud truly revolutionised thinking about the mind, and his specific impact was on the importance of the unconscious, the role of childhood sexuality, the force of the irrational, and he was a formative influence on developmental psychology. He moved from Vienna in 1939, when the Nazis took over, and lived for the last year of his life in London.

What is common to both these and the social structuralists is the belief that surface events are to be explained by structures lying below or above the surface. The explicit and obvious is but a manifestation of something implicit and hidden and so the job of social theory is, as Richard and Fernande De George express it, to 'uncover deep structures, unconscious motivations, and underlying causes which account for human actions at a more basic and profound level than do individual, conscious decisions, and which shape, influence and structure those decisions' (1972a, p. xii).

It's an unfair analogy, but if man were an automobile, a behaviourist would want to know how the fuel is converted into power, an interactionist would want to know what it's like to drive the vehicle, but a structuralist would want to strip its bodywork and see how the parts fit together. The analogy, distorted as it is, isn't too far away from the conception of Sigmund Freud, for whom the mind was a 'mental apparatus' driven along by nervous energy and governed by the principle of keeping excitation at a constant level.

Stuart Hughes observes that, to the end of his life, Freud used a mechanistic vocabulary, and that sometimes his metaphors were hydraulic but more often were drawn from the field of electricity (1974, p. 134). Having published in physiology and neurology, and trained as a natural scientist, it is hardly surprising that Freud saw his theories of mind as natural scientific. Marie Jahoda notes that he 'held fast to this self-image' as a natural scientist and was disturbed, as he says in his early publications, with Bruner, that Freud's case studies seemed to lack 'the serious stamp of science'. He grudgingly admitted that they sounded like fiction (1977, p. 14).

Before the first of Freud's publications, there was also a growing record of interest in, and speculation on, sexual pathologies and the sexual origins of psychopathological conditions. Havelock Ellis and R. Van Krafft-Ebing had directed attention to such phenomena. Also, as Jerome Bruner argues 'Freud is inconceivable without Darwin' and indeed Darwin is a 'necessary condition' for Freud and for his success (1973, p. 139). As the summit of an evolutionary process, man could still view himself with smug satisfaction as the final, perfect product. It remained for Freud to present the image of man as the unfinished product of nature: 'struggling against unreason, impelled by driving inner vicissitudes and urges that had to be contained if man were to live in society, host alike to seeds of madness and majesty, never fully free from an infancy anything but innocent' (Bruner, 1973, p. 140). What Freud was thus proposing was that man at his best and man at his worst is subject to a common set of explanations, that good and evil grow from a common process.

Daniel N. Robinson summarizes the antecedents well, when he describes Freud's conceptualization of psychological man: an animal whose mental apparatus emerged from the primitive roots of the lower orders; an animal whose mission is to survive as an individual and a species, and whose survival is inextricably tied to 'sexual arousal and conquest'; a machine of sorts in which the 'flux and flow of energies seek equilibrium and cannot be eliminated as long as life goes on'; a machine, too, in which pressures diverted from one region unfailingly surface elsewhere in the system; but a developing machine, each of whose 'stages' brings new demands and new means with which to meet them (1979, p. 228). The instinctive past is ever present in this creature even if now steeped in high culture. The old voices still speak, even if heard only at unconscious levels – levels in which survival itself is rooted. Like Skinner, Freud gives us a hedonistic impulse even to the most selfless of our actions. Man seeks gratification; seeks to avoid pain; seeks to express the ageless urges of his species.

Freud's most definitive psychological model of the mind was published in 1923, in *The Ego and the Id*, where he introduced his division of the mind into *id, ego,* and *super-ego*. According to Freud's conception, the human mind is constantly beset by three different kinds of demands that usually conflict with one another, and require some sort of compromise solution, says Fancher (1979, p. 240). To begin with there were the demands arising from within the body itself – the biologically-based needs for nourishment, warmth, physical or sexual gratification. These instinctual drives seeking immediate satisfaction constituted what he termed the id. The second major element within the human mind he termed the ego, which deals with the real world outside the person, mediating between it and the id. Obviously, there occur countless occasions when instinctive demands and the constraints of social reality come into conflict, where instinctive gratification must be delayed, modified, or abandoned altogether because of the realities of the world.

The final structural component within the human mind is the superego, a special part of the ego which contains the conscience, the social norms acquired in childhood. As Leslie Stevenson notes, the super-ego – like the id – can confront the ego, this time with moral rules; the ego thus has to 'reconcile the conflicting demands of id, super-ego, and external reality (1974, p. 66). Whatever can become conscious is in the ego, although even in it there may be things which remain unconscious, whereas everything in the id is permanently unconscious. (Note the superficial resemblance to Mead's three-part structure of I, Me and Self.)

The instinctual drives of the id are the *source* of all of the 'mental energy' of the mind. This energy flows into, and helps shape, the mind, developmentally, through a succession of 'stages'. Like Piaget, as we shall see, Freud believed that people had to pass through a number of 'stages' which were invariant, although the exact time of onset and termination might vary. The stages which he classified as *oral, anal, genital* and *phallic* were based on erogenous zones of the body. What mattered was the experience of the bodily changes that took place at such zones, parental reaction to both the child's experience of, and demands arising from, such experiences, and finally the child's experience of possible parental reactions. Depending on such criteria, energy might be released – and in varying quantities – or blocked; a child might pass on to another stage or may get fixated on the current one, and so on. The important point to note is that the energy had to go somewhere. This strongly deterministic conception is, as we have seen, common to other structuralists who saw whole societies passing through set development stages in history.

It is clear then, that at the centre of Freud's theories is the notion of unconscious motivation or determination. Alasdair MacIntyre observes that for Freud, the unconscious is an 'omnipresent background to conscious and overt mental life and to behaviour', and it exerts a continual 'causal influence upon conscious thought and behaviour' (1958, p. 31). The form of Freud's concept of the unconscious derives partly from Freud's assumption of total determinism; put simply, the unconscious is the place in which behaviour is determined. Jahoda argues that Freud's determinism is total and unrelenting, nothing occurs by chance or by accident (1977, p. 15). Freud talks of the thorough-going meaningfulness and determinism of even the apparently most obscure and arbitrary mental phenomena (MacIntyre, 1958, p. 90). In *The Psychopathology of Everyday Life*, for example, he discussed the 'forgetting' of names and words. An example which illustrates the motive of 'unpleasure' (Freudian *Unlust*) in unconscious forgetting is as follows, as reported to Freud by his one-time colleague Carl Gustav Jung. A certain Herr Y fell in love with a woman, but the woman failed to return his love and instead married Herr X. Herr X was well known personally to Herr Y from prior business dealings. For a long time after the marriage, however, Herr Y found himself repeatedly unable to recall the name of Herr X whenever he had to correspond with him. Similarly, in terms of 'slips of the tongue', a favourite of Freud's was a slip committed by the President of the Lower House of the Australian Parliament during opening formalities. The President, who apparently had reason to expect a stormy and unfruitful session, greeted the assembly with the words 'Gentlemen, I take notice that a full quorum of members is present and herewith declare the sitting *closed*!' (in Sulloway, 1980, p. 355).

Jahoda points to two other aspects of Freud's determinism. To begin with, the psychologically determining factors can be established retrospectively only, and once discovered cannot be used predictively in other cases. The explanation for this is simple: we cannot yet measure exactly the relative strength of various psychological factors, with the result that in a circular fashion 'we only say at the end that those which succeeded must have been the stronger' (1977, p. 15). The technique of psychoanalysis can recognize causality retrospectively with certainty whereas prediction is impossible. The other aspect of Freud's determinism, is that psychological events are overdetermined in two ways. First, the chain of causation can be extended backwards in time. 'Hysterical symptoms, for example, can be explained by a relatively recent event, but there is one before which determines the power of subsequent events and is, therefore, also an explanation' (Jahoda, 1977, p. 15). Overdeterminism refers, secondly, to the fact that several simultaneous factors, each of them with some explanatory power, contribute to the formation of symptoms. So, a child may be scared of black hair: the cause of this is traced to a hatred of his father who has black hair, and this is caused by his father's leaving him alone when a child, which in turn was caused by his father's having an affair with his secretary which was caused by ungratifying sexual relations with his wife... and so on. On the other hand, the child also hates blackness which is based on a fear of spiders, beetles and other black insects. These are the two forms of overdetermination.

MacIntyre points to the extent of Freud's determinism, when he states that for Freud the difference between the obsessional ritual of a compulsion neurosis and normal behaviour lies only in the normality of the behaviour; for 'he could not have done other than he did' can truly be said of the person in both cases. Indeed, MacIntyre adds there is a sense in which the non-neurotic is more deluded than the neurotic. For, in obsessional neuroses, the patient is aware of the compulsion to perform his ritual whereas the normal person has the – if the determinist is right – illusion of free decision (MacIntyre, 1958, p.91). Recall Skinner's similar views.

One of the difficulties in attempting to evaluate Freud is his emphasis on clinical evidence. As Philip Rieff puts it, as a strategist in the 'wars of truth', Freud habitually insisted that theory and therapy are really the same, and that interpretation can be properly administered only in the setting of therapy (1979, pp. 102–3). Through the technique of psychoanalysis, and with such procedures as dream interpretation and 'free association' (saying whatever comes into the mind), Freud the clinician would attempt to excavate the unconscious. Though the goal of psychoanalytic treatment may be summarized as self knowledge this is hardly likely to be easy as psychoanalytic practice, as in psychoanalytic theory, is all about tension- and conflict-resolution. The confusion that this engenders together with some of the more exotic elements of Freud's scheme leads to the conclusion that 'the patient speaks in vain', as S. Y. Timpanaro puts it (1976, p. 46). Everything the person says can be interpreted as caused by previous events beyond the patient's recognition.

A contemporary approach to Freud is offered by Jacques Lacan who considers that the real subject of psychoanalysis is the *un*conscious, and particularly the discourse of the unconscious. This discourse is structured like a language, and its grammar can be unravelled. Indeed, the best known of Lacan's pronouncements is *'L'inconscient est structuré comme un language'* (the unconscious is structured like a language). As Malcolm Bowie observes, the relationship between language and the unconscious may be looked at broadly in two ways. First, it is clearly possible that psychical tensions and conflicts could have played their part in determining the structure of human language in the first place. Second, language is the sole medium of psychoanalysis: 'For the patient as he speaks his dreams and his fantasies, and for the analyst as he punctuates the patient's discourse and places constructions upon it, the unconscious is available only in a linguistically mediated form' (Bowie, 1979, pp. 125–6). Lacan has little patience with the first approach, and rather sees it as language creating the unconscious. And he sees linguistic mediation as extending far beyond the analytic dialogue. Lacan points out that the human subject, as he acquires speech, is inserting himself into a pre-existing symbolic order and thereby submitting his libido (*désir*) to the systemic pressures of that order: 'in adopting language he allows his free instinctual energies to be operated upon and organized' (Bowie, 1979, p. 126). It is the peculiar privilege of man the language-user to remain oblivious, while making things with words, of the extent to which words have made, and continue to make, him.

In a nutshell, for Lacan, the unconscious is the record of its transformation into a human subject (Callinicos, 1982, p. 36), and structural linguistics is the most appropriate *methodology* for the scientific study of it (Miel, 1970, p. 98). Lacan is not alone in stressing the importance of language as an avenue to our minds and indeed, all the other theorists in this chapter have made use, in different degrees, of this uniquely human facility.

## Schemes of thinking: Piaget

An 'epigenetic spiral' was how Jean Piaget described psychological and biological development, stressing that this was not a predetermined unfolding of innate properties. He maintained that the human organism, like all other biological entities, including animals and plants, has an internal organization and that this organization, or inner structure, is present from birth to death. Both infant and adult share the same unique human mode of cognitive functioning – the mind's functions operate through the same structures, in other words. Generally, Piaget was concerned with the changes in quality which take place in humans' mental make-up.

Crucially, for Piaget, the organism was not a passive reflector but rather possessed active potentialities which could unfold to a greater or lesser extent, depending upon the nature of the interaction with the environment. Piaget, seeking the essential property or capacity of organisms, concluded that it was 'action'. As Howard Gardner puts it, although casual talk treats feeling, thinking, seeing or understanding as discrete processes, the 'scientist must appreciate that they are all and equally forms of action' (1972, pp. 59–60). Activity, in fact, is a crucial

### Jean Piaget (1896–1980)

Born in Neuchâtel in Switzerland, he first published in 1907 (on the albino sparrow) and received his doctorate for a thesis on molluscs in 1918. In 1921, he became Director of Studies at Jean-Jacques Rousseau Institute in Geneva and two years later published his first psychology book *The Language and Thought of the Child*. From 1940–71 he held a chair in experimental psychology, University of Geneva. Revolutionised thinking about the development of children's thought, which he argued grew through qualitative changes in biological structures emanating from interaction with the environment.

idea for Piaget in two senses. Firstly, he believed that it is only by way of the baby's overt (bodily) actions and the older child's internalized (mental) actions that knowledge of objects (actual or symbolic) is possible. Thinking is activity, thought is action. Secondly, his view was that our knowledge of ourselves, others and the world, and the learning process are not so much discovery as contruction: 'the active creation of novel structures that did not previously exist – either in the world or in the mind' (Boden, 1979, p. 18).

We can begin by looking at the invariant function of 'adaptation' which can be sub-divided into 'assimilation' and 'accommodation'. 'Assimilation' means that the human being takes in that which is external in accordance with its internal organization, just as, say, the digestive system can assimilate animal fats but not large pieces of metal. At the same time, the organism 'accommodates' itself to what it has 'assimilated'; the organism changes by assimilating the external and accommodating itself to this assimilation. And the adaptation seeks a progressive 'equilibrium'.

As we have already observed, for Piaget, knowing is action. Initially the organism acts when it comes into contact with the environment, and these initial actions are all overt and swiftly become co-ordinated into sets; for example, the set of actions related to sucking. These sets of co-ordinated actions form what Piaget called 'schemes' (or 'schemas') and the various schemes which the human has developed at any particular time form a structure.

As the organism develops, its cognitive structures change from the 'instinctual' through the 'sensori-motor' to the 'operational' structure of adult thought and Piaget maintained that these three forms of cognitive structure represent different levels of knowing. The process of knowing is not a matter of sensory data rushing into the mind, but an activity in which the human organism, through experience, makes sense of the environment. The ability to make sense is directly linked to the particular cognitive stage (or level) reached and the order of the stages is invariant and universal; their structure never changes and every human being passes through them, although the age of onset and termination may vary. A child or adult may operate at one level or another, although generally each stage represents a different way of dealing with a particular aspect of the environment. So we would anticipate that most of a child's thinking would be characteristic of the stage he has reached.

The first phase, 'sensori-motor' period, is between birth to 18 months approximately when – as in all the stages – profound changes are taking place. For example Piaget claimed that the child is unable to make any distinction between himself and the rest of the world; 'he is profoundly egocentric', writes Margaret Donaldson (1978, p. 134). It must be remembered that this egocentrism is unconscious. In the course of this period, the child slowly manages to reduce this lack of awareness, and he begins to distinguish himself from the rest of the world. 'By the end of the period, he has constructed the notion of a world of objects (and of persons) which are independent of him and of his actions. He knows that things go on existing when he cannot see them or sense them in any way' (Donaldson, 1978, p. 134). Evidence that this fundamental change takes place during the period is held to be provided by the child's behaviour when an object with which he is playing is hidden from him, say, by a cloth which is placed over it. Up to the age of six months or so, he makes no attempt to recover the object. This is taken to mean that he still has no 'object concept', no idea of the independent existence of other things. Piaget cited the case of Laurent:

> At six months and nineteen days Laurent immediately began to cry from hunger and impatience of seeing his bottle (he was already whimpering as he does quite regularly at mealtime). But at the very moment when I make the bottle disappear behind my hand or under the table – he follows me with his eyes – he stops crying. As soon as the object reappears, a new outburst of desire; then flat calm after it disappears. I repeat the experiment four more times; the result is constant until poor Laurent, beginning to think the joke bad, becomes violently angry. (1954, p. 30).

The second stage is termed the 'concrete operational period' (18 months to 11 years approximately), which is divided into two sub-periods, the 'pre-operational period' and 'concrete operations'. An example here of change is that of 'irreversibility'. While the child at the pre-operational subperiod is to some extent able to transform mentally the present state of things into some future state, he is unable yet to realize that the transformation he has brought about is reversible by a series of changes in the opposite direction. Reversibility, however, is a property exclusive to operational thought. For example, a four year old child was asked, 'Do you have a brother?'. 'Yes, he's called Jim'. 'Does Jim have a brother?', 'No!'. The relationship was conceived as acting in one direction only, from the subject to the brother, and so was not reversible.

The final period is the 'formal operational' one and the thinking of this period, once it has been consolidated, is the thinking of the intelligent adult. Its most marked feature is the ability to reason logically. Piaget observes that while the concrete operational thinker is still concerned to manipulate things even if he does this 'in the mind', the formal operational thinker has become able to manipulate propositions, or ideas. We can reason on the basis of verbal statements. Piaget quoted, as an example, the following problem: Edith is fairer than Susan. Edith is darker than Lily. Who is the darkest? This problem gives considerable difficulty to many children of ten. Yet if it were a question of arranging three dolls in serial order the task would be easy for them (Donaldson, 1978, p. 139).

There have been many criticisms of Piaget's model: for example, the experimental work of Peter Bryant which suggests that children are more able at making certain types of inferences than Piaget believed (1975, pp. 149-58). The notion of 'stages' has also come under criticism, and many deny the existence of a distinct type of sensori-motor intelligence. Piaget was also commonly accused of ignoring the social and motivational aspects of the mind. For instance, the personal interactions between mother and baby prior to and during the baby's acquisition of language have only recently become the focus of developmental research, and the current questions about their function in cognitive organization have not arisen out of a specifically Piagetian approach. More importantly, maybe, the social phenomenon of language, which is closely related to knowledge, has not been studied too closely by Piaget. Piagetians, of course, as Boden notes, believe that the basic organizing principles of knowledge arise prior to language and that logic structures language rather than *vice versa*. (1979, p. 152). This is a deeply important point and one which has aroused controversy. Piaget's position was that we all have a fixed psychic structure and so language acquisition fits in with the existing organization, proceeding through set levels. The structure determines our ability to talk. In contrast to this view, people like Benjamin Whorf whose research was conducted amongst other cultures rather than in experimental laboratories, have argued for linguistic determinism: that the way we talk orders our conceptions of the world and, therefore, logically precedes knowledge. The knowledge we possess is determined by the language we use for making sense of the world. So some cultures have many different terms for different types of snow; they don't see anything

## Noam Chomsky (1928– )

Born in Philadelphia, was educated at the University of Pennsylvania where he studied linguistics, mathematics and philosophy. He was awarded his Ph.D. in 1955. Since 1955 he has taught at the Massachusetts Institute of Technology, where he now holds the Ferrari P. Ward Chair of Modern Languages and Linguistics. His first book published in 1957, *Syntactic Structures,* revolutionized the scientific study of language by stressing the biological, universal nature of language. Also known as an articulate and radical critic of American foreign policy, he risked imprisonment by refusing to pay taxes and gave support to anti-Vietnam movements. Has written on politics and 'technical experts' in such books as *American Power and the New Mandarins* (1969).

different from western cultures, but their conception of reality with multiple phenomena of snow is different because of the difference in their language (1956).

Piaget's developmental model was conceived in the context of traditional philosophical positions. He sets out the historical opposition between empiricism and nativism. Empiricism, he says, describes the growth of knowledge in terms of genesis without structure, whereas nativism offers us structuralism without genesis. Classical nativists and empiricists share two philosophical biases that set them at odds with Piaget. First, many of them ignore mental processes and structures which are not consciously introspective. Secondly, classical nativists and empiricists underplayed the role of bodily action in the growth of knowledge. Piaget's epistemological synthesis was a genetic structuralism. Another theorist, Noam Chomsky, a mathematician and linguist, developed propositions concerning the mind and language, which also posed empiricist vs. nativist issues.

## The innate blueprint

Interest in Noam Chomsky's work arises from its originality in subjecting the creativity or 'generativity' of human uses of language to rigorous analysis. The thrust of what Chomsky calls 'transformational theory' is: humans are basically creative beings, born with a sort of blueprint for language. This innate mental plan contains rules which equip them to talk effectively even though they, as children, may have had very little linguistic experience. Grammar is a natural capacity unique to humans and, in holding to this view, Chomsky enters the traditional empiricist vs. nativist debate, supporting the latter in arguing that we are born with innate ideas.

The question Chomsky's theory sets out to answer is: how do individuals the world over generate the capacity to speak, recognize and understand normal sentences? How, for example, is a 5-year-old child who falls in the mud able to say: 'Today, I falled in the mud'? 'Falled' instead of 'fell' is obviously incorrect, but the organization of the actual sentence seems to be a grammatically competent construction indicating a knowledge of the rules governing the English past tense. Briefly stated, Chomsky's answer is that the mind possesses an innate blueprint complete with rules which is the basis for linguistic competence. The essential creativity of humans is given in the capacity to transform or generate new words, concepts and ever more complicated sentence structures. Though appearing to harbour a highly voluntaristic model of man, however, we are forced to reckon with the biological determinism implied by the allowance of innate structures of mind; these are biological 'givens' – we are born with them.

Of course this hybrid determinism contrasts with the brand espoused by

Skinner whose work was anathema to Chomsky. The basic assumption appears to have been that child language was adult language filtered through a great deal of cognitive noise, and starved of vocabulary. For Skinner, all one needs to do in order to understand language is to identify the 'controlling variables' which will enable us to predict specific utterances. For example, in the same way as it is possible to say that a rat's (or pigeon's) bar-pressing behaviour is partly under the control of a flashing light, so the presence of a bad smell might cause one to exclaim 'Oh what a terrible smell'. And if a child said 'Hickory Dickory Dock', you are likely to continue 'the mouse ran up the clock'. In theory then, as Jean Aitchison argues, Skinner sees no difficulty in 'linking up any particular set of words which a human might wish to produce with an identifiable external happening' (1976, p. 19). Chomsky demonstrates, however, that in practice the matter is considerably more complex.

For example, take Skinner's notion of reinforcement: children, unlike his rats and pigeons, do not receive pellets of food when they make a correct utterance. Similarly, studies undertaken by Roger Brown and his associates demonstrate that parents tend to approve statements which are true rather than those which are grammatically correct. So a child who said 'Teddy sock on' and showed his mother a teddy bear wearing a sock would probably meet with approval. But if the child said the grammatically correct utterance 'Look, Teddy is wearing a sock', and showed his mother a bear without a sock, he would meet with disapproval. In other words, if approval and disapproval worked in the way Skinner suggests, 'you would expect children to grow up telling the truth, but speaking ungrammatically'; in fact the opposite seems to happen, says Aitchison (1976, p. 21).

It does not follow of course that no aspects of language acquisition can reasonably be described in behaviourist terms. For example, some people invariably say 'shit' if they miss a bus. But there is little doubt, however, that the behaviourist account fails to come to grips with the problem posed by what Chomsky called 'creativity'.

It is quite impossible to assume that we gradually accumulate strings of utterances throughout life and store them ready for use on an appropriate occasion. As well as producing novel grammatical sequences, anyone who has mastered a language is automatically able to discard deviant utterances which he may never have met before; 'Giraffe under in walks Gorilla the' will be rejected instantaneously. Chomsky also uses 'creativity' in a second sense to mean that utterances are not controlled by external happenings. Aitchison puts it well when she notes that the 'appearance of a daffodil does not force a human to shriek "daffodil". He can say whatever he likes: "What a lovely colour" (or) "Why do flowers always give me hay fever?"' (1976, p. 29).

Given the child's ability, the next question is 'how do they do it?' To Chomsky, human infants 'know' in advance what languages are like. As he puts it: 'the child must acquire a generative grammar of his language on the basis of a fairly restricted amount of evidence. To account for this achievement, we must postulate a sufficiently rich internal structure – a sufficiently restricted theory of universal grammar that constitutes his contribution to language acquisition' (in Aitchison, 1976, p. 31). In other words there are internal rules or principles at work. Indeed children are extremely adept at constructing generalizations that go beyond the available data, and having once arrived at a generalization, children are also extremely resistant to explicit correction from adults. Deirdre Wilson and Neil Smith offer the following example as a usual one:

'child: I bringed you a sweetie.
parent: No. Say, "I brought you a sweetie".
child: I brought you a sweetie – and I bringed you a lollie'. (1980, p. 169)

Chomsky's notion of internal structures does not literally mean that children are born with language in their heads ready to be spoken. It means that a blueprint is there, which is not necessarily brought into use until the behaviour is 'triggered' by other aspects of the environment and the child's development. Before continuing to describe Chomsky's account it is perhaps worth noting Judith Greene's point that, far from helping psychologists to solve the language problem, Chomsky's work has been designed rather to 'induce a healthy respect for the complexities of language behaviour, thereby cutting off some attractive avenues of oversimplification' (1972, p. 189).

Chomsky points out that children are to some extent in the same situation as a linguist faced with an unknown language, in that both are surrounded by a superficially unintelligible confusion of sound which they must somehow sort out. A child, according to Chomsky, constructs in internalized grammar in the same way that a linguist attempts to understand an unknown language. The child looks for regularities in the speech he hears going on around him, then makes guesses as to the rules which underlie the patterns. The guesses will move from simple ones to complex ones, and gradually his mental grammar will become more sophisticated. Eventually his internalized rules will cover all the possible utterances of his language. As Aitchison argues, if this hypothesis-testing view of language acquisition is correct, a child must be endowed with an innate *hypothesis-making device* which enables him, like a miniature scientist, to construct increasingly complex hypotheses' (1976, p. 92).

However, there are differences between a linguist working on an unknown language, and a child acquiring language for the first time, in particular the fact that the linguist has considerably more help at his disposal. He can ask the native speaker of the unknown language questions concerning meaning and grammar. Yet the child acquires the complete grammar. This suggests that by itself, an internal hypothesis-making device is not sufficient to account for the acquisition of language. The child must have rather more information at his disposal, and accordingly Chomsky comes up with the wired-in knowledge of language universals, writes Aitchison: 'Children learn language so fast and so efficiently because they "know" in outline what languages look like. They know what is, and what is not, a possible language. All they have to discover is *which* language they are being exposed to' (1976, p. 94).

According to Chomsky, language universals are of two types, *substantive* and *formal*. Substantive universals represent the fundamental 'building blocks' of language, the substance out of which it is made. For illustration, a child might know instinctively the possible sets of sounds to be found in speech; he would automatically reflect sneezes and belches, but accept B,O,G,L, and so on. He would dismiss PGPGPG as a possible word, but accept POG, PIG, PEG, or PAG. Formal universals on the other hand, are concerned with the form or shape of a grammar. According to Chomsky, children would 'know' in advance how their internalized grammar must be organized. It must have a set of phonological rules for characterizing sound patterns, and a set of semantic rules for dealing with meaning, linked by a set of syntactic rules dealing with word arrangement.

Linked to these abilities, Chomsky also assumes that every sentence has an inner hidden 'deep structure' and an outer manifest 'surface structure'. These two levels are linked by what Chomsky calls 'transformation rules'. As Greene notes, Chomsky cites three main types of examples all aimed at demonstrating that the actual surface order of words often positively distorts the underlying meaning relationships which all native speakers are aware of (Greene 1975, pp. 97–8).

1 pairs of sentences which have quite different surface structures and yet everyone knows that they have the same underlying meaning relationships. For example, the active and passive sentences Jane hit the boy, and the boy was hit by Jane;
2 two sentences which have similar surface structures and yet everyone knows that they have quite different underlying relationships. For example, John is easy to please and John is eager to please have similar surface orders of words and yet in the first *John* is the object of the verb *to please*, while in the second he is the subject; making it possible to say 'it is easy to please John' but not 'it is eager to please John';
3 single sentence which has two different underlying meaning. For example the ambiguity of 'visiting aunts can be a nuisance', can only be expressed by deriving it from two different underlying deep structures, one indicating that the first surface noun phrase means 'to visit aunts' and the other that it means 'that aunts visit one'.

As stated earlier, the rules expressing the relation of deep and surface structure are called grammatical transformations, or transformation rules. Chomsky assumes that children somehow 'know' about deep structures, surface structures and transformations. They realize that they never have to reconstruct for themselves deep structures which are never visible on the surface. So far then we have noted Chomsky's notions of the innate hypothesis-making device, the wired-in knowledge of language universals, and, in particular, the formal universals which enable children to know automatically that language involves two levels of syntax – a deep and a surface level, linked by 'transformations'. With this innate help a child can speedily sift through the babble of speech he hears around him, and hypothesize plausible rules which will account for it. Additionally, Chomsky suggests that children must be equipped with an *evaluation* procedure which will allow them to choose between a number of possible grammars. Children must have some kind of mechanism which enables them to weigh up one grammar against another, and discard the less efficient.

In summary then, the three elements of a hypothesis-making device, linguistic universals, and an evaluation procedure, constitute an innately endowed language acquisition device (LAD). With the aid of LAD any child can learn any language with relative ease, and indeed without such an endowment language acquisition would be impossible. *Ergo* biological determinism. As Gardner puts it, with such 'inborn structures', the learning of language 'becomes as unproblematic as a duck's following his mother or a squirrel's burial of nuts' (1972, p. 241).

We noted earlier that Chomsky is in the forefront of the empiricist vs. nativist debate and in order to be able to comment on this it is important to evaluate Chomsky's linguistic evidence. To begin with, as Aitchison notes, his proposals are not necessarily an 'all-or-nothing' package deal. He may be right in some respects and wrong in others (1976, p. 103). For example, on the question of whether Chomsky is correct in assuming that children are geared to looking for two levels of structure, a deep level and a surface one, the evidence is not too supportive (Aitchison, 1976, p. 203). On the other hand there is strong evidence that children do know instinctively that language is rule-governed.

Lyons points out that Chomsky's nativist case rests upon the alleged universality of certain formal principles of sentence construction in natural languages. But, he adds, this notion is 'not subject to direct empirical verification', for it is obviously impracticable to 'bring up a child from birth with no knowledge of any natural language, exposing him only to utterances in an artificial language spoken in a full range of "normal" situations' (1970, p. 46).

Aitchison prefers the suggestion that children have an 'inbuilt ability for *processing* linguistic data – though it is not clear whether this ability is specific to language or dependent on other general cognitive abilities' (1976, p. 232). Donaldson argues that the 'Chomskyan revolution' was a revolt against behaviourism; a child with LAD had need of experience indeed, but only to set going processes which were destined to depend upon it very little thereafter (1978, p. 36). She now sees another revolt, and against Chomsky. The argument now is that children are able to learn language precisely because they possess certain other skills, and specifically because they have a relatively well-developed capacity for making sense of certain types of situation involving direct and immediate human interaction. As Donaldson puts it, the 'primary thing is now held to be the grasp of meaning – the ability to "make sense"of things, and above all to make sense of what people do, which of course includes what people say' (1978, p. 38). It is no longer being claimed that when the child learns languages he is using skills highly specific to that task. On the contrary, language learning is now presented as being closely bound up with all the other learning that is going on. Donaldson muses that perhaps the idea that words mean anything – in isolation – is a highly sophisticated adult notion, and a Western adult notion at that. She adds: 'Heinz Werner tells the story of an explorer who was interested in the language of a North American tribe and who asked a native speaker to translate into his language the sentence: "The white man shot six bears today." The Indian said it was impossible. The explorer was puzzled, and asked him to explain. "How can I do that?" said the Indian. "No white man could shoot six bears in one day." ' (1978, p. 38).

Donaldson concludes that Chomsky's LAD is a formal data processor and in its way just as automatic and mechanical as processes of a behaviourist kind. The 'living child does not seem to enter into the business very actively (not to say fully) in either case. What does the warm blood in the veins matter?' (1978, pp. 38–9). Lyons sees it a little differently. He reads the Chomskyan view to be that we are endowed with a number of specific faculties ('mind') which play a crucial role in our acquisition of knowledge and enable us to act as 'free agents', undetermined (though not necessarily unaffected) by external stimuli in the environment (1970, pp. 126–7). Related to this as Aaron Cicourel's criticism that Chomsky's formulation gives no room to the context in which language acquisition takes place: to subsume human meaning under syntactic components which are ultimately derived from universal, context-free rules is inadequate because this does not account for the way in which meaning is generated in actual social interaction (1973). Indeed, this kind of accusation would be levelled at every theorist in this chapter.

Chomsky's model of man is a blend of biological determinism and human creativity. As such, it is criticized by behaviourists for being too biologically obscure and unscientific, by interactionists for being devoid of social content and psychologists for being overdeterministic. Yet, as Gardner points out, Chomsky is objected to by Claude Lévi-Strauss, the 'high priest of structuralism' for painting a picture of man of 'infinite capacity for original thought' (1972, p. 242). So what does Lévi-Strauss offer instead?

## Universals

Chess is an actual game, played by real people. It is also an abstract set of rules and conventions that exist above and beyond each individual game. Yet chess only ever acquires concrete form in the relationship developing between the pieces in individual games.

Similarly, with language: we identify two dimensions, as did the French linguist Ferdinand Saussure who called the abstract *langue* (language) and the actual *parole* (speech). 'The nature of the *langue* lies beyond and determines the nature of each manifestation of *parole*, yet it has no concrete existence of its own except in the piecemeal manifestations that speech affords' (Hawkes, 1977, p. 21). *Parole* then is the small part of the iceberg that appears above the water, while *langue* is the larger mass that supports it, and is implied by it, both in speaker and hearer, but which never itself appears.

Another distinction Saussure made was between *signifier* and the *signified*. For Saussure any word in a language is a *sign*, and indeed that language functions as a complex of signs. And he analyzed the sign into two components, the sound which he termed signifier and a mental (or conceptual) component, the signified. To make the matter a little clearer, Sturrock points out that we have experience, in our daily lives, of a great

---

**Claude Levi-Strauss (1908– )**

Born in Belgium, the son of an artist and grandson of a rabbi. Moved to Versailles in 1914. As a child he was lonely, given to introspection and reading. Educated in law at the University of Paris. He moved to University of Sao Paulo as professor of anthropology in 1934. In 1939, he returned to France to serve in army and later left for New York, where he met and came under the influence of Roman Jakobson, one of the founders of the 'Prague School' of structural linguistics. In mid-50s his *Tristes Tropiques* became a best-seller in France and he followed this up with more systematic theoretical works of his version of structuralism. Along with Althusser, he is the most influential modern structuralist.

many signs that are not verbal ones, of pictures and diagrams for example. Any object, be it natural or artificial, can become a sign provided that it is employed to communicate a message, i.e. to *signify* (1979a, p. 7).

The nature of the message conveyed by signs, such as wreaths of flowers, is one determined by the culture in which the sender and recipient live. Flowers have no natural significance, only a cultural or conventional one. When they are employed as signs they enter into what is often referred to as a *code*, a channel of communication linking the two parties to any such cultural transaction. (Note: the sign is roughly the equivalent of what symbolic interactionists called a symbol).

For Saussure, language is arbitrary at the level of the signified (as well as signifier), for each native language divides up in different ways the total field of what may be expressed in words; one language has concepts that are absent from another. The extremely important consequences which Saussure draws from this is that language is a system not of fixed, unalterable essences, but of changing forms. 'It is a system of relations between its constituent units, and those units are themselves constituted by the differences that mark them off from other, related units. They cannot be said to have any existence within themselves, they are dependent for their identity on their fellows' observes Sturrock (1979a, p. 10). It is thus the place which a particular unit (phonetic or semantic) occupies in the linguistic system which alone determines its value. In short, without difference there can be, for example, no meaning. Sturrock states that it would be possible, if rudimentary, to 'differentiate the entire contents of the universe by means of a two-term code or language, as being either *bing* or *bong* perhaps. But without the introduction of that small phonetic difference, between the two vowel sounds, we can have no viable language at all' (1979a, p. 10).

Roman Jakobson looked at the rules for the determination, classification and combination of phonemes, and indeed reduced all oppositions of sound to binary oppositions. His emphasis on binary relations and oppositions has been remarkably influential both in and out of linguistics. The study solely of signs and of the operation of the vast numbers of codes in any culture which enable us to interpret these signs satisfactorily, is now practised under the name of semiology (France) and semiotics (USA).

One of the leading proponents of semiology is Roland Barthes, who used Saussure's basic model to expose what he felt to be the hidden or concealed meanings of everyday life through the study of signs (1967). Like Whorf, he stressed that concepts are not formed in the human mind independently of the terms we use to express them. Yet, there is no necessary relationship between the sound-image, or signifier, of 'car' and the metal things we drive around in; the relationship is arbitrary so that the word 'car' means the metal thing, because the structure of language *makes* it mean that:

there are no real or natural car-like qualities that exist beyond language. We experience the reality of a car through language: we 'encode' the word and apply meaning to it.

So: the meanings we have of things are structured by signs about, rather than our experience of, things: the human world is not experienced as a series of facts, but encoded signs about facts which we can decode to take out the meanings. The world strikes us as natural and 'right' but Barthes argues that it's possible to uncover unseen codes and conventions through which the meanings of experience, as depicted by groups in power (the bourgeoisie), are accepted by the whole of society. He does this by examining many levels of everyday life, but, in particular, literature. For Barthes, writing is not a simple transmission of reality through the use of words: it is a complex social and political process performed at specific times in specific places and in a specific way – what Barthes called *écriture*.

Simply stated, Barthes argued that literature, film and, indeed, all levels of life are saturated in an 'anonymous ideology' so that humans accept a certain version of reality, a bourgeois one, unquestioningly. We are not conscious of the ideology for it cannot present itself to the consciousness; rather, it is embedded in consciousness; it is taken for granted as commonsense. But Barthes says that what we accept as inevitable is the bourgeois version of reality as conveyed by, for example, literature which employs specific relationships between the signifiers and the signified and uses them as reflections of reality. For Barthes, there can be no neutral reflection of reality – it all depends on the *écriture*. 'In fact it *shapes* reality in its own image, acting as the institutionalized carrier, transmitter or encoder of the bourgeois way of life and its values,' writes Hawkes (1977, p. 107).

*Mythologies* (1973) is Barthes' analysis of the 'myths' (images and beliefs) generated by the French mass media to portray a particular view of reality where bourgeois values surface as natural and right: the society authenticates its own being. Barthes uses the example of a *Paris-Match* photograph of a black soldier saluting the French flag; at one level this is a gesture of loyalty and, at another, it signifies to the viewer that France is a great Empire without any colour discrimination and that blacks faithfully serve it; thus it authenticates colonialism in showing how blacks serve their so-called oppressors. The thought control is not a conspiracy organized by groups in power, but is a subtle, all-pervasive ideology, unseen and undetected. Books, films, all of mass culture, is ideological.

The photograph has no single meaning nor simply reflects reality any more than a written text has one neutral meaning. The world, for Barthes, cannot be reduced to just one dimension or a single version. The belief that we can do this is bound up with notions of human beings as individuals, a bourgeois notion suggesting that individuals can interpret and project reality from their own point of view.

'The authors of this book are Cashmore and Mullan', we might say, but, for Barthes, this statement is part of the bourgeois emphasis on individuals as creators of their own products; that humans are separate entities with inviolable wills and personalities. Barthes' structuralist conception is of the production of literature as a collective process of reality manufacture and authentification through the codes that shape the meanings we make of words and images – so that it is always a conservative force in presenting reality 'the way it is' and thus justifying the status quo. Authors, like other people, are not individuals but part of a social complex and their products are also totally social. The numerous other people, historical factors, political influences etc. on the text's production are masked if we assume that the author is the source of the text.

Using Saussure's model, Barthes used the examination of signs to debunk the notion of the individual and show how analysis must proceed at other levels, beyond the grasp of the human. Semiology was one area of application; anthropology was another.

Claude Lévi-Strauss, for instance, tried to reduce much ethnographic data to binary oppositions. He approached human societies using the methods and models of structural linguistics. Ultimately his concern is to establish facts about the 'human mind', rather than about the organisation of societies. Leach notes that Lévi-Strauss's search for 'fundamental properties' is a recurrent theme in his writings and for Lévi-Strauss what is 'fundamental and universal must be the essence of our true nature' (1970, p. 18).

Lévi-Strauss' aim then is to discover the universal, basic structure of man which is hidden below the surface and which manifests itself in language, cooking, dress, table manners, art, myths, and all the other expressions of social life. Lévi-Strauss believes that the deep structure of a set of different activities in any society will be the same for them all. Since the table manners, cooking customs, kinship patterns, and so on of a particular society are all ways in which that society expresses itself, they should all, as manifestations of that society, have something in common. If we proceed to compare two different societies, each of which with its own myths, table manners, and so on, Lévi-Strauss argues that there will be a basic similarity between them, such that if one could uncover the proper 'rules of transformation', one could transpose the one set of patterns into the other set.

Lévi-Strauss describes Geology, Psychoanalysis and Marxism as his 'three mistresses'. All three showed that understanding consists in 'the reduction of one type of reality to another; that true reality is never the most obvious of realities... in all these cases the problem is the same: the relation... between reason and sense-perception' (in Leach, 1970, p. 13).

In terms of the empiricism vs. nativism debate, Lévi-Strauss is representative of the latter position.

Lévi-Strauss sees it as a universal requirement of the human mind to divide, to categorize and to classify phenomena; and he argues that the fundamental form of our categorization is binary. Our minds process what we observe in the form table/not-table, blue/not-blue, and so on. He was influenced here by the work of Jakobson who, as we saw earlier, reduced all sound oppositions to binary oppositions. Mennell makes the point that Lévi-Strauss seems merely to assume that, if our minds process sounds in this fashion, they must process everything else that way too: 'his debt to linguistics is limited to an analogy, and analogies are always suspect' (1980, p. 62).

Indeed, a number of structural-linguistic theories are prominent in Lévi-Strauss' writings. For instance, the priority of the collective and universal over the individual and contingent; an emphasis on the relational at the expense of the isolated unit; and acceptance of the application of the sign to non-linguistic phenomena. As Giddens observes, the implication of the latter point, as construed by Lévi-Strauss, is 'not just that concepts employed by linguistics can be applied to the study of social and cultural phenomena; but that these are phenomena whose inmost nature is the same as that of language' (1979, p. 19). The structure of each corresponds to the grammar of a language. Thus, as the grammar of English is to spoken English, so the grammar or structure of, say, modes of fashion or table manners is to dressing or eating.

Leach notes that Lévi-Strauss's selection of culturally significant binary oppositions, the equivalents of vowel/consonant, compact/diffuse oppositions in phonology, often 'seems rather arbitrary but they fit with the ethnographic data surprisingly well' (1973, p. 47). For example: left hand vs. right hand; every human individual is aware of the difference between his left and his right. Our two hands are alike in being hands, opposite in being left and right. Similarly, raw vs. cooked; human beings characteristically eat part of their food cooked. The use of fire for cooking is what distinguishes men from beasts. Lévi-Strauss has argued that the worry about what it is that distinguishes 'true men' from mere beasts is an anxiety shared by all humanity everywhere. If this is true, then concern with the opposition culture/nature is basic even when the concepts as such do not exist. Lévi-Strauss postulates that raw vs. cooked is a universal metaphor for nature vs. culture.

Ethnographic data is of interest to Lévi-Strauss only in so far as it can be used as evidence of mental processes valid for all human minds. Take the cultural data of the myth. Working primarily with the myths of Brazilian Indians, the Sherente and Bororo, for instance, he brought order out of the previous chaos by treating the myths as interconnected parts forming a system; not as discrete units. In analysing myths he has grouped them into sets, and analysed them structurally. For Lévi-Strauss, the structure of the various sets are homologous, and one set can be transformed into another set by making certain transformations throughout. He believes that, by adjusting the contents and characters of myths we can see them as structurally equivalent. Mennell points out that: 'he compares a complex of myths to a musical score, which can be read simultaneously for the melodic sequence (horizontally) and for the harmonic structure (vertically). The counterparts to melody and harmony in the study of myth he calls the syntagmatic and paradigmatic dimensions' (1980, p. 64). The syntagmatic chain refers to the actual sequence of elements in a particular myth, while the paradigmatic dimension links the similar elements in alternative and related versions of the myth. Not surprisingly, Lévi-Strauss believes that the units of myth invariably come in pairs of opposites, indeed that the opposition self/other is a prototypical category of thought (Mennell, 1980, p. 66).

For Lévi-Strauss, the practice of bestowing animate properties to inanimate objects, known as totemism, is a particular instance of a much more general phenomenon, one indeed that all societies have to face in one way or another. As Peter Worsley shows: 'the problem of how men perceive, select, intellectually order and socially structure the similarities and differences in both the natural and cultural realms respectively, and how connections are established between these two orders' (1970, p. 205).

Lévi-Strauss dismisses all theories of totemism except those that posit some sort of resemblance between totem groups and the names they choose. Such a resemblance, he stresses, is analogical, not literal. It is not that, for example, members of the beaver clan look like beavers or that members of the eagle clan look like eagles; rather these names mark off differences between such clans. Thus, one clan lives on the mountainside, and has high social prestige, while the other lives in the valley, and has lower prestige, and this difference is captured in their names, with the higher group having the same relationship to the lower one as eagles are seen to have to beavers. In Lévi-Strauss' formula, 'it is not the resemblances but the differences which resemble each other' (in Gardner, 1972, p. 135).

Lévi-Strauss uses the term *bricolage* to refer to the means by which the non-literate, non-technical mind of the so-called 'primitive' man responds to the world around him. The process involves a 'science of the concrete' which, far from lacking logic, in fact carefully and precisely 'orders, classifies and arranges into structures the *minutiae* of the physical world in all their profusion by means of a "logic" which is not our own' (Hawkes, 1977, p. 51). These improvized structures, *ad hoc* responses to an environment, then serve to establish homologies and analogies between the ordering of nature and that of society, and so satisfactorily 'explain' the world and make it habitable. As Hawkes puts it, a significant feature of *bricolage* is clearly the ease with which it enables the non-literate *bricoleur* to establish satisfactory analogical relationships between his own life and the life of nature, instantaneously and without puzzlement or hesitation: 'as a result, the "savage" or better, the "multi-conscious" mind, able and willing to respond to an environment on more than one level simultaneously, and constructing in the process an elaborate and to us a bewildering complex "world picture", builds mental pictures which facilitate an understanding of the world in as much as they resemble it' (1977, p. 52).

As an instance, Lévi-Strauss cites this account from the Phillipines:

> Almost all the Hanunóo's activities require an intimate familiarity with local plants and a precise knowledge of plant classification. Contrary to the assumption that subsistence-level groups never use but a small segment of the local flora, ninety-three per cent of the total number of native plant types are recognized by the Hanunóo as culturally significant... The Hanunóo classify all forms of the local avifauna into seventy-five categories... they distinguish about a dozen kinds of snakes... sixty-odd types of fish... the thousands of insect forms present are grouped by the Hanunóo into a hundred and eight name categories, including thirteen for ants and termites. (in Gardner, 1972, p. 137).

Lévi-Strauss defines 'savage' thought then as analogical thought. What is involved here is a 'reciprocity of perspectives in which man and the world mirror each other by means of 'classificatory systems' which operate as 'systems of meaning' (Lévi-Strauss, 1966, p. 222). Analogical thought works by imposing on the world a series of structural contrasts or oppositions to which all the members of the culture tacitly assent; Lévi-Strauss proposes that these oppositions are analogically related in that their differences are felt to resemble each other. As a result an analysis of the analogical relationship between, say, raw and cooked will offer insights into the nature of the particular reality that each culture perceives.

Lévi-Strauss's conclusion? The principles of human thought are universal. Lévi-Strauss believes, as Philip Pettit puts it, 'that the human mind... is *determined* in its expressions by the unconscious laws of the semiological systems it puts into operation' (1977, p. 77). What seems to be Lévi-Strauss's view is that the mind develops classificatory and organizational principles that, in turn, work as a structure; this then operates to determine the modes human thought can take.

C.R. Badcock points to the essentially functionalist nature of Lévi-Strauss' model and argues that his analysis of myth brings him close to the conclusions of another prominent social theorist, Talcott Parsons, in that 'both seem to conclude that the psychological basis of society is a vast interlocking system of mutually supporting ideas' (1975, p. 114).

We will look at Parsons next, but, before closing, let us note that all the theorists of this chapter have made sizeable contributions to our conceptions of the structure of the human mind, though not necessarily to our knowledge of that phenomenon. In their own ways, each has produced an extreme and provocative model though none has actually presented methodological apparatus with which we can practicably test the theories. For that matter, many of the other theorists of the structuralism strain suffer from the same flair and expect us to accept their models as articles of faith. None more so than the theorists we encounter in the next chapter.

### Technical Terms

**Epistemology:** The study of the status of knowledge, its sources, scope and, probably most importantly, the reliability of claims to knowledge.

**Ethnography:** Research of the customs, beliefs, practices, generally, the way of life of groups in different cultures.

**Discourse:** A multi-dimensional mode of communication involving language and gesture as well as the more stylized media of arts, literature, film etc.

**Neurosis:** A psychological disturbance characterized by exaggerations and unrealistic anxieties, the condition having no organic cause and the sufferer being aware of his condition, yet not able to control it.

**Libido:** Freud's term for sexual energy, the driving force or motor of all human behaviour. In later works, Freud used the word to cover all forms of psychic energy.

**Psychopathology:** The study of psychological disturbances and their origins as opposed to *Social Pathology*, in which whole societies are disturbed by such things as high crime or suicide rates (see section on Durkheim).

**Verification:** A procedure carried out to discover whether a statement is true or false. Falsifiability refers to the statement's potentiality for being made into a testable form. Karl Popper repudiated the positivists' use of verifiability as a criterion to distinguishing science from non-science. In other words, scientific statements cannot be tested for their truth, but they can be tested to see if they are false.

### Further Reading

*The Structuralists: from Marx to Lévi-Strauss* (1972) by Richard and Fernande De George, includes extracts from a variety of authors together with an excellent and clear introduction.

*Lévi-Strauss* (1970) by Edmund Leach, is a clear and scholarly account of Lévi-Strauss's contribution to both anthropology and social science generally.

*Piaget* (1979) by Margaret A. Boden, is a continually stimulating essay on Piagetian psychology.

### Advanced Reading

*Freud and the Dilemmas of Psychology* (1977) by Marie Jahoda, discusses Freud's

achievements in the context both of science and history.
*Chomsky* (1970) by John Lyons, is the best non-technical account of Chomsky's work available.
*Structuralism and Semiotics* (1977) by Terence Hawkes, includes a brief but clear account of the importance of Saussure.

# 9

# Mistrust of Consciousness

**Systems**

'The System is to blame!' This type of accusation is common. The idea that particular individuals can be exonerated from responsibility and their actions seen as only insignificant gestures when confronted by the more powerful, overarching scheme of things has grown in popularity. 'You can't beat the system' is an acknowledgement of the impotence of individuals in modern times.

We think in terms of systems: value systems, personality systems, systems of rules and, of course, social systems. The concept pervades our thought so that we are always aware that we're part of a system over which no single person has control: systems aren't so much governed as self-governing: we think of them as having a life of their own – and immortality, in some cases.

The concept of system has not escaped the attentions of social theorists. In particular, Talcott Parsons has done much to elevate it to a most elaborate and sophisticated interpretation of the human condition. Though often criticized, Parsons, during the course of his academic career, produced an exhaustive, often complicated but always ingenious elaboration of what was to be called systems theory (1951). For all the abstruse language, the irritating circularity of argument and the obvious conservative bias, Parsons' is a theory of immense proportions, seeking to explain not only the nature of human action and the course of social change, but also the relationship between society and the cosmos, always stressing the paramount importance of the system.

So, what is it exactly? In abstract, the system is viewed as a set of related and interdependent phenomena which have boundaries that are maintained; it exists in a state of equilibrium or balance with its environment and has certain mechanisms for maintaining this state. Whether we study planetary movements or human conduct, or even thought processes, we can discover the existence of continuous, logically related elements that function as a system. For Parsons, all phenomena that are accessible to human senses are systemic: they can be grasped by using abstract concepts in an ordered, related way (1968).

His analysis begins with the fundamental unit of human action, all of

### Talcott Parsons (1902–1980)

Born in Colorado, his father was a Congregational clergyman. He studied biology at Amherst College as an undergraduate but, in 1923, changed to social science. In a year of study at the London School of Economics and Political Science, he became interested in Malinowski's functionalism and this was reflected in his later theories on social systems. His first major work, *The Structure of Social Action,* was published in 1937 and began a monumental academic life's work spanning in total fifty years with over 150 books and articles, mostly on social theory.

which is seen to be directed towards attaining goals. Starting from Weber's view of action as always oriented towards some objective, Parsons theorized that a person, in striving to reach a goal, must have information about relevant objects plus some personal feelings or values about them in relation to his needs and the ability to make certain choices (1951). Rather like a soccer player who needs:

1 Information about where the goal posts, his team-mates and opposition defenders are;
2 An emotional commitment to scoring a goal;
3 Options about which route to take, or passes to make. Yet always within the system of play.

The soccer example also resembles Parsons' scheme in the sense that players are always compelled to take into account the actions of others. A forward confronting a burly defender expects him to present a stern challenge *en route* to goal. But he also expects that an unmarked team-mate on the wing is waiting to receive the ball and carry through the progress to goal. A pattern of mutual expectations emerges and this becomes a norm that can exert a binding control on the players; the action is controlled, so the interaction between two forwards becomes bound by the norm of passing in front of goal. Imagine the scene when the norm is broken and the forward 'goes it alone' only to be dispossessed: the expectant partner angrily gestures, asking furiously: 'why didn't you pass?'

The answer might be related to what Parsons called 'situational conditions': 'I couldn't quite reach the ball' (a biological constraint) or 'the ball got stuck in the mud' (an ecological constraint). Or it could be in terms of his subjective ideas: 'I thought I could do better by myself'.

Parsons was no Brian Clough, but he argued that the emergence and acceptance of norms comes about through each partner's weighing-up the advantages and disadvantages of courses of action. Individuals have the capacity to make choices, but they have vested interests in stabilizing some sets of relationships rather than constantly looking for alternatives. The quick interaction of the two forwards can reap rewards which would not come if the man with the ball paused to ponder on the choices available to him elsewhere. The actions of players are reasonably predictable to each other, as they are to an observer once he has discovered the norm which regulates the play, or, to use Parsons' term, the unit act.

Now, if the interaction of the two players becomes a series of botches, it is unlikely whether the norm will hold, for, according to Parsons, humans need to extract gratification from each other's actions. To continue to participate in a relationship, people need to be motivated to adhere to norms. Where motivation is missing, they will not. Where the adulation of the crowd, the congratulations of team members and the win bonuses are absent, there will be no motivation to stick to the norms and, of course, Parsons is very much in agreement with the exchange theorists on this point.

The importance of the interaction between two individuals, known as a dyad, lies in the fact that Parsons believed it held all the elements of a social system, except on a small-scale; it was a microcosm, a miniature representation of a larger complex of interactions (1951). Any individual performing a social act faces five sets of possibilities, which Parsons called 'pattern variables', and these are seen also to be characteristic of whole social systems. Parsons split each possibility in two like this: affectivity vs. affective neutrality, where the choice is between gaining immediate gratification from an act (such as one motivated by impulsive lust) or deferring this in favour of longer term satisfactions, such as marrying and raising a family; diffuseness vs. specificity, meaning that the person can base his relationship on a broad number of interests or a specific, narrow number (a husband-wife relationship is obviously diffuse whereas a doctor-patient relationship is specific); particularism vs. universalism, the choice being whether a person should relate to another for certain purposes in terms of particular standards (say a mother and her child, whom she would judge according to specific standards) or general, universal criteria (the same mother might be a judge in a 'beautiful baby' competition and impartially apply a set of uniform, accepted standards); ascription vs. achievement, dealing with how assessments of others are made, on the basis of what he is (say, a black man) or what he does (plays football with proficiency); self vs. collectivity, posing the dilemma of whether to orient action to one's own interest or to those of the wider collectivity (like the football forward opting, for his own self-interest, to score a goal in preference to passing the ball to a team-mate and giving his team a better overall chance).

Parsons argued that the dominant emphasis in small-scale societies lies with the first halves of the pattern variables, whereas modern industrial societies are characterized by such things as affective neutrality and self-interest. There are a number of objections to this rather inflexible categorization, not the least of which is that the distinction between the variables is never as clear-cut as Parsons suggests. However, it was Parsons' intention to stress the penetration of personal choices in decision-making for action by the social norms of the social system, that is, the regulating, controlling role of the system.

Parsons spells out what he calls 'mechanisms' through which this is done, the first one being socialization, through which the child acquires language, beliefs, values and norms of conduct. The second is a control mechanism of society used to minimize deviations in stable, normal patterns of behaviour. Together, the mechanisms work to integrate the individual personality into the social system and, thereby, promote equilibrium. Like the functionalists, whom he acknowledged as great influences, Parsons saw societies as smoothly coordinated, persistent entities, each part fitting neatly into the whole system. This is not to detract from his recognition of conflicts, or, to be Parsonian, tensions, but the concepts on offer, as Turner puts it, 'weight analysis in the direction of looking for processes that maintain the integration and, by implication, the equilibrium of social systems' (1982, p. 49).

So, Parsons presents a model of a social system which has its basis in the interaction of two or more people, but which develops what Cohen calls 'emergent' properties, a norm being a good example as it takes on a regulating, controlling function independent of any particular person (1968, p. 101). The system as a whole has a different ontological status to human beings and, therefore, has 'needs' of its own, the central one being 'integration'.

Following the leads of Durkheim and Radcliffe-Brown, Parsons saw a society's survival as depending on its ability to adapt to the natural environment, extracting and distributing necessary resources. The system must also have goals, and clearly established methods for reaching them; and it must have methods of socializing its members and bringing them under control. This exemplifies Turner's point because Parsons' concern is squarely with the problem of how the total system survives through integrating personality and cultural systems into the social system. There is no attention given to how the actual system itself is responsive to the perceived needs of specific groups. For example, one could argue quite plausibly that a capitalist social system is manipulated in such a way as to perpetuate the influence and power of groups which have access to certain scarce resources, and that socialization and control mechanisms are geared to the requirements of these groups rather than the system as a whole. Equilibrium may, indeed, be maintained, but it favours the interests of the powerful, not the powerless.

The system itself comprises four subsystems, each of which fulfils a requisite function. For example, the economy deals with the provision and distribution of material resources, the polity determines goals and motivates members of society to achieve them, kinship functions to produce socially competent members through socialization, and culture serves to reinforce values and norms through various agencies, including religion, education and the media. The subsystems are all interrelated, and are related to the dominant values of any society. Like Durkheim, Parsons placed a great importance on agreements in society: that people were of a like mind on certain matters. This made possible a common value system and gave rise to consensus. Parsons is sometimes called a 'consensus theorist' in contrast to the Marxian conflict theorists; this is because

Parsons, in formulating his model of society as a system, tended to disguise many of the often severe oppositions of interest and disagreements on values which pervade societies.

So, a Marxian analyst might explain the overthrow of the Shah of Iran, and the sudden rise to power of the religious leader Ayatollah Khomeini in 1980, by documenting the polarization and opposition of two classes precipitated by the Shah's westernization policies and the ensuing disjunction of the relations and forces of production; whilst a Parsonian would point to the presence of deeply and widely held Islamic values which held the system together but were placed under stress by the Shah's actions. The usurpation came with the surfacing of the values and the restoration of a man who personified them – the Ayatollah – thus re-establishing equilibrium. The changes were due more to the discordance of the *ancien regime* with cultural values than to the vitality of revolutionary forces.

The Parsonian analysis emphasizes the primacy of cultural values in maintaining order or prompting change. Hence the insistence on studying socialization, the way in which values are imparted, and control, the method through which deviations from them are held in check. A Marxian can allow for the pervasiveness of values, but would see the socialization agencies, like family and educational systems, and the control agencies, such as the legal and religious systems, as regulating and supporting the total system but, in the final analysis, controlled by dominant groups, whose positions of power give them access to the agencies. The system does not regulate itself so much as it is manipulated by power-holders.

Phenomena such as economic inequality, political domination, ideological control and material oppression are given little room in the Parsonian model, so that it would be taxed severely to explain the sequence of events in Poland in 1981. Where were the shared cultural values? The majority of people reputedly shared a system of values totally at variance with those who held power by military force and quite openly tried to suppress majority values, as articulated collectively through the trade union Solidarity, and personally through its leader Lech Walesa. The examples of Iran and Poland reveal the weaknesses of studying social systems as evolving organic wholes.

'Who now reads Spencer?' asked Parsons before proposing a grand theory of social change in which the total world system was said to evolve through primitive and intermediate into modern stages (1968; 1971). Thus, in common with previous progress theorists, Parsons allowed only a very limited role for actual human beings in instigating social change, for the motor of change is somehow out of control and grinds on remorselessly, independently of individuals. This has been a feature not only of Parsons' work but of a whole tradition known as general systems theory (GST).

## GST: the manic drive for unity

In GST, as in Parsons, the focus of inquiry stays with the total configuration rather than living individuals and the effort is to promote broad nomothetic inquiry designed to produce general, universal propositions (see Laszlo, 1975). Parsons' study was directed primarily at social reality, though all levels of reality from neurophysiology to world systems and planetary systems can and have been studied in terms of relations between elements. Richard Ball likens the topic of GST analysis to gravity: 'There is no such "thing" as gravity. It is not even a force. Gravity is a set of relationships' (1978, p. 66). That is the way in which particular events connect with each other in the system. Every system then (1978):

1. Has material elements which occupy physical space and have an energy which makes the relations between them alive; connecting them is a flow of information;
2. Has a tendency towards degeneration or entropy, so that all systems whether social, organic or physical are never more than temporary arrangements;
3. Can be broken down into smaller subsystems or be built into a larger system, like a human being can be analyzed as a series of psychological and biological subsystems or as part of a family, religious, or world system;
4. Is either closed when boundaries are impermeable and there are no connections with surrounding environments, or open when there is a constant flow of exchange of information, matter and energy with the environment, thus operating a feedback which makes possible adaptation;
5. Is cybernetic if it can receive feedback, change as a result of it and, thus become self-regulating and totally adaptive;
6. Is always part of a distinct level of system.

On the final point, James Miller has theorized seven levels of living systems: cell, organ, group, organization, society and super-national (1971; 1978). Each exists as part of a hierarchy and is composed of further series of subsystems, each having unique properties but uniting with others to form wholes.

Miller's effort to produce a grand systems theory of all living things and build conceptual bridges across natural and social sciences with elaborate classifications exemplifies GST. Also working in this area is Ludwig von Bertalanffy, a biologist who originally defined the GST programme, believing that, once the universal principles of systems was uncovered, 'a stupendous perspective emerges, a vista towards a hitherto unsuspected unity of the conception of the world. Similar general principles have evolved everywhere, whether we are dealing with inanimate things, organisms, mental or social processes' (1952, p. 199).

The attempt to formulate gargantuan systems theories encompassing all living matter predates von Bertalanffy and rests philosophically on the same holistic conception as the other theories of this section. P.K.

M'Pherson suggests the Greek ideal to 'see life steadily, see it whole' provides the imperative for contemporary systems theory (1974, p. 220). Rejected are the reductionism of the behaviourist and the specialization of the interactionist strains, as well as dualistic philosophies which saw man as separated from the natural world. Man was part of the natural order and could not meaningfully be studied except as one element in the gigantic whole. This view has also informed the theories of Comte, Hegel and Marx, whom Donald McQuarie and Terry Amburgie describe as 'a forerunner of the modern systems approach' (1978, p. 17).

These older works, as well as the modern GST, are motivated by what Kenneth Boulding calls the 'manic drive for unity... to break out of the confines of particular disciplines' (1973, p. 952). While the ambition and scope of GST are huge, there are hazards in trying to analyze systemically what is often a most unsystemic social reality.

'Apparently, one is supposed to reason by analogy from the assumed relations of the [system] elements to the relations between the individual human begins', comments David Hull (1970, p. 362). Observable natural phenomena do operate coherently in terms of systems and so do aspects of human behaviour. But humans *act*: they have purposes behind their behaviour and meanings attached to it. No systems theory can do full justice to the complexity of unique human behaviour. It may be patterned and regulated so that it appears very similar to the movements of molecules or planets, but it is guided by internal states.

Now, of course, this type of criticism is easily countered by the deterministic systems theorists who would argue that to analyze human action by reference to subjective states is misleading. The real determinants of those states lie outside the control of any single individual. They are in the system, individual products of socialization. Subjective states are not inadmissable, but they must be seen as derived from the system. Consensus is maintained through roughly equivalent subjective states over such fundamental issues as values.

As we have mentioned, this facet of systems theory smacks strongly of conservatism because it masks conflict. But this does not necessarily destroy the whole thrust of the analysis. Other theorists have accepted certain philosophical principles of systems theory; like conceding the inconsequential nature of man, his impotence and the decisive role of social factors beyond his reach in shaping him, his thoughts and behaviour. But with a difference. In the alternative analysis, the apparent cultural consensus is linked to the crucial concept of ideological domination.

## The two Marxisms

Many point to the similarities between Parsons and Louis Althusser, a

French philosopher (or 'Marxist mandarin' as he is sometimes called), and indeed as Nicos Mouzelis puts it, Althusserian Marxists appreciate the 'systematicity' and rigour in Parsons' writings (1975, p. xviii; see also Sklair, 1977). Before describing aspects of Althusser's version of Marx's model it is important to note some of the features and problems involved in understanding Marx.

David McLellan comments that views as to what constituted the kernel of Marx's doctrine have been widely different. Until well on in this century, Marx was viewed as an economist, the author of *Capital*, who had claimed, by his analysis of the contradictions of capitalist society, to have demonstrated its inevitable collapse. But by around 1930, with the first publication of Marx's 'early writings' particularly his *Paris Manuscripts*, there was a remarkable change of emphasis. As McLellan puts it, 'Marx was discovered to be really a humanist' (1980, p. 1). This obviously raised the problem of the relationship of Marx's earlier to his later writings: was there one Marx or two? Indeed, 'schools' of Marx formed. Some saw the young Marx in the old Marx, that is saw continuities, others saw the young Marx and the early writings as a transitory stage, and so on. Althusser himself holds strong views on the matter, which we return to.

Peter Worsley asserts that there is no 'real or true' Marx, for there is no such thing as Marxism, as Marxism is not so much a thing as a process, a 'series of linked historical emergencies: Marxisms' (1980, p. 1). Marxism, that is, is a plural phenomenon. This to us is not too satisfactory. We share with Gouldner the view that there are two distinct tendencies. 'One conceiving Marxism as "critique" and the other conceiving it to be some kind of "science" '. Marxism has been divided then between critical Marxists and scientific Marxists' (1980, p. 32). Gouldner sees this tension

---

### Jürgen Habermas (1929–    )

Brought up in Nazi Germany he is considered to be the leading contemporary 'critical theorist' following on from the work of people like Max Horkheimer, Erich Fromm, Theodor Adorno, Walter Benjamin and others of the 'Frankfurt School' of the Institute of Social Research (1923–50). He taught at Heidelberg and then in 1964 obtained a chair in philosophy and sociology at the University of Frankfurt. In 1971 he moved to the Max Planck Institute in Starnberg, West Germany, where he is currently working. Was once a leading spokesman for the student groups of the 1960's, but whilst he saw them as moving away from original democratic goals they saw him as becoming disinterested in actual as opposed to theoretical struggles.

as between voluntarism and determinism but, he adds, this is not the special plight of Marxism. It is, in fact, only the expression within Marxism of a 'larger condition common to social theory, to academic sociology no less than Marxism' (1980, p. 36). Indeed: a point we ourselves have continuously stressed.

Critical Marxism leads toward a perspective in which human decisions can make a difference, that is toward a voluntarism in which human determination counts. For example, the Frankfurt School retains confidence in the power of human rationality and has 'developed a series of concepts intended to go beyond Marx to interpret the changes that have taken place in the world since his death' (McLellan, 1975, p. 81). These consist mainly of adding the dimension of social psychology to Marx's work, as well as that of Freud. Critical Marxists also emphasize the basic proposition that, if society is increasingly under the artificial control of so-called technical experts, then any purely empirical approach to social theory must end up as a defence of that control.

Critical theories for Raymond Geuss consist of three theses: they have special standing as guides for human action in that they are firstly aimed at producing enlightenment in the agents who hold them, making them see what their true interests are, and secondly are inherently emancipatory; they are *forms* of knowledge; they differ epistemologically from theories in natural science in that they are 'reflective' rather than 'objective' (1981, pp. 1-2).

The difference between reflective and objective theories is highlighted in the dispute over positivism which, for our purposes, originated with the Theodor Adorno and Karl Popper debate in 1961 (Adorno *et al*, 1976). It later became clear that what was troubling Adorno was Popper's 'scientism' - the view that the logic of the natural sciences was the supreme form of rationality. Jürgen Habermas can be regarded as the leading contemporary 'critical theorist' because he reiterates Geuss's three theses, and echoes Adorno's concern over scientistic rationality.

Essentially, Habermas conceives of his work as an attempt to develop a theory of society with a practical intention: the self-emancipation of people from domination. As David Held puts it, critical theory remains designed to help in the making of history 'with will and consciousness' (1980, p. 250).

For Habermas, late capitalism is beginning to produce a technological ideology that will dehumanize the world: 'men are coming to be seen and treated as objects, not agents' (Hall, 1981, p. 49). Habermas talks of 'technology and science as ideology', of the 'scientization of politics' (1971), and in *Knowledge and Human Interests* (1972) he offers a classification of knowledge based on three different social 'interests': an interest in technical control which manifests itself in empirical science, or 'scientific knowledge'; an interest in social interaction and self-understanding which manifests itself in hermeneutic knowledge (interpretation); and an emancipatory interest which is conceived as bringing together theoretical and practical reason as critical theory.

Habermas takes psychoanalysis as his model in explaining the concept of an emancipatory theory. Psychoanalysis is seen as creating the conditions in which the individual, by coming to reflect on his determinations, frees himself. As Anthony Giddens puts it, 'if successful, psychoanalytic therapy translates unconscious processes, which cause the person to behave in ways not subject to his own voluntary control, into conscious modes of action which are subject to his rational mastery' (1976, p. 59). Habermas argues that this procedure can be applied to whole societies.

The theory of interests represents Habermas' initial attempt to specify the relation between knowledge and human activity. In his more recent theory of 'communicative competence' he argues that all speech is oriented to the idea of a genuine consensus which is rarely realized. As Held notes, 'the end result of this argument is that the very structure of speech is held to involve the anticipation of a form of life in which truth, freedom and justice are possible' (1980, p. 256). On Habermas's account, critical theory makes this its starting point. It is Habermas's contention that in every communicative situation in which a consensus is established under coercion, we are likely to be confronting instances of systematically distorted communication. This therefore is his formulation of ideology. The process of emancipation entails the transcendence of such systems of distorted communication, and 'this process, in turn, requires engaging in critical reflection and criticism' (Held, 1980, 256).

Much of the criticism of Habermas stems from the use of psychoanalysis as a model (see our earlier discussion of the practice). To begin with, the relationship between analyst and patient is an authoritarian one. More importantly psychoanalytic therapy is an encounter between individual persons attempting to uncover motives, and as important as this may be, 'it gives us little clue as to how to connect the explication of human action with the properties of social institutions as *structures*' (Giddens, 1976, p. 70). Another problem is the question, to whom is critical theory addressed? Who is to enlighten whom, how, and in which situations? These issues are only treated by Habermas at an abstract level.

Critical theory developed, then, as a response to positivistic, 'scientistic' interpretations of human action which paid scant attention to issues of will, consciousnes and the power of human rationality. However, scientific Marxism, on the other hand, stresses the 'lawful regularities that inhere in things and set limits on human will counter-posing determinism to voluntarism' says Gouldner (1980, p. 59). Unlike the 'going beyond of

Marx' attempted by the Frankfurt School, scientific Marxism – that is Althusser – represents itself as a direct interpretation of Marx. It is the aim of Althusser to 'rehabilitate' Marx as a structuralist before his time.

A fundamental idea of Althusser's is that of the nature of science as a theoretical activity which consists, above all, in the construction of a 'problematic'. Relevant here is the influence of the French philosophers of science, Bachelard and Canguilhem (see Lemert, 1981a, p. 228 and Glucksmann, 1974, pp. 97-9), who provided Althusser with his idea of the 'epistemological break' (or rupture) which divides pre-science (ideology) from science. Utilizing this idea, Althusser argues that Marx should be divided into four: 1840-44, early works; 1845, works of transition; 1845-57, works of maturation; and 1857-83, works of maturity. This is held to separate the young Marx as a humanist philosopher sharply from the mature Marx (after 1845) who was a social scientist (see Bottomore, 1981a, p. 14).

Althusser is fundamentally opposed to any distinction between 'theory' and 'facts' which treats external empirical reality in opposition to a knowing subject. Theory is not a collection of propositions which can be arrived at by observation of reality, since reality can never be apprehended without theory. The 'facts' are never theory-neutral. All knowledge is the effect of theoretical practices which take place inside thought itself; scientific practice has no object existing outside its own activity. In other words, as Paul Walton and Andrew Gamble put it, for Althusser 'the object of knowledge is never the real, the concrete' (1976, p. 108).

Knowledge is thus the outcome of theoretical practice on raw materials, but the 'raw material' is not constituted by what we can observe or

**Louis Althusser (1918–    )**

Born in Algeria, in 1948 he received a degree in philosophy from Ecole Normale Supérieure. He began teaching there and at the same time joined the Communist Party. Previously he had been in the Resistance and Catholic student organisations. In 1976, he denounced Soviet repression and Stalinism as he felt it limited individual freedom in the same way as Fascism. Although a committed Marxist, he rejected the humanistic interpretations of the early Marx and advocated a 'scientific' analysis based on his writings after 1856. His impulse was to cleanse Marxian analysis of any taint of Hegelian idealism. His extreme structuralist version of Marx attracted followers, at first, in third world countries and later in the USA and UK, where he became something of an academic cult figure in the late '70s.

experience. For example, Althusser makes an analogy between human labour on the raw material of nature and theoretical work on the raw material of pre-scientific conceptualization. Science emerges from a process of labour based on three generalities. As Bryan Turner notes, for Althusser, science: 'takes existing common-sense, intuition and ideological ideas (Generalities I) as raw material which is then transformed by theoretical work (Generalities II) into systematic, elaborate scientific knowledge (Generalities III)' (1981, p. 36). Hence new knowledge does not result from the discovery of hitherto unknown facts, and knowledge cannot therefore be the product of observation and experimentation. Rather, scientific knowledge is not cumulative, but involves epistemological breaks which separate science from ideology.

According to Althusser, Marx broke with pre-scientific notions in the period 1845 and 1857 by formulating a theory of history based on the radically new concepts of social formation, mode of production and superstructure. Before continuing it is worth noting, as Tom Bottomore does, that Althusser's demarcation between ideology and science is simply an assertion. It raised more questions than it answers (1981a, p. 17).

The social formation ('society' for bourgeois sociologists) for Althusser is a system, a complex whole, the complexity of the whole depending on the fact that it consists of a number of distinct but interrelated 'instances' or elements, apart from the economy itself – the political, the ideological, the theoretical – none of which are reducible to the economic. The complexity of the whole, the social totality, possesses a structure – a structure in dominance. As Alex Callinicos puts it: 'The contradiction within the economic between the social relations of production and the forces of production determines the character of the social totality because it determines which of the other instances is to be the dominant instance; thus, under feudalism, the political was the dominant instance, although the economy was determinant in the last instance' (1976, p. 41). That is to say that the determination of the economy consists precisely of assigning to a particular instance the role of the dominant instance.

Thus, these specific instances possess 'relative autonomy' within the overall structure in dominance determined by the economy in the last instance. The complex unity of the social totality is one, then, in which the superstructure – the political and the ideological – are treated as 'consisting of specific, distinct instances of the whole, articulated upon each other and upon the economy, but in which they are ordered by the economy in a specific relation of domination and subordination', according to Callinicos (1976, pp. 42-3). In other words, although 'in the final instance' – which of course might never come – the economy determines the whole, at any particular time it might order and shape the whole in such a way that the ideological or political, say, might be dominant, but never determinant. From the necessary unity of all the contradictory levels composing the social totality, and the autonomy that each level possesses, it follows that the unity of the totality is the unity of a complex of instances at uneven stages of development relative to each other. It is in this connection that Althusser uses Freud's notion of 'overdetermination': the unity of the whole is the unity of the essentially uneven instances. It reflects the relative autonomy of the different instances.

The unity of the social totality can only be grasped at any one moment by understanding it as a unity of related, necessarily uneven instances. Althusser employed the notion of 'conjuncture' to express this necessary co-existence of necessarily uneven instances at a given moment. As Callinicos puts it: 'the conjuncture is the specific complex unity that a social formation reveals to analysis at any one point in time' (1976, p. 47).

The next important notion to grasp is that of 'structural causality'. Overdetermination, we recall, is the idea of a structure whose complexity, the mutual distinctness and interdependence of its elements, is expressed through the way in which the economy displaces the dominant role within the structure to a particular instance, organizing the other instances in terms of this structure in dominance. 'Clearly, then, given these displacements, the causality governing each element is not one that can be attributed to any discrete cause, but rather to the structure of the whole as determined by the economy in the last instance' (Callinicos, 1976, p. 52). The role of the economy then, can only be understood by the relations constituting the structure of the whole, only through the mode in which the elements of the whole are articulated on each other.

Althusser assigns a central role to ideological structures whose specific role is to mystify the working of social formations. Paul Hirst and Penny Woolley talk about the means by which subjects are constituted and given the capacity to act 'as if', through the operation of 'Ideological State Apparatuses' (ISAs). ISAs create subjects with conceptions and capacities appropriate to their places as agents in the (exploitative) social division of labour (1982, p. 134). Ideology, in other words, plays its part in the reproduction of the conditions of production, including the reproduction of an amenable labour-force, through the ISAs, which Althusser distinguishes from the 'repressive state apparatus' (RSA). The RSA functions mainly by repression and consists of, for example, the government, army, police, prisons, and so on. The ISAs, on the other hand, function predominantly by ideology, that is by the propagation and inculcation of beliefs favourable to the reproduction of the mode of production. Among the many ISAs to be found in advanced capitalist societies, Althusser lists the religious ISA, the educational ISA, the family ISA, the political ISA (including political parties), the cultural ISA, and so on. Mennell notes that it is 'striking that many of these institutions coincide with those which Talcott Parsons tended to identify with his functional exigency of pattern maintenance' (1980, p. 88).

In the feudal mode of production, the coupled institutions of church and family conditioned individuals to accept their lot. In the capitalist mode of production the Church is superseded by educational institutions. The Church's role as a justifier was simpler than education's is in modern society. Why? Because modern societies are characterized by a much more complex division of labour: 'They must distribute individuals in roughly the right proportions required by a much more complex division of labour based formally not on status but on ability and acquired skill. The educational system must produce so many people capable of functioning as managers, so many as technicians, skilled workers, unskilled workers, etc., and who accept and conform to their allotted role in this (exploitative) social division of labour' (Hirst and Woolley, 1982, p. 135). ISAs then, must make subjects both accessible to exploitation whilst being kept unaware of the process.

In other words, an ISA is identified in terms of its function in maintaining the prevailing order. Hence, Althusser's theory has 'functionalist tendencies' (Callinicos, 1982, p. 75). Althusser's social wholes, which he sees as coherent systems with their own internal logic and capacities for self-maintenance or reproduction, do not help him too much with the problem of explaining social change. As Mennell argues, the 'immanent contradictions between the economic forces of production and the social relations of production, which for Marx provided the engine of history, for Althusser appears mysteriously to produce not continuous processes of development varying in pace, but a number of abrupt and discontinuous historical ruptures' (1980, p. 89). Transformations from one self-maintaining mode of production to another apparently occur in cataclysmic structural 'breaks'. If such an interpretation does not match historical evidence, no matter, for Althusser considers historical evidence to be empiricist and therefore unscientific. As E.P. Thompson notes, Althusser confuses the 'necessary empirical dialogue with *empiricism*' (1978, p. 196). Thompson adds that Althusser's structuralism is a structuralism of *statis*: 'Althusser's conceptual universe has no adequate categories to explain contradiction or change – or class struggle' (1978, p. 197).

This problem of explaining social change is exacerbated by Althusser's notion of history as 'a process without a subject'. For Althusser, as Geoffrey Hawthorn notes, 'men were not subjects. The illusion of subjectivity was the illusion of the younger, and even the middle-aged Marx' (1976, p. 228). Rather for Althusser, 'the structure of the relations of production determines the *places* and *functions* occupied and adopted by the agents of production, who are never anything more than the occupants of those places, insofar as they are supports (*Träger*) of those functions' (in Connolly, 1981, p. 45).

Human choice and decision-making abilities are thus illusory notions. Our thoughts and actions seem to be inviolably our own, but ultimately they are determined by powers lying beyond our control: those emanating from the structure in dominance of the social formations, but, ultimately, the economic instance. But, Callinicos asks, must 'we accept that men and women as the active agents of history are necessarily the prisoners of ideology?' (1976, p. 71). Certainly all the theorists of the section would argue so, and this includes Michel Foucault who, like Althusser, is concerned with ideology, knowledge and power. We complete this section with a consideration of his *oeuvre*.

### Power-knowledge: Foucault

'When I was studying during the early 1950s, one of the greatest problems that arose was that of the political status of science and the ideological functions which it would serve... a whole number of interesting questions were provoked. These can all be summed up in two words: power and knowledge'. Thus began the intellectual quest of Michel Foucault (1980, p. 109).

His work is as challenging and provocative as any contemporary social theorist and, in a way, defies summary as a distinct strand of thought: Foucault resists categorization as any particular type of theorist and switches his attentions frequently. There are few unifying themes or theoretical thrusts save for the power-knowledge relationship which he uses as a means to analyze the changing epistemological forms in different social structures.

It seems fitting, then, to close this section with an examination of a

### Michel Foucault (1926–    )

Born in Poitier, France, Educated in a local state school and then a Catholic school. Studied philosophy at the Ecole Normale Supérieure and later took courses in psychology. Joined Communist Party but broke with them in 1951. During the '50s, he taught at Uppsala in Sweden, Warsaw and Hamburg. During this time he completed his *History of Madness*, which earned him his doctorate and reflected his multi-diciplinary approach to scientific study. In 1960, he returned to France to become head of the philosophy department at the University of Clermont-Ferrand for six years.

theorist who writes not only of humans and society, but of those who theorize about humans and society and on the nature of theory itself.

Though often called a structuralist, Foucault, since about 1969, has objected to having his work classified with that of, for example, Lévi-Strauss, Althusser and Lacan. Despite this, there is, in Foucault, a selective use of the concepts of structural linguistics and what Giddens calls 'a mistrust of consciousness or "subjectivity" ' (1979, p. 38). Together, they give Foucault's enterprise a clear affinity with French structuralism.

The forms of knowledge, or *epistemes*, of which Foucault writes are not the property of any individual or group of individuals: they have independent status and, crucially, can never be known by those working within them. They can only be analyzed reflectively and as totalities disconnected from individuals. Then Foucault's work is history? Not quite: it is what he calls 'archaeology' (1972).

Were a historian to investigate a particular epoch when a certain configuration of theories, ideas and beliefs was dominant, he might trace inventions, and their inventors, changes, and the progressive evolution of truth and clarity from error and obscurity. But, according to Foucault: 'Archaeology is not in search of inventions... not to draw up a list of founding saints; it is to uncover the regularity of a discursive practice' (1972, p. 188). A discursive practice is how Foucault refers to cultural life – arts, sciences, philosophies and so on.

Foucault is out to uncover the underlying unity of discourses in historical periods and analyze both how these gel together in one epoch, yet are transformed totally in another. Like an archaeologist, his initial dig is for isolated items, but his eventual aim is to analyze how they all fit together – in Foucault's case, to comprise a code of knowledge.

In *Madness and Civilization*, for example, he describes how the definition of madness among the elite groups depended on the composition of the elite itself, as well as on society's need for outcasts; and how madness appeared only when leprosy had gone (1965). In a Durkheimian way, Foucault argues that all societies need out-people because their exclusion promotes everyone else's feelings of inclusion and solidarity; the mad themselves were perceived as less than human. Foucault is not so much concerned with the nature of madness itself as the way it was apprehended by the sane, and this can be seen to change drastically in the seventeenth century. Previous beliefs about the inhumanity of the mad gave way to a new apprehension. Confinement of the mad in hospitals, often disused leprosariums, accompanied what Foucault believes to be a rise of scientific knowledge and a decline of religion. Mad people came under the scrutiny of scientific practitioners and were regulated by legal controls.

But, while Foucault's focus is madness, he is, all the time, making statements about sanity: about the power of hospital directors, vested with scientific authority, to define, diagnose and treat the mad. He links to the prevailing knowledge of the epoch the way in which the mad were brutalized, chained, and made to share insanitary dungeons with rats; the mad were cast alongside criminals. Prevailing knowledge of madness was connected to the power held by certain groups. In the nineteenth century, madness became associated with sickness and therefore gained access to medical treatment. The distinction between madness and sanity was weakened in this century with the spread of medicalization.

In subsequent works, Foucault extends this type of analysis, trying to show how such concepts as disease and sexuality are parts or elements of the form of knowledge in which they are embedded; that the way people thought about them was based on a total social consciousness (1973; 1979).

Foucault's archaeological method means to study knowledge 'vertically', working from texts, or extracts of texts, produced in a given period and analyzing them with the aim of identifying distinctive discursive modes shared by the works of that particular age. He shows no particular concern with the people who wrote them nor with the personal influences on the writers. For Foucault shares with the other French structuralists the conviction that the texts, like languages, have independent statuses; they can be seen to form a coherent whole apart from the individuals producing them. Collectively, the texts stand apart from their authors.

So Foucalt is averse to studying, as some historians may be, the development of certain areas of knowledge, like economics or biology, for objects to be studied and concepts to be used within each discipline change so profoundly with epistemological 'mutations' (total transformations in codes of knowledge) which occur periodically. It is more relevant to study the relations between economics and biology *inside an epoch*, Foucault contends. At stages in history, knowledge is transformed and so, generally, is consciousness. So fundamental are the rearrangements that new lines of unity or connections appear. One of Foucault's examples is the change in thinking at the end of the eighteenth century, a change perhaps personified by Comte. Previously, things were perceived, studied and classified according to characteristics, but after the change, the world became more visible as a set of internal relations performing functions. The world didn't change; but perceptions of it did.

Elements internal to the *episteme* are always discussed in connection with each other and not elements from other epistemes, so that Foucault builds internally coherent 'structures of knowledge'. 'Such a search for structures of knowledge, however, when combined with Althusser's concept of "epistemological ruptures", tends to "dehistorize" history. But Foucault introduces "historical blocks of time", arguing that this allows him to study "periods dominated by a specific knowledge", while moving back and forth in time and space within each period he defines as self-contained' notes Edith Kurzweil (1980, p. 194).

The question Foucault asks is: 'How is it that, at certain moments and in certain orders of knowledge, there are these sudden take-offs, those hastenings of evolution, these transformations which fail to correspond to the calm, continuist image that is normally accredited?' (1980, p. 112).

Foucault is interested in what he calls 'the problem of the regime': 'It is a question of what governs statements, and the way in which they govern each other so as to constitute a set of propositions which are scientifically acceptable, and hence capable of being verified or falsified by scientific procedures' (1980, p. 112).

All our knowledge is fired by the 'will to truth', but this truth doesn't impose itself on a pure receptive human mind – Locke's *tabula rasa*. It is created and disseminated by people and can never be neutral or pure. It is always a case of who said it and how it was said, rather than what was said and whether it could be verified.

So when Foucault looks closely inside his 'historical blocks', he concentrates on religion, philosophy and science, always trying to expose the changing role of power as articulated through such figures as priests, lawyers, judges and physicians – the victuallers of 'truth'. Knowledge was thought to reside with these figures; they diffused it. This gave them the facility to exercise power and, at the same time, that power was reproduced in their knowledge. Foucault shows how their knowledge and, therefore, power was formed and operated in actual working places rather than being imposed from above by some state or institution.

This is a political conception of knowledge but not simply one that implies that knowledge 'reflects' power relations, as some Marxian interpretations might have it, for as Foucault points out: 'Power produces knowledge.... Power and knowledge directly imply one another' (1977, p. 27). Knowledge can never be true or false for it is always contingent on power. And, conversely, there can be no power without a knowledge of it. Alan Sheridan gives a Foucault example:

> 'Crime produced the prison; the prison the delinquent class; the existence of a delinquent class an excuse for the policing of the entire population. This policing led to the extraction and recording of information about groups and individuals... The exercise of power over the population and the accumulation of knowledge about it are two sides of a single process; not power and knowledge, but power-knowledge' (1980, p. 162).

This view of the inseparability of power and knowledge is given detailed substantiation in Foucault's varied studies in which he accounts for the constitution of knowledge with continual reference to power relationships. The relationships themselves must be explored because, as Foucault insists: 'Power in the substantive sense, le 'pouvoir, doesn't exist... power means relations' (1980, p. 198).

Foucault takes a nominalist approach, meaning that the question of his enquiry is not 'what is knowledge'. That is not as important as: 'Under what conditions is power-knowledge possible?' Or, 'How is power-knowledge operationalized in practical activities?' His answers involve locating certain categories of people, like the mad, prisoners, or children, whose ability to exercise power is very restricted, although only a small number do not somehow actually find ways of exercising power – if only on each other.

So, there is in his work a challenge to both individualist, or interactionist, and Marxian notions of power in which the 'mechanics', as he calls them, are left unexplicated: 'Power is everywhere; not because it embraces everything, but because it comes from everywhere... power is not an institution, nor a structure, nor a possession' (1979, p. 93).

For Foucault, power does not reside in a state apparatus, where it ensures the subordination of the proletariat, as Althusser theorizes it. Nor is it the ability of one individual or group to impose their will over another, as Weber would argue. Sheridan echoes Foucault; 'Power should be understood as "the multiplicity of power relations" at work in a particular area.' They are 'transformed, strengthened and, sometimes reversed' (1980, p. 183). Foucault studies not the possession of power because it is not a thing to be possessed, but rather a facility to be exercised; he examines what Sheridan calls 'an infinitely complex network of "micro-powers", of power relations that permeate every aspect of social life' (1980, p. 139). Power is everywhere as knowledge is everywhere; to know is to exercise power.

Clearly then, Foucault's position is in contrast to Marxian stances. Ideology, for instance, which is so central to Marxian theory, does not appear in Foucault if only because, as he points out: 'it always stands in virtual opposition to something else which is supposed to count as truth' (1980, p. 118). And what counts as 'truth' is always wrapped up with power relations; it is never neutral. To believe in ideology is also to believe in its opposite: truth. Foucault rejects this duality.

There is also the question of change. Foucault analyses gigantic mutations in forms of knowledge and, therefore, consciousness, but never gives an explanation of the dynamic or motor behind them upon which a historical materialist theory would insist when noting the critical modes of production. There are sudden changes from one *episteme* to another because human thought is creative and unpredictable. Foucault does not deny the parts played by material factors in the production and shaping of human thought, but, for him, they are not complete explanations in themselves as some Marxian theorists would believe. But Foucault's brand of idealism is not based on the notion of an autonomous, active subject *à la* symbolic interactionism. The human is always governed by underlying sets of rules dictating what he is able to think and do because he exists with an *episteme* – and this is simply not reducible to anything less than a totality.

Foucault is acknowledging the role of consciousness in spurring social change, yet denying its independence as a unit for social analysis. For humans don't say what they mean, nor mean what they say; they do things that are not intended – their thoughts are not transparent to themselves. Consciousness cannot be interpreted as a 'given' and analyzed as if independent. So, what is change? Where does it come from? Who does it?

It's almost self-defeating to systematize Foucault, particularly on this point, for he simply does not have a theory of history and society in the same sense as most of the other figures in this book. He provides masses of intricate, disparate analyses which cannot possibly be presented as 'truth' – the way things are – if only because his own work is situated in the *episteme* of this age. Foucault can only present provocations to debate. But this is not a shortcoming, for any attempt at social theorizing will always be subjected to the same necessary limitation, according to Foucault.

In an attention-demanding way, Foucault's work is anti-social theory. We seem to have travelled a very long way from Parsons, the social theorist *par excellence* with whom we started this chapter. Yet Foucault shares with the others a desire to find a new way of connecting things together so that they form wholes – sometimes coherent, sometimes not. It is the curiosity about such connections which bonds this chapter: the search for new patterns, new spaces in which to see them and new angles from which to describe them. For Foucault, it was through archaeology; for Althusser, through structures; for the others, through systems analysis. All looked for the complete set of elements rather than individual items: man does not come into the picture as an active, operational being; the structure or system in which he lives is always, in one way or another, self-contained and independent of his volition.

We have simplified and, at times, caricatured the thinkers of this chapter in our efforts to stress what we feel to be the most fundamental issue in social theory. That issue crops up in various guises: as free will vs. determinism, as agent vs. structure, as history vs. the individual. We believe it deeply affects the entire theoretical enterprise and, therefore, social science generally. What remains is to see if we can distil the insights of past chapters into a model of and programme for social theory. Our conclusion will be aimed at precisely this.

## Technical Terms

**Epistemological Break:** First coined by the French philosophers of science Bachelard and Canguilhem, who argued that knowledge proceeds, not cumulatively, but rather through the process of discernible, sharp breaks.

**Generalities I, II, III:** This refers to Althusser's notion that science emerges from a process of labour. The levels of activity are, I: common sense, intuition and ideological ideas, II: theoretical work, III: systematic, elaborate scientific knowledge.

**Historicism:** The view that no historical situation can be understood except on its own terms; that events have to be understood in relation to other events surrounding it. History is seen to have a 'logic' of its own, independent of men's volition . This unfolds through a series of stages, the development of which cannot be interrupted.

**Ideology:** There are 2 basic conceptions of this. One holds that it represents a distortion of truth and a deliberate obscuring of reality (eg. Althusser). The other holds that there is no absolute truth or 'pure' reality, so all apprehensions of it are, in a sense, ideological (eg. Foucault).

**Nominalism:** The view that the world has no real essence apart from the labels we attach to it with words. Against this *realism* (or essentialism) asserts that the world has an essential nature or essence and that the task of science is to uncover the real nature of things.

**Problematic:** A conceptual or theoretical system as outlined by Althusser, it sets limits to what questions can be posed and examined.

**Reproduction:** The process by which a society makes itself over and over again through the organized practical and intellectual activities of its members.

**Hermeneutics:** The term first developed by Dilthey (see chapter 4) used to denote the discipline concerned with the investigation and interpretation of human speech, behaviour, institutions as intentional.

## Further Reading

*The Structure of Sociological Theory* (1982 edition) by Jonathan Turner, has a very clear and up-to-date exposition of Parsons' theories.

*Sociological Theory* (1981) by Doyle Paul Johnson devotes half a chapter to Parsons' approach and a full concluding chapter to what Johnson calls 'Open Systems Theory' which equates to GST.

*Structuralist Analysis in contemporary social thought* (1974) by Miriam Glucksmann compares the theories of Lévi-Strauss and Althusser.

## Advanced Reading

*Structuralism and Since* (1974) edited by John Sturrock is a useful alternative to the frequently obscure French structuralist writers.

*Michel Foucault: the will to truth* (1980) by Alan Sheridan is undoubtedly the most accessible account of the life and works of one of the most bewildering modern thinkers.

*Althusser's Marxism* (1976) by Alex Callinicos is the clearest account of Althusser, while E. P. Thompson's *The Poverty of Theory* (1978) is a polemical account.

*Introduction to Critical Theory* (1980) by David Held is a comprehensive and authoritative account of critical theory.

## Theory into action

## The Capitalist State

In both his book *Political Power and Social Classes* (1973) and his debate with Ralph Miliband following the publication of the latter's *The State in Capitalist Society* (1969), Nicos Poulantzas has attempted to describe the nature of the state in capitalist societies in structuralist terms. Poulantzas and Miliband do agree on certain points. For example, they are both committed to providing a fully-fledged theory of the workings of the state in terms consistent with those outlined by Marx in *Capital* (though Marx himself never developed such a project with any rigour). As such, both are opposed to the conception of the state proposed by 'pluralist-democratic' theories: here the idea is that the state is a neutral body, acting as a mediator of different, possible contrasting, interest groups and keeping democracy intact by sifting through, and arbitrating on, interests in a system of 'checks and balances'. Implied in this conception is the existence of more than one elite group – that is, small powerholding circles – and managers or administrators who perform as 'go-betweens' for the central state authority, the private business sector and the rest of the population (as such the managers enjoy a degree of independence from the dictates of each of these three groups).

Perhaps the crucial point shared by Poulantzas and Miliband is that the state must not be seen in terms of a strict, direct 'reflection' of the economic interests of one single group in society. This idea is inspired by Althusser who, when discussing the overlapping structures of society, referred to three different levels, or 'instances' (economic, political and ideological), each of which affect each other in some measure and each of which is determined 'in the last instance' by the economic level. However, although they exist in a unified system, each level has a certain amount of independence from the others. In other words, it is not completely independent of the system, but has 'relative autonomy'.

Drawing on Althusser's total theory, Poulantzas tries to develop what he calls a 'regional theory', or a theory of one level, in this case, the political. But where, as we have seen, Althusser's conception of society was strongly reminiscent of Parsons' model in the sense that the social formation was a self-enclosed system, Poulantzas introduced struggle between social classes as a relatively, but not wholly, autonomous agent of change. The state is a crystallization of this class struggle: it mirrors the conflicts in the broader society rather than the specific interests of only one class. In sum, the social system's contradictions, so important to the Marx-Engels theory, give rise to class conflicts and the state responds to such conflicts by intervening in them. Thus, it functions to maintain the whole system by intervention and, although that intervention may sometimes favour working class interests, the maintenance of the total system is ultimately in the interests of the ruling classes. It follows that the state in itself does not have power, but rather reflects the imbalance of power in society generally. So although the state is not neutral, neither is it 'under the thumb' of ruling groups – yet it inevitably reflects those groups' interests rather than those of the working class.

In Marxian style, he depicts the state as subordinated to the interests of objective economic classes. These are themselves not reducible to individual people or even groups of people, who are merely bearers of classes, or *trager*. Whereas Miliband would want to agree with most of Poulantzas' argument, and then set about proving it by researching the actual operations of the state through the actions of and relationships between people, Poulantzas insists that such objects as classes and the state are not amenable to empirical investigation simply because they do not refer to the actions of people. They exist beyond them, are not visible and therefore cannot be apprehended. Miliband's mistake in assuming that social phenomena can be analyzed by looking at individuals with motives, intentions, desires etc. derives from what Althusser called 'the problematic of subject'.

In contrast to Poulantzas, Miliband tries to demonstrate the contingency of connections between the ownership of wealth and political domination; that under certain conditions, the two coincide. He also documents the contingency, or incidence, of the connections between elite groups. Again, the assumption is that classes and other social phenomena are composed of people. For Poulantzas, they are not: they exist objectively and independently of people.

If, for example, we turn to the role of bureaucracy, one of the major State institutions, Miliband argues that members of the capitalist class directly participate in the State apparatuses and in government – this is established as a matter of fact; that the social origins of those at the summit of the bureaucracy are the same as those of the ruling class – public schools, Oxbridge, etc.; and, finally, that personal ties of influence exist between the ruling class and members of the State bureaucracy – this, too, is established as a matter of fact.

Against this Poulantzas argues that the demonstration of direct participation of members of the capitalist class in the bureaucracy and the government, either through informal influence or through formal ties (due to economic power, etc.) is irrelevant to the analysis of the relationship between economically dominant classes and the state. This relationship is an objective relationship which exists independently of particular spheres of influence which can be empirically discerned. Thus Poulantzas argues that if the function of the state in a social formation and the interests of the dominant class coincide, this is by reason of the system – it it not necessary to the analysis of the functions of the state to demonstrate empirically the presence of interests of the dominant class within it. The class origins of the members of the bureaucracy are not necessarily relevant to the role it establishes for itself, and indeed it may be deceptive to assume so. The bureaucracy is a servant of the ruling class, not because of the class origins of its members, nor the personal relations among the members of dominant class and bureaucracy, but by virtue of its part in integrating the state in the total social formation.

What Miliband does is effectively to obscure the analysis, according to Poulantzas. His 'discoveries' of connections based on empirical research are fragmentary, ill-conceived and show only limited elements of the social formation. So, the research fails to take account of the totality and is therefore deceptive.

Like most of the other social structuralists, Poulantzas is hostile to this type of empirical investigation for failing to account for the totality, a phenomenon which is not apprehensible to the human senses and can only be grasped through theoretical practice (Althusser's Generality III). Observation is necessarily flawed and the human subject is irrelevant. As such, Poulantzas' work is structuralist in the very extreme and presents itself as the ultimate example of a theory based on the mistrust of human consciousness and on faith in the presence of a determining structure.

# Epilogue

Imagine we are watching a puppet show. The puppets are moving about jerkily, their motion activated by agitations of the strings that are attached to their limbs. They enact a drama, but are never actually in that drama. Their behaviour is governed by the strings.

Then we move back in the hall to a position from which it is not possible to see the strings. Now, the puppets seem to move about of their own accord: their manœuvres are not precipitated by the jerking of strings, but are prompted by their own wishes. They appear to be uncontrolled.

On moving further back in the hall, we find their precise actions less visible. It becomes hard to discern the intricacies of the movements. The man next to us in the audience then whispers to us that he has X-ray vision. 'Prove it,' we say, but he can't. 'But believe me,' he insists. 'Those puppets look as if they're moving freely, but, inside their heads they have nothing but computer circuits.' He says they only seem to have free will, but are really programmed for action. 'From the moment they're made,' he reckons. Has he got X-ray vision? There's no way of telling.

Disillusioned, but intrigued we leave the hall and make our way outside. Round the back of the theatre we see that its back wall has been demolished, leaving only a skeleton of a scaffold. But without the scaffold, the whole building would fall apart; the hall would fall, as would the puppet stage, as would the puppets. We think so, anyway; but there's no way of knowing.

Social theory presents us with a similar problem: is there any way of knowing? Or is all theory destined to remain just that: theory, and not knowledge. In a way, we have tried the patience of the readers. We have asked that they accept the theories presented, yet have only on occasion attempted to say whether they are true or not.

The question the whole book begs is: is there any kind of knowledge that is either true or false, or are all kinds of knowledge derived from a particular way of looking at the world. Do our conclusions about the nature of man and his relationship to society ultimately hinge on the basic assumptions we make about him in the first place?

If we assume man is free, uncontrolled and untrammelled by such invisible forces as structure or unknown factors like stimuli, then we can construct all manner of theories based on his sense of freedom and inviolable will to that freedom. In spite of all attempts to constrain him, he is able to assert himself and his essential creativity and freedom. Jean-Paul Sartre goes so far as to assert that: 'Man is nothing else but what he makes of himself' (1973, p. 601). Thus man is condemned to his freedom.

But we can never prove this nor indeed demonstrate this to another who believes that the existence of structures is incontestable. Man acts in certain, predictable ways, thinks in almost uniform patterns and generally lives in a manner that suggests he is not the motive force we sometimes take him to be. Quite the opposite. He is restricted, some would say totally restricted, in his movements, either by the structure of a society which encases him or by the structure of a mind which canalizes his thought and behaviour. In this view, he cannot even think for himself: 'he is unceasingly modified by causes, whether visible or concealed, over which he has no control, which necessarily regulate his mode of existence, give the hue to his way of thinking, and determine his manner of acting' (Holbach, 1973, p. 585).

Others would say neither view is completely right: it is just a matter of suspending assumptions about his creativity or lack of it and trying to look more closely at the actual physical influences on his behaviour. What looks to be free action or reflection of some structure is, on analysis, an elaborate series of responses to stimuli in the environment. Something happens; he responds.

All social theory is, as we have seen, committed to an X-ray view of society: dismissing what seems obvious and certain and trying to uncover what goes on beneath the surface of reality. It is about the removal of the obvious, and the presentation of the hidden. Structuralists are perhaps the most extreme proponents of this in their insistence that appearance is not reality. Further, reality is not apprehensible to the human senses. Thus empiricism, the gathering of facts about the world from research schedules, is permissible but only as elaborations of the world as we see it. Beneath the surface lurks a deeper, more profound, yet intangible, reality. It may be in the mind; it might be in society; it may even be beyond human comprehension. We are asked to believe it is there.

The results of empirical research may certainly look insignificant from the dizzying levels of the structuralist's office desk. In a way, a lot of atheoretical empirical work is not enlightening and designed only to tell us what we already know – or, at least, suspected. Is there an alternative to the grand theories of structuralists and the fact-grubbing empiricism of much research?

In an attempt to strike a balance, Robert Merton developed what he called middle-range theories (with the accent on the plural). No one single theory of society was possible for Merton, but multiple theories couched at a lower level of abstraction than those of his mentor, Parsons. Merton's project was to encourage research, taking selected portions from the more abstract theories while reformulating some of their concepts so as to make theoretically-informed statements about the world verifiable and, conversely, falsifiable through empirical research (1949).

Similar in spirit, if not letter, was the critique of C. Wright Mills who issued a warning against what he saw as inconsequential atheoretical research but also against the vast theoretical edifices that seemed to have no necessary relation to reality (1959). Mills stressed the need to account for the history of a society and the biography of an individual, for neither can be understood without an understanding of both. Mills held a vision of man as a shaper of his own destiny, though severely influenced by his place in history and his location in the hierarchy of power. In spite of these, there remained a vision of a potent being, exerting influences.

The problem with Mills' and, for that matter, Merton's approach is that they are both unquestioningly reliant upon empirical data. There is no critical questioning of the way in which that data, culled from research, is appreciably affected, some would say polluted, by the dominant theoretical strains. It is impossible to conduct research meaningfully without engaging some sort of theoretical apparatus and this, as we have relentlessly emphasized, necessitates making assumptions about what are uncertain and, indeed, unknowable features of man. We believe that facts are encrusted in assumptions about man and his essential creativity or his ultimate determination by outside (or inside) forces.

We have not detailed the theories of the three strains to argue for the dismissal of research nor for the abandonment of pure theory. We feel that most research has been guided by one or more of the strains. Hence our 'theory into action' illustrations. Research must not only be theoretically informed, it must be saturated in theoretical assumptions about the nature of man. All our illustrations we feel to be brilliant examples of research in their own right. They cannot be tested against an objective 'real' world for the world they suppose is *in* the theoretical model they assume. Nor can they be tested against theories of another strain: so diverse are the models of man that they are incomparable.

We feel that we should evaluate theories not by testing against something called reality (with Berger and Luckmann, we agree that reality is a distinctly human artefact, anyway): but by assessing its plausibility and its fruitfulness in supplying information that can be used to emancipate man.

Is the assailant who is kicking the black youth merely responding to the stimulus of the skin colour? Or does he actually believe that blacks are taking over the country and thereby acting consciously on that belief? Or is he subservient to an unseen force that has affected his mind and action? Or is he all of these? Perhaps it is impossible to know. Yet that doesn't stop our wanting to use theory and research to minimize such conflicts and thus promote at least a degree of emancipation based on understanding.

We feel that we can assume that man is willed and potentially creative, even though the theories considered in two thirds of this book would suggest the contrary. They may have something in insisting that, in the last instance, man is somehow determined. However, we are not certain of this. We feel that from this moment to the last instance offers a wide latitude and range for man's possibilities. Besides, the last instance is a point at which we may never arrive.

# Bibliography

ABERCROMBIE, Nicholas (1980), *Class, Structure and Knowledge,* Oxford: Basil Blackwell.
ADORNO, Theodor W., ALBERT, Hans, DAHRENDORF, Ralf, HABERMAS, Jurgen and POPPER, Karl R. (1976), *The Positivist Dispute in German Sociology,* London: HEB.
AITCHISON, Jean (1976), *The Articulate Mammal.* London: Hutchinson.
ALLPORT, Gordon (1955), *Becoming,* Newhaven: Yale University Press.
ALTHUSSER, Louis (1969), *For Marx,* Hardmondsworth: Allen Lane, The Penguin Press.
ALTHUSSER, Louis (1971), *Lenin and Philosophy and other essays,* London: NLB.
ANDERSON, Perry (1980), *Arguments Within English Marxism,* London: New Left Books.
ASHWORTH, D. D. (1979), *Social Interaction and Consciousness,* London: Wiley.
BADCOCK, C. R. (1975), *Lévi-Strauss,* London: Hutchinson.
BALDWIN, James Mark (1906), *Mental Development in the Child and the Race,* New York: Macmillan.
BALL, Richard A. (1978), 'Sociology and general systems theory', *The American Sociologist,* vol. 13 (February), pp. 65–72.
BANDURA, Albert (1973), *Aggression: a social learning analysis,* Englewood Cliffs, New Jersey: Prentice-Hall.
BANDURA, Albert (1977), *Social Learning Theory,* Englewood Cliffs, New Jersey: Prentice-Hall.
BANDURA, A., ROSS, D. and ROSS, S. A. (1961), Transmission of aggression through imitation of aggressive models, *Journal of Abnormal and Social Psychology,* vol. 63, pp. 575–82.
BANNISTER, D. (1966), A New Theory of Personality, pp. 361–371 in Brian M. Foss ed. (1966), *New Horizons in Psychology.*
BANNISTER, D. and TRANSELLA, Fay (1971), *Inquiring Man,* Harmondsworth: Penguin.
BARTHES, Roland (1967), *Elements of Sociology,* London: Cape.
BARTHES, Roland (1973), *Mythologies,* London: Paladin.
BEECH, H. R. (1969), *Changing Man's Behaviour,* Harmondsworth: Penguin.
BECKER, Howard S. (1963), *Outsiders,* New York: Free Press.
BERGER, Peter L. (1969), *The Social Reality of Religion,* London: Faber & Faber.
BERGER, Peter L. (1971), *Invitation to Sociology,* Harmondsworth: Penguin.
BERGER, Peter L. and BERGER, Brigitte (1981), *Sociology: a biographical approach,* Harmondsworth: Penguin.

BERGER, Peter L. and LUCKMAN, Thomas (1972), *The Social Construction of Reality,* Harmondsworth: Penguin.
BERGER, Peter L. and PULLBERG, Stanley (1965), 'Reification and the Sociological Critique of Consciousness', *History and Theory,* vol. 4, pt. 2, pp 196-211.
BIENKOWSKI, Wladyslaw (1982), 'The difficult escape from dogma', *Times Higher Education Supplement,* No. 481 (22 January), pp 12-13.
BIERMAN, A.K. and GOULD, James A. eds. (1973), *Philosophy for a new generation,* New York: Macmillan.
BIERSTEDT, Robert (1975), 'Sociological thought in the eighteenth century', pp 3-38 in Tom Bottomore and Robert Nisbet, eds. (1979), *A History of Sociological Analysis.*
BILTON, Tony, BONNETT, K., JONES, P., STANWORTH, M., SHEARD, R. and WEBSTER, A. (1981), *Introductory Sociology,* London: Macmillan.
BLACK, Max (1973), 'Some aversive responses to a would-be reinforcer', pp 125-134 in Harvey Wheeler ed. (1973), *Beyond the Punitive Society.*
BLACKBURN, Robin ed. (1972), *Idealogy in Social Science,* Glasgow: Fontana.
BLAU, Peter M. (1964), *Exchange and Power in Social Life,* New York: Wiley.
BLAU, Peter M. (1971), 'Justice in social exchange', pp 56-68 in H. Turk and R. L. Simpson eds. (1971), *Institutions and social exchange: the sociologies of Talcott Parsons and George C. Homans.*
BLUMER, Herbert (1962), 'Society as Symbolic Interaction', pp 179-92 in A. M. Rose ed. (1962), *Human Behaviour and social processes.*
BLUMER, Herbert (1966), 'Sociological implications of the thought of G. H. Mead', *American Journal of Sociology,* vol. 71 (March), pp 535-44.
BLUMER, Herbert (1969), *Symbolic Interactionism,* Englewood Cliffs, New Jersey: Prentice-Hall.
BODEN, Margaret A. (1972), *Purposive Explanation in Psychology,* Harvard University Press: Cambridge, Massachusetts.
BODEN, Margaret (1979), *Piaget,* Glasgow: Fontana.
BORING, Edwin G. (1957), *A history of experimental psychology,* Englewood Cliffs, New Jersey: Prentice-Hall, Inc.
BOTTOMORE, Tom ed. (1981), *Modern Interpretations of Marx,* Oxford: Basil Blackwell.
BOTTOMORE, Tom (1981a), Introduction, pp 1-22, in Tom Bottomore ed. (1981), *Modern Interpretations of Marx.*
BOTTOMORE, Tom and NISBET, Robert eds. (1979a), *A History of Sociological Analysis,* London: Heinemann Educational Books.
BOTTOMORE, Tom and NISBET, Robert (1979b), 'Structuralism', pp 557-98 in T. Bottomore & R. Nisbet eds. (1979), *A History of Sociological Analysis.*
BOULDING, Kenneth E. (1973), 'General systems as an integrating force in the social sciences', pp. 951-67 in Gray, N. C. and Rizzo, N. (1973), *Unity Through Diversity,* 2 vols, New York: Gordon & Breach.
BOWER, Tom (1975), Competent Newborns, pp. 112-26, in Roger Lewin ed. (1975), *Child Alive.*
BOWIE, Malcolm (1979), Jacques Lacan, pp 116-53, in John Sturrock ed. (1979), *Structuralism and since: From Lévi Strauss to Derrida.*
BRODBECK (1973), On the philosophy of the social sciences, pp 91-110, in John O'Neill ed. (1973), *Modes of Individualism and Collectivism.*
BRUNER, Jerome S. (1973), 'Freud and the image of man', pp 138-46, in Frank Cioffi ed. (1973), *Freud.*
BRY, Adelaide (1975), *A primer of Behavioural Psychology,* New York: Mentor.
BRYANT, Peter (1975), Children's Inferences, pp. 149-58, in Roger Lewin ed. (1975), *Child Alive.*

CALLINICOS, Alex (1976), *Althusser's Marxism,* London: Pluto Press.
CALLINICOS, Alex (1982), *Is there a future for Marxism?*, London: Macmillan.
CAPLAN, Arthur L. ed. (1978), *The Sociobiology Debate,* New York: Harper & Row.
CASTANEDA, Carlos (1973), *A separate reality,* Harmondsworth: Penguin.
CHAPMAN, Anthony J. and JONES, Dylan M. eds. (1980), *Models of Man,* Leicester: British Psychological Society.
CHEIN, Isidor (1981), The problem of the image of man, pp 385–391, David Potter et al eds. (1981), *Society and the social sciences.*
CHOMSKY, Noam (1965), *Aspects of the theory of syntax,* Cambridge, Mass: MIT Press.
CHOMSKY, Noam (1970), Recent Contributions to the theory of innate ideas, pp 79–89, in Liam Hudson ed. (1970), *The Ecology of human intelligence.*
CHOMSKY, Noam (1972), *Language and Mind* New York: Harcourt Brace Jovanovich.
CIBA Foundation Symposium 33 ed. (1975), *Parent–Infant Interaction,* Amsterdam: Associated Scientific Publishers.
CICOUREL, Aaron V. (1968), *The Social Organization of Juvenile Justice,* New York: Wiley.
CICOUREL, Aaron V. (1973), *Cognitive Sociology,* Harmondsworth: Penguin.
CIOFFI, Frank ed. (1973), *Freud,* London: Macmillan.
COHEN, David (1977), *Psychologists on Psychology,* London: Routledge & Kegan Paul.
COHEN, David (1979), *J. B. Watson: the founder of Behaviourism,* London: Routledge & Kegan Paul.
COHEN, Percy S. (1968), *Modern Social Theory,* London: H.E.B.
COMTE, Auguste (1853), *The Positive Philosophy of Auguste Comte,* 2 volumes translated by Harriet Martineau, London: Chapman.
CONNERTON, Paul ed. (1976), *Critical Sociology,* Harmondsworth, Penguin.
CONNERTON, Paul (1976a), Introduction, pp 11–40, in Paul Connerton ed. (1976), *Critical Sociology*
CONNOLLY, William E. (1981), *Appearance and Reality in politics,* Cambridge: C.U.P.
COOLEY, Charles Holton (1909), *Social Organization,* New York: Charles Scribners Sons.
COOLEY, Charles Holton (1964), *Human Nature and the Social Order,* New York: Schaken.
COSER, Lewis A. ed. (1965), *Georg Simmel,* Englewood Cliffs, New Jersey: Prentice-Hall.
COSER, Lewis A. (1977), *Masters of Sociological Thought,* 2nd ed., New York: Harcourt, Brace & Jovanovich.
COSER, Lewis, A. and ROSENBERG, Bernard eds. (1969), *Sociological Theory: A book of readings,* London: Macmillan.
COULTER, Jeff (1979), *The Social Construction of Mind,* London: Macmillan.
CUZZORT, Ray P and KING, Edith W., (1980), *Twentieth Century Social Thought,* 3rd ed., New York: Holt, Rinehart & Winston.
DAVIS, Kingsley and MOORE, Wilbert E. (1945), 'Some principles of stratification', *American Sociological Review,* vol. 10, No. 2, pp 242–9.
DAWE, Alan (1973), 'The underworld view of Erving Goffman', *British Journal of Sociology,* vol. 24, No. 2 (June), pp 246–53.
DAWE, Alan (1979), 'Theories of Social Action', pp 362–417 in T. Bottomore and R. Nisbet eds. (1979), *A History of Sociological Analysis.*
DE GEORGE, Richard T. and FERNANDE, M. eds. (1972), *The Structuralists: From Marx to Lévi-Strauss,* Garden City, New York: Anchor Books.

DE GEORGE, Richard T. and FERNANDE, M. (1972a), Introduction, pp xi–xxix, in Richard T. De George and Fernande M. De George eds. (1972), *The Structuralists: From Marx to Lévi-Strauss.*
DENNETT, Daniel C. (1981), *Brainstorms: philosophical essays on mind and psychology,* Brighton: Harvester Press.
DESMONDE, William H. (1975), 'G.H. Mead and Freud: American social psychology and psychoanalysis', pp. 329–48 in C.J. Jesser (1975), *Social Theory Revisited.*
DEWEY, John (1896), 'The reflex arc concept in psychology', *Psychological Review,* 3 (July), pp 357–70.
DEWEY, John (1922), *Human Nature and Conduct,* New York: Holt.
DILTHEY, Wilhelm (1976), *Selected Writings,* translated by H. & P. Rickman, Cambridge: C.U.P.
DITTON, Jason ed. (1980), *The View from Goffman,* London: Macmillan.
DIXON, Keith (1973), *Sociological Theory,* London: Routledge & Kegan Paul.
DODWELL, P.C. ed. (1972), *New Horizons in Psychology 2,* Harmondsworth: Penguin.
DONALDSON, Margaret (1978), *Children's Minds,* Glasgow: Fontana.
DOUGLAS, Jack D. (1967), *The Social Meanings of Suicide,* Princeton: University Press.
DURKHEIM, Emile (1952), *Suicide,* London: Routledge & Kegan Paul.
DURKHEIM, Emile (1963), *Montesquieu and Rousseau,* Ann Arbor: University of Michigan Press.
DURKHEIM, Emile (1964a), *The Division of Labour in Society,* New York: Free Press.
DURKHEIM, Emile (1964b), *The Elementary Forms of the Religious Life,* London: Allen & Unwin.
DURKHEIM, Emile (1965), *The Rules of Sociological Method,* New York: Free Press.
ECCLES, John C. (1977), *The Understanding of the Brain,* New York: McGraw-Hill.
EHRMANN, Jacques ed. (1970), *Structuralism,* Garden City, New York: Anchor Books.
EKEH, Peter (1974), *Social Exchange Theory,* London: H.E.B.
ELSTER, Jon (1978), *Logic and Society,* Chichester: John Wiley.
EMMET, Dorothy and MACINTYRE, Alasdair eds. (1970), *Sociological Theory and Philosophical Analysis,* London: Macmillan.
ENGELS, Frederick (1973), 'Speech at the graveside of Karl Marx', pp 429–30 in K. Marx and F. Engels (1973), *Selected Works.*
ESTES, William K. (1972), Learning, pp. 15–35, in P.C. Dodwell ed. (1972), *New Horizons in Psychology 2.*
EYSENCK, H.J. and NIAS, D.K.B. (1980), *Sex, Violence and the Media,* St. Albans: Granada.
FANCHER, Raymond E. (1979), *Pioneers of Psychology,* New York: W.W. Norton.
FARRELL, B.A. (1970), Psychoanalytic Theory, pp 19–28, in S.G.M. Lee and Martin Herbert eds. (1970), *Freud and Psychology.*
FARRELL, B.A. (1970a), The scientific testing of psychoanalytic findings and theory, pp 371–381, in S.G.M. Lee and Martin Herbert eds. (1970), *Freud and Psychology.*
FISHER, Bernice M. and STRAUSS, Anselm (1979), 'Interactionism', pp 457–98, in T. Bottomore and R. Nisbet eds. (1979), *A history of sociological analysis.*
FLAVELL, J.H. (1963), *The developmental psychology of Jean Piaget,* Princeton: Van Nostrand.
FLETCHER, Ronald (1972), *The Making of Sociology,* vol. 2, London: Nelson.

# Bibliography

FOSS, Brian M. ed. (1966), *New Horizons in Psychology,* Harmondsworth: Penguin.
FOSS, B. M. ed. (1978), *Psychology Survey, No. 1,* London: George Allen & Unwin.
FOUCAULT, Michel (1965), *Madness and Civilization,* New York: Random House.
FOUCAULT, Michel (1970), *The Order of Things,* London: Tavistock.
FOUCAULT, Michel (1972), *The Archaeology of Knowledge,* London: Tavistock.
FOUCAULT, Michel (1973), *The Birth of the Clinic,* New York: Pantheon.
FOUCAULT, Michel (1977), *Discipline and Punish,* London: Allen Lane.
FOUCAULT, Michel (1979), *History of Sexuality,* vol. 2, London: Allen Lane.
FOUCAULT, Michel (1980), *Power/Knowledge,* ed. by Colin Gordon, Brighton: Harvester Press.
FOX, Robin (1970), The Cultural Animal, *Social Science Information,* vol. 9, pp 7-25.
FRISBY, David (1981), *Sociological Impressionism,* London: H.E.B.
GARDNER, Howard (1972), *The Quest for Mind,* London: Quartet.
GARFINKEL, Harold (1967), *Studies in Ethnomethodology,* Englewood Cliffs, New Jersey: Prentice-Hall.
GERTH, H. H. and MILLS, C. Wright (1961), *From Max Weber: essays in sociology,* London: Routledge & Kegan Paul.
GEUSS, Raymond (1981), *The idea of a critical theory: Habermas and the Frankfurt School,* Cambridge: Cambridge University Press.
GEWIRTH, Alan (1973), Subjectivism and Objectivism in the social sciences, pp 111-118, John O'Neill ed. (1973), *Modes of Individualism and Collectivism.*
GIDDENS, Antony (1976), *New Rules of Sociological Method,* London: Hutchinson.
GIDDENS, Anthony (1979), *Central Problems in Social Theory,* London: Macmillan.
GILLIN, Charles Talbot (1975), 'Freedom and the limits of social behaviourism', *Sociology,* vol. 9, No. 1, pp. 29-47.
GLUCKSMANN, Miriam (1974), *Structuralist Analysis in contemporary social thought,* London: Routledge & Kegan Paul.
GOFFMAN, Erving (1961), *Asylums,* Harmondsworth: Penguin.
GOFFMAN, Erving (1967), *Interaction Ritual,* Harmondsworth: Penguin.
GOFFMAN, Erving (1969), *The Presentation of the Self in Everyday Life,* Harmondsworth: Penguin.
GOFFMAN, Erving (1971), *Relations in Public,* London: Allen Lane.
GOFFMAN, Erving (1972), *Encounters,* Harmondsworth: Penguin.
GOFFMAN, Erving (1975), *Frame Analysis,* Harmondsworth: Penguin.
GOFFMAN, Erving (1981), *Forms of Talk,* Oxford: Blackwell.
GONOS, G. (1977), Situation versus frame, *American Sociological Review,* 42, pp 854-67.
GOULDNER, Alvin W. (1960), The norm of reciprocity: a preliminary statement, *American Sociological Review,* vol. 25, pp 161-78.
GOULDNER, Alvin W. (1971), *The Coming Crisis of Western Sociology,* London: Heinemann.
GOULDNER, Alvin W. (1980), *The Two Marxisms,* London: Macmillan.
GRAY, Jeffrey A. (1979), *Pavlov,* Glasgow: Fontana.
GREENE, Judith (1972), *Psycholinguistics,* Harmondsworth: Penguin.
GREENE, Judith (1975), *Thinking and Language,* London: Methuen.
HABERMAS, Jürgen (1970), Towards a theory of communicative competence, *Inquiry,* No. 13, pp 360-75.
HABERMAS, Jürgen (1971), *Towards a Rational Society,* London: Heinemann Educational Books.

HABERMAS, Jürgen (1972), *Knowledge and Human Interests,* London: Heinemann Educational Books.
HABERMAS, Jürgen (1974), *Theory and Practice,* London: Heinemann Educational Books.
HABERMAS, Jürgen (1976), *Legitimation Crisis,* London: HEB.
HABERMAS, Jürgen (1976), Systematically Distorted Communication, pp 348-63, in Paul Connerton ed. (1976), *Critical Sociology.*
HABERMAS, Jürgen (1979), *Communication and the Evolution of Society,* London: HEB.
HAHN, Frank and HOLLIS, Martin eds. (1979), *Philosophy and Economic Theory,* Oxford: Oxford University Press.
HAHN, Frank and HOLLIS, Martin (1979a), Introduction, pp 1-18, in Frank Hahn and Martin Hollis eds. (1979), *Philosophy and Economic Theory.*
HALL, John A. (1981), *Diagnoses of Our Time,* London: HEB.
HAMILTON, Peter (1974), *Knowledge and Social Structure,* London: Routledge & Kegan Paul.
HARRÉ, R. and SECORD, P. F. (1972), *The Explanation of Social Behaviour,* Oxford: Basil Blackwell.
HARRIS, Marvin (1969), *The Rise of Anthropological Theory,* London: Routledge & Kegan Paul.
HAWKES, Terence (1977), *Structuralism and Semiotics,* London: Methuen.
HAWTHORN, Geoffrey (1976), *Enlightenment and Despair,* London: C.U.P.
HEATH, Anthony (1976), *Rational Choice and Social Exchange,* Cambridge: C.U.P.
HEIM, Alice (1970), *Intelligence and Personality,* Harmondsworth: Penguin.
HELD, David (1980), *Introduction to Critical Theory: Horkheimer to Habermas,* London: Hutchinson.
HERGENHAHN, B. R. (1976), *An introduction to theories of learning,* Englewood Cliffs, New Jersey: Prentice-Hall.
HILL, Winifred F. (1972), *Learning,* London: Methuen.
HIRST, Paul and WOOLLEY, Penny (1982), *Social relations and human attributes,* London: Tavistock.
HOLBACH, Baron (1973), The Natural Determination of Man, pp 585-93 in Bierman, A. K. and Gould, James A. eds. (1973), *Philosophy for a new generation.*
HOMANS, George C. (1950), *The Human Group,* New York: Harcourt, Brace and World.
HOMANS, George C. and SCHNEIDER, David, M. (1955), *Marriage, Authority, and Final Causes: A Study of Unilateral Cross-cousin marriage,* New York: Free Press.
HOMANS, George C. (1961), *Social Behaviour: Its elementary forms,* New York: Harcourt, Brace & World.
HOMANS, George C. (1962), *Sentiments and Activities,* New York: Free Press.
HOMANS, George C. (1964), Bringing men back in, *American Sociological Review,* vol. 29 (5), pp 809-18.
HOMANS, Goerge C. (1964a), 'Commentary', *Sociological Inquiry,* vol. 34, (Spring), pp 221-31.
HOSPERS, John (1956), *An introduction to philosophical analysis,* London: Routledge & Kegan Paul.
HOWE, Michael, J. A. (1978), Human Learning, pp 143-155, in B. M. Foss ed. (1978), *Psychology Survey No. 1.*
HUDSON, Liam ed. (1970), *The ecology of human intelligence,* Harmondsworth: Penguin.
HUDSON, Liam (1975), *Human Beings,* London: Jonathan Cape.

HUDSON, Liam (1976), *The Cult of the Fact,* London: Jonathan Cape.
HUGHES, H. Stuart (1974), *Consciousness and Society,* St. Albans: Paladin.
HULL, David L. (1970), 'Systemic dynamic social theory', *Soiological Quarterly,* vol. 11, no. 3, pp 351–65.
IONS, Edmund (1977), *Against Behaviouralism,* Oxford: Blackwell.
JOHODA, Marie (1977), *Freud and the Dilemmas of Psychology,* London: Hogarth Press.
JAHODA, M. (1980), One model of man or many?, pp 277–387, in Anthony J. Chapman and Dylan M. Jones eds. (1980), *Models of Man.*
JAMES, William (1890), *Principles of Psychology,* 2 volumes, New York: Holt.
JAMES, William (1948), *Psychology,* Cleveland, Ohio: World Publishing.
JARVIE, I. C. (1972), *Concepts and Society,* London: Routledge & Kegan Paul.
JAY, Martin (1973), *The Dialectical Imagination,* London: H.E.B.
JESSER, Clinton Joyce (1975), *Social Theory Revisited,* Hinsdale, Illinois: Dryden Press.
JOHNSON, Doyle Paul (1981), *Sociological Theory,* New York: Wiley.
JOYNSON, R. B. (1974), *Psychology and common sense,* London: Routledge & Kegan Paul.
JOYNSON, R. B. (1980), Models of Man: 1879–1979, pp 1–13, in Anthony J. Chapman and Dylan M. Jones eds. (1980), *Models of Man.*
JUNG, John (1971), *The experimenter's dilemma,* New York: Harper & Row.
KAPLAN, David and MANNERS, Robert A. (1972), *Culture Theory,* Englewood Cliffs, New Jersey: Prentice-Hall.
KEAT, Russell and URRY, John (1975), *Social Theory as Science,* London: Routledge & Kegan Paul.
KELLY, George (1981), A psychology of man himself, p 360, in David Potter *et al* eds. (1981), *Society and the social sciences.*
KIERNAN, Chris (1978), Behaviour modification, pp 131–142, in B. M. Foss ed. (1978), *Psychology Survey, No. 1.*
KOESTLER, Arthur (1967), *The ghost in the machine,* London: Hutchinson.
KOESTLER, Arthur and SMYTHIES, J. R. eds. (1969), *Beyond Reductionism,* London: Hutchinson.
KING, Dave (1981), 'Gender Confusions', pp 155–83, in Kenneth Plummer ed. (1981), *The Making of the Modern Homosexual,* London: Hutchinson.
KOLAKOWSKI, Leszek (1972), *Positivist Philosophy,* Harmondsworth: Penguin.
KOLB, William L. (1967), 'A critical evaluation of Mead's "I" and "Me" Concepts', in J. G. Manis and B. N. Meltzer eds. (1967), *Symbolic Interaction.*
KUHN, Manford H. (1954), 'Factors in personality', pp 43–60, in F. L. K. Hsu ed. (1954), *Aspects of Culture and Personality,* New York: Abelard-Schuman.
KUHN, Manford H. (1954), 'Kinsey's view on human behaviour', *Social Problems,* vol. 7, pp 119–25.
KUHN, Manford H. (1964), 'Major trends in symbolic interaction theory in the past twenty five years', *Sociological Quarterly,* vol. 5 (Winter), pp 61–84.
KUHN, Manford H. and McPARTLAND, Thomas S. (1954), 'An empirical investigation of self-attitudes', *American Sociological Review,* vol. 19 (February), pp 68–76.
KURZWEIL, Edith (1980), *The Age of Structuralism,* New York: Columbia University Press.
LUCAN, Jacques (1979), *The Four Fundamental Concepts of Psychoanalysis,* Harmondsworth: Penguin.
LAING, R. D. (1967), 'Sanity and Madness', *New Statesman,* vol. 16, no. 6.
LAKATOS, Imre and MUSGRAVE, Alan eds. (1970), *Criticism and the Growth of Knowledge,* Cambridge: C.U.P.
LACLAU, Ernesto (1975), The specificity of the political: the Poulantzas-Miliband

debate, *Economy and Society*, Volume 4(1), pp 87-110.
LANE, Michael ed. (1970), *Structuralism: a reader,* London: Jonathan Cape.
LANGER, Jonas (1969), *Theories of development,* New York: Holt, Rinehart & Winston.
LARSON, Calvin J. (1977), *Major Themes in Sociological Theory,* New York: David McKay.
LASZLO, Ervin (1973), 'Ludwig von Bertalanffy and Claude Lévi-Strauss', pp 143-167 in Gray, N.C. and Rizzo, N. eds. (1973), *Unity Through Diversity,* 2 vols, New York: Gordon & Breach.
LASZLO, Ervin (1975), 'The meaning and significance of general system theory', *Behavioural Scientist,* vol. 20, pp 9-24.
LEACH, Edmund (1969), 'Vico and Lévi-Strauss on the origins of history', pp 309-18 in Giorgio Tagliacozzo and Hayden V. White eds. (1969), *Gambiattista Vico.*
LEACH, Edmund (1970), *Lévi-Strauss,* Glasgow: Fontana.
LEACH, Edmund (1970a), Telstar and the Aborigines or La pensée suavage, pp 183-204, in Dorothy Emmet and Alasdair MacIntyre eds. (1970), *Sociological theory and philosophical analysis.*
LEACH, Edmund (1973), Structuralism in social anthropology, pp 18-32, in David Robey ed. (1973), *Structuralism: an introduction.*
LEACH, Edmund (1976), *Culture and Communication,* Cambridge: C.U.P.
LEE, S.G.M. and HERBERT, Martin eds. (1970), *Freud and Psychology,* Harmondsworth: Penguin.
LEMERT, Charles C. ed. (1981), *French Sociology: rupture and renewal since 1968,* New York: Columbia University Press.
LEMERT, Charles C. (1981a), Knowledge and social order: beyond the education debate, pp 225-31, Charles C. Lemert ed. (1981), *French Sociology: rupture and renewal since 1968.*
LÉVI-STRAUSS, Claude (1966), *The Savage Mind,* London: Weidenfield & Nicolson.
LÉVI-STRAUSS, Claude (1969), *The Elementary Structures of Kinship,* London: Eyre & Spottiswoode.
LEWIN, Roger ed. (1975), *Child Alive,* London: Temple Smith.
LEWIN, Roger (1975a), Brain development and the environment, pp 193-208, Roger Lewin ed. (1975), *Child Alive.*
LEWIS, J. David and SMITH, Richard (1981), *American Sociology and Pragmatism,* Chicago: University of Chicago Press.
LICHTMAN, R.T. (1970), 'Symbolic interactionism and social reality', *Berkeley Journal of Sociology,* vol. 15, pp. 75-94.
LICHTMAN, Richard (1973), 'Symbolic interactionism and social reality', *Berkeley Journal of Sociology,* vol. 15, pp 75-94.
LUKES, Steven (1973), *Emile Durkheim: his life and work,* London: Allen Lane.
LUKES, Steven (1973a), *Individualism,* Oxford: Basil Blackwell.
LUKES, Steven (1974), *Power: a radical view,* London: Macmillan.
LUKES, Steven (1981), Fact and Theory in the social sciences, pp 396-405, in Potter *et al* eds. (1981).
LYONS, John (1970), *Chomsky,* Glasgow: Fontana.
LYONS, John (1973), Structuralism and linguistics, pp 5-20, David Robey ed. (1973), *Structuralism: an Introduction.*
MacALPINE, Ida (1973), Tribute to Freud, pp 124-38, in Frank Cioffi ed. (1973), *Freud.*
McGUIRE, R.J., CARLISLE, J.M. and YOUNG, B.G. (1965), Sexual deviations as conditioned behaviour: a hypothesis, *Behaviour Research and Therapy,* vol. 2, pp 185-190.

MacINTYRE, A C. (1958), *The Unconscious,* London: Routledge & Kegan Paul.
MacINTYRE, Alasdair (1969), 'The Self as a work of art', *New Statesman,* 28 March.
MACKSEY, Richard and DONATO, Eugenio eds. (1970), *The Structuralist Controversy,* London: The John Hopkins University Press.
MADGE, John (1963), *The Origins of Scientific Sociology,* London: Tavistock.
MAHER, Brendan (1972), Experimental Psychopathology, pp 148–168, in P. C. Dodwell ed. (1972), *New Horizons in Psychology 2.*
MALINOWSKI, Bronislaw (1922), *Argonauts of the Western Pacific,* London: Routledge & Kegan Paul.
MALINOWSKI, Bronislaw (1944), *A Scientific Theory of Culture,* Chapel Hill: University of North Carolina Press.
MANIS, J. G. and MELTZER, B N. eds. (1967), *Symbolic Interactionism,* Boston: Allyn & Bacon.
MARX, Karl (1904), *A Contribution to the Critique of Political Economy,* Chicago: Kerr & Co.
MARX, Karl (1961), *Economic and Philosophical Manuscripts of 1844,* Moscow: Foreign Languages Publishing House.
MARX, Karl (1973), *Grundrisse,* Harmondsworth: Penguin.
MARX, Karl (1976), *Capital,* 3 volumes, Harmondsworth: Penguin.
MARX, Karl and ENGELS, Friedrich (1930), *The Communist Manifesto,* New York: International Publishers.
MARX, Karl and ENGLES, Friedrich (1959), *Basic Writings on Politics and Philosophy,* edited by Lewis Feuer, Garden City: Doubleday/Anchor.
MARX, Karl and ENGELS, Friedrich (1960), *The German Ideology,* New York: International Publishers.
MARX, Karl and ENGELS, Friedrich (1968, reprinted 1973), *Selected Works,* London: Lawrence & Wishart.
MARTINDALE, Don (1970), *The Nature and Types of Sociological Theory,* London: Routledge & Kegan Paul.
MAUSS, Marcel (1954), *The Gift,* New York: The Free Press.
McCALL, George J. and SIMMONS, J. L. (1966), *Identities and Interactions,* New York: Free Press.
McDERMOTT, John J. (1981), *The Philosophy of John Dewey,* London: University of Chicago Press.
McGUIRE, R. J., CARLISLE, J M. and YOUNG, B. G. (1965), 'Sexual Deviations as conditioned behaviour: a hypothesis', *Behaviour Research and Therapy,* vol. 2, pp 185–90.
McLELLAN, David (1975), *Marx,* Glasgow: Fontana.
McLELLAN, David ed. (1980), *Marx's Grundrisse,* London: Macmillan.
McQUARIE, Donald and AMBURGEY, Terry (1978), 'Marx and modern systems theory', *Social Science Quarterly,* vol. 59, no. 1 (June), pp 3–19.
MEAD, George Herbert (1934), *Mind, Self and Society,* Chicago: University of Chicago Press.
MEAD, George Herbert (1964), *On Social Psychology* (ed. Anselm Strauss), Chicago: University of Chicago Press.
MEAD, George Herbert (1967), *The Mind, Self and Society,* Chicago: University of Chicago Press.
MEAD, George Herbert (1981), *The Philosophy of the Present,* edited by Arthur E. Murphy, London: University of Chicago Press.
MELTZER, Bernard N., PETRAS, John W., REYNOLDS, Larry, T. (1975), *Symbolic Interactionism,* London: Routledge & Kegan Paul.
MENNELL, Stephen (1980), *Sociological Theory: uses and unities,* 2nd edition, London: Thos. Nelson.

MERBAUM, Michael and STRICKER, George eds. (1975), *Search for Human Understanding,* New York: Holt, Rinehart & Winston.

MERTON, Robert K. (1949), *Social Theory and Social Structure,* Glencoe, Illinois: Free Press.

MIDGLEY, Mary (1980), *Beast and Man: the roots of human nature,* London: Methuen.

MIDGLEY, Mary (1981), Have we a nature?, pp 348-49 in David Potter *et al* eds. (1981), *Society and the social sciences.*

MIEL, Jan (1970), Jacques Lacan and the structure of the unconscious, pp 94-101, in Jacques Ehrmann ed. (1970), *Structuralism.*

MILIBAND, Ralph (1969), *The State in Capitalist Society,* pp 253-262, in London: Weidenfeld & Nicolson.

MILIBAND, Ralph (1972), The problem of the capitalist state, pp 253-262, in Robin Blackburn ed. (1972) *Ideology in Social Science.*

MILLER, George A. (1965), Some preliminaries to psycholinguistics, *American Psychologist,* vol. 20, pp 15-20.

MILLER, George A. (1969), *Psychology: the science of mental life,* Harmondsworth: Penguin.

MILLER, James G. (1971), 'The nature of living systems', *Behavioural Science,* vol. 16, pp 277-301.

MILLER, James G. (1978), *Living Systems,* New York: McGraw-Hill.

MILLS, C. Wright (1959), *The Sociological Imagination,* New York: O.U.P.

MILLS, C. Wright (1964), *Sociology and Pragmatism,* New York: Paine-Whitman.

MISCHEL, Theodore ed. (1977), *The self: psychological and philosophical issues,* Oxford: Basil Blackwell.

MISCHEL, Theodore (1977a), Conceptual issues in the psychology of the self: an introduction, pp 3-28, in Theodore Mischel ed. (1977), *The self: psychological and philosophical issues.*

MISIAK, Henryk and SEXTON, Virginia Standt (1968), *History of Psychology: an overview,* New York: Grune & Stratton.

MOMMSEN, W.J. (1965), 'Max Weber's political sociology and his philosophy of world history', *International Social Science Journal,* vol. 17, pp 23-45.

MORICK, Harold ed. (1980), *Challenges to empiricism,* London: Methuen.

MORICK, Harold (1980a), Introduction: the critique of contemporary empiricism, pp 1-28, in Harold Morick ed. (1980), *Challenges to empiricism.*

MOUZELIS, Nicos P. (1975), *Organization and Bureaucracy,* London: Routledge & Kegan Paul.

M'PHERSON, P. K. (1974), 'A perspective on systems science and systems philosophy', *Futures,* vol. 6 (June), pp 219-39.

MURCHISON, C. ed. (1926), *Psychologies of 1925,* Worcester, Mass: Clark University Press.

NISBET, Robert (1970), *The Sociological Tradition,* London: H.E.B.

NISBET, Robert (1980), *The History of the Idea of Progress,* London: H.E.B.

NYE, Robert D. (1975), *Three Views of Man,* Belmont: Wadsworth.

NYE, Robert D. (1979), *What is B. F. Skinner really saying?,* Englewood Cliffs, New Jersey: Prentice Hall.

O'CONNOR, D. J. (1971), *Free Will,* Virginia: Doubleday.

O'NEILL, John (1972), *Sociology as a Skin Trade,* London: Heinemann Educational Books.

O'NEILL, John ed. (1973), *Modes of Individualism and Collectivism,* London: H.E.B.

O'NEILL, W. M. (1968), *The beginnings of modern psychology,* Harmondsworth: Penguin.

ORNSTEIN, Robert E. (1977), *The Psychology of Consciousness,* New York:

Harcourt Brace & Jovanovich.
PACKARD, Vance (1978), *The people shapers,* London: McDonald & Jane's.
PARKIN, Frank (1979), *Marxism and Class Theory; a bourgeois critique,* London: Tavistock.
PARSONS, Talcott (1951), *The Social System,* New York: Free Press.
PARSONS, Talcott (1968), *The Structure of Social Action,* New York: Free Press.
PARSONS, Talcott (1971), *The System of Modern Societies,* Englewood Cliffs, New Jersey: Prentice-Hall.
PASSMORE, John (1968), *A hundred years of philosophy,* Harmondsworth: Penguin.
PETTIT, Philip (1977), *The concept of structuralism: a critical analysis,* Berkeley: University of California Press.
PHILLIPS, Derek L. (1973), *Abandoning Method,* London: Jossey Bass.
PHILLIPS, John L. (1969), *The origins of intellect: Piaget's Theory,* San Francisco: W. H. Freeman.
PIAGET, J. (1954), *The construction of reality in the child,* New York: Basic Books.
PIAGET, Jean (1971), *Structuralism,* London: Routledge & Kegan Paul.
PLATT, John R. (1973), The Skinnerian Revolution, pp 22-56, in Harvey Wheeler ed. (1973), *Beyond the Punitive Society.*
PLUMMER, Kenneth (1975), *Sexual Stigma: an interactionist account,* London: Routledge & Kegan Paul.
PLUMMER, Kenneth ed. (1981), *The Making of the Modern Homosexual,* London: Hutchinson.
PLUMMER, Kenneth (1981), 'Pedophilia: constructing a sociological baseline', pp 221-50, in M. Cook and K. Howells eds. (1981), *Adult Sexual Interest in Children,* London: Academic Press.
PODGÓRECKI, Adam and LOS, Maria (1979), *Multi-dimensional Sociology,* London: Routledge & Kegan Paul.
POLOMA, Margaret M. (1979), *Contemporary Sociological Theory,* New York: Collier-Macmillan.
POMPA, Leon (1975), *Vico: a study of the 'New Science',* Cambridge: C.U.P.
POMPA, Leon (1982), *Vico's Theory of the causes of historical change,* London: Octagon Press.
POPE, Kenneth S. and SINGER, Jerome L. (1978), *The Stream of Consciousness: scientific investigations into the flow of human experience,* New York: John Wiley.
POPE, Kenneth S. and SINGER, Jerome L. (1978a), Introduction: The flow of human experience, pp 1-6, in Kenneth S. Pope and Jerome L. Singer eds. (1978), *The Stream of Consciousness: scientific investigations into the flow of human experience.*
POPPER, Karl (1959), *The Logic of Scientific Discovery,* London: Hutchinson.
POPPER, Karl R. (1963), *Conjectures and Refutations,* London: Routledge & Kegan Paul.
POPPER, K. R. and ECCLES, J. C. (1977), *The Self and its Brain,* London: Springer-Verlag.
POTTER, David *et al* eds. (1981), *Society and the social sciences,* London: Routledge & Kegan Paul.
POULANTZAS, Nicos (1972), The problem of the capitalist State, pp 238-253, in Robin Blackburn ed. (1972), *Ideology in Social Science.*
POULANTZAS, Nicos (1973), *Political power and Social Classes,* London: New Left Books.
PRIBRAM, Karl H. (1973), Operant Behaviourism: Fad, Fact -ory, and Fantasy, pp 101-112, in Harvey Wheeler ed. (1973), *Beyond the Punitive Society.*

RACHLIN, Howard (1970), *Introduction to Modern Behaviourism,* San Francisco: W. H. Freeman.
RACHMAN, S. (1966), Sexual Fetishism: an experimental analogue, *Psychological Record,* vol. 16, pp 293-6.
RADCLIFFE-BROWN, A. R. (1948a), *The Andaman Islanders,* Glencoe, Illinois: Free Press.
RADCLIFFE-BROWN, A. R. (1948b), *A Natural Science of Society,* New York: Free Press.
RADCLIFFE-BROWN, A. R. (1958), *Structure and Function in Primitive Society,* Glencoe, Illinois: Free Press.
REX, John (1961), *Key Problems in Sociological Theory,* London: Routledge & Kegan Paul.
REX, John (1980), A tale of two cities, *New Society,* 7 August, pp 277-78.
RHEA, Buford ed. (1981), *The Future of the Sociological Classics,* London: Allen & Unwin.
RICHARDS, Janet Radcliffe (1982), *The Sceptical Feminist,* Harmondsworth: Penguin.
RICKERT, Heinrich (1962), *Science and History,* New York: Van Nostrand.
RIEFF, Philip (1979), *Freud: the mind of the moralist,* Chicago: The University of Chicago Press.
RITZER, George, *Sociology: a multiple paradigm science,* Boston: Allyn & Bacon.
ROBEY, David ed. (1973), *Structuralism: an introduction,* Oxford: Clarendon Press.
ROBEY, David (1973a), Introduction, pp 1-5 in David Robey ed. (1973), *Structuralism: an introduction.*
ROBINSON, Daniel N. (1976), *An intellectual history of psychology,* New York: Macmillan.
ROBINSON, Daniel N. (1979), *Systems of Modern Psychology,* New York: Columbia University Press.
ROCK, Paul (1979), *The Making of Symbolic Interactionism,* London: Macmillan.
ROSE, Arnold M. ed. (1962), *Human Behaviour and Social Processes,* London: Routledge & Kegan Paul.
ROSE, Arnold M. (1962), 'A systematic summary of symbolic interaction theory', pp 3-19 in A. M. Rose ed. (1962), *Human Behaviour and Social Processes.*
ROSEN, Robert (1973), Can any behaviour be conditioned?, pp. 135-148, in Harvey Wheeler ed. (1973), *Beyond the Punitive Society.*
ROSENTHAL, R. (1966), *Experimenter effects in Behavioural Research,* New York: Appleton Century-Crafts.
SACKS, Harvey, SCHEGLOFF, Emmanuel and JEFFERSON, Gail (1974), 'A simplest semantics for the organization of turn-taking', *Language,* vol. 50, no. 4 (part 1), pp 696-735.
SARTRE, Jean-Paul (1973), The existential man, pp 600-7, in A. K. Bierman and James A. Gould eds. (1973), *Philosophy for a new generation.*
SCHEGLOFF, Emmanuel (1974), 'Notes on a conversational practice: formulating place' in David Sudnow ed. *Studies in Social Interaction,* New York: Free Press.
SCHUTZ, Alfred (1972), original 1932, *The Phenomenology of the Social World,* London: Heinemann.
SHERIDAN, Alan (1980), *Michel Foucault: the will to truth,* London: Tavistock.
SHOTTER, John (1975), *Images of Man in Psychological Research,* London: Methuen.
SIEGEL, A. E. (1956), Film-mediated fantasy aggression and strength of aggressive drive, *Child Development,* 27, pp 365-78.
SIMMEL, Georg (1910), 'How is society possible', *American Journal of Sociology,* vol. 16 (November), pp 372-91.

SINGLEMAN, Peter (1972), 'Exchange as symbolic interaction', *American Sociological Review*, vol. 47 (August), pp 414–24.
SKIDMORE, William (1979), *Theoretical thinking in sociology*, Cambridge: Cambridge University Press.
SKINNER, B. F. (1953), *Science and Human Behaviour*, New York: Macmillan.
SKINNER, B. F. (1964), Behaviourism at fifty, pp 79–109, in T. W. Wann ed. (1964), *Behaviourism and phenomenology*.
SKINNER, B. F. (1971), *Beyond Freedom and Dignity*, New York: Bantam/Vintage Books.
SKINNER, B. F. (1973), *Beyond Freedom and Dignity*, Harmondsworth: Penguin.
SKINNER, B. F. (1973a), *Answers for my critics*, pp 256–266, in Harvey Wheeler ed. (1973), *Beyond the Punitive Society*.
SKINNER, B. F. (1974), *About Behaviourism*, New York: Knopf.
SKINNER, B. F. (1976), *Walden Two*, Macmillan: New York.
SKINNER, B. F. (1976a), *Particulars of my life*, London: Jonathan Cape.
SKINNER, B. F. (1978), *Reflections on Behaviourism and Society*, Englewood Cliffs, New Jersey: Prentice-Hall.
SKLAIR, Leslie (1977), 'Ideology and the sociological utopias', *Sociological Review*, vol. 25 (1), pp 51–72.
SMITH, Neil and WILSON, Deidre (1979), *Modern Linguistics*, Harmondsworth: Penguin.
SOROKIN, Pitirim (1928), *Contemporary Sociological Theories*, New York: Harper & Row.
SPENCER, Herbert (1966), *The Works of H. Spencer, volume 6*, Osnabruck: Zeller.
SPENCER, Herbert (1969), *The Principles of Sociology*, London: Macmillan.
SPERBER, Dan (1979), Claude Lévi-Strauss, pp 19–51, in John Sturrock ed. (1979), *Structuralism and since: from Lévi Strauss to Derrida*.
STEVENSON, Leslie (1974), *Seven Theories of Human Nature*, Oxford: Oxford University Press.
STRANGER, Jack R. (1978), A search for the sources of the stream of consciousness, pp 9–29, in Kenneth S. Pope and Jerome L. Stringer eds. (1978), *The stream of consciousness: Scientific investigations into the flow of human experience*.
STRAUSS, Anselm S. (1977), *Mirrors and Masks: the search for identity*, London: Martin Robertson.
STRYKER, Sheldon (1980), *Symbolic Interactionism: a social structural version*, Menlo Park, Ca.: Benjamin/Cummings.
STURROCK, John ed. (1979), *Structuralism and since: From Lévi Strauss to Derrida*, Oxford: O.U.P.
STURROCK, John (1979a), Introduction, pp 1–19 in John Sturrock ed. (1979), *Structuralism and since: From Lévi Strauss to Derrida*.
SUGGS, R. C. (1966), *Marquesan Sexual Behaviour*, New York: Harcourt, Brace & World.
SULLOWAY, Frank J. (1980), *Freud, biologist of the mind*, Glasgow: Fontana.
SUTHERLAND, Stuart (1977), *Breakdown*, St Albans, Granada.
TAGLACOZZO, Giorgio and WHITE, Hayden V. (1969), *Giambattista Vico*, Baltimore, Mass.: John Hopkins Press.
TART, Charles T. ed. (1975), *Transpersonal Psychologies*, London: Routledge & Kegan Paul.
TART, Charles T. (1975a), Introduction, pp 1–9, in Charles T. Tart ed. (1975), *Transpersonal Psychologies*.
TAYLOR, Charles (1964), *The explanation of behaviour*, London: Routledge & Kegan Paul.

TAYLOR, Daniel M. (1970), *Explanation and Meaning,* Cambridge: Cambridge University Press.
TAYLOR, Laurie (1977), Freud, *New Society,* 8 December, pp 515-518.
TERRACE, H. S. (1982), Can animals think?, *New Society,* March 4, pp 339-43.
THOMAS, M. H., HORTON, R. W., LIPPINCOTT, E. C. and DRABMAN, R. S. (1977), Desensitization to portrayals of real life aggression as a function of exposure to television violence, *Journal of Personality and Social Psychology,* vol. 35, pp 450-8.
THOMAS, W. I. and ZNANIECKI, Florian (1918), *The Polish Peasant in Europe and America,* 5 volumes, Chicago: University of Chicago Press.
THOMAS, William Isaac and THOMAS, Dorothy S. (1928), *The Child in America,* New York: Knopf.
THOMPSON, E. P. (1978), *The Poverty of Theory,* London: Merlin Press.
TIMPANARO, S. Y. (1976), *The Freudian Slip: psychoanalysis and textual criticism,* London: New Left Books.
TURK, H. and SIMPSON, R. L. eds. (1971), *Institutions and social exchange: the sociologies of Talcott Parsons and George C. Homans,* New York: Bobbs-Merrill.
TURNER, Bryan S. (1981), *For Weber,* Routledge & Kegan Paul.
TURNER, Johanna (1975), *Cognitive Development,* London: Methuen.
TURNER, Jonathan H. (1974), *The Structure of Sociological Theory,* Homewood, Illinois: The Dorsey Press.
TURNER, Jonathan H. (1982), *The Structure of Sociological Theory,* 3rd ed., Homewood, Illinois: The Dorsey Press.
TURNER, Jonathan H. and MARYANSKI, Alexandra (1979), *Functionalism,* Mengo Park, Ca.: Benjamin Cummings.
TURNER, Ralph H. (1962), 'Role-taking: process versus conformity', pp 20-40 in A. M. Rose ed. *Human Behaviour and Social Processes.*
TURNER, Ralph H. (1976), 'The real self: from institution to impulse', *American Journal of Sociology,* vol. 81, no. 5, pp 989-1016.
TURNER, Ralph H. (1978), 'The role and the person', *American Journal of Sociology,* vol. 84, pp 1-23.
TURNER, Roy ed. (1974), *Ethnomethodology,* Harmondsworth: Penguin.
von BERTALANFFY, Ludwig (1952), *Problems of Life,* London: Watts & Co.
WALLACE, Ruth A. and WOLF, Alison (1980), *Contemporary Sociological Theory,* Englewood Cliffs, New Jersey: Prentice-Hall.
WALTON, Paul and GAMBLE, Andrew (1976), *From Alienation to Surplus Value,* London: Sheed & Ward.
WANN, T. W. ed. (1964), *Behaviourism and Phenomenology,* Chicago: The University of Chicago Press.
WATSON, John B. (1913), 'Psychology as the Behaviourist Views it', *The Psychological Review,* vol. 20, pp 158-177.
WATSON, J. B. (1926), Experimental Studies on the growth of the emotions, pp 7-27 in C. Murchison ed. (1926), *Psychologies of 1925.*
WATSON, John B. (1970), *Behaviourism,* New York: W. W. Norton.
WATSON, John B. and RAYNER, Rosalie (1920), Conditioned emotional reactions, *Journal of experimental psychology,* vol. 3, pp 1-14.
WATSON, Robert I. (1971), *The Great Psychologists,* Philadelphia: J. B. Lippincott.
WEBER, Marianne (1975), *Max Weber: a biography,* New York: Wiley.
WEBER, Max (1930), *The Protestant Ethic and the Spirit of Capitalism,* London: Allen & Unwin.
WEBER, Max (1947), *Theory of Social and Economic Organization,* New York: Free Press.

WEBER, Max (1968, original 1922), *Economy and Society*, 3 volumes, New York: Bedminster.
WEIGEL, John A. (1977), *B. F. Skinner*, Boston: Twayne.
WESTLAND, Gordon (1978), *Current crises of psychology*, London: Heinemann Educational Books.
WHEELER, Harvey ed. (1973), *Beyond the Punitive Society*, London: Wildwood House.
WHEELER, Harvey (1973a), Introduction: a nonpunitive world?, pp 1–21 in Harvey Wheeler ed. (1973), *Beyond the Punitive Society*.
WHORF, Benjamin Lee (1956), *Language, thought and reality*, Cambridge, Mass: MIT Press.
WHYTE, Hayden (1979), 'Michel Foucault', pp 81–115 in John Sturrock ed. (1979), *Structuralism and Since*.
WIEDER, D. Lawrence (1974), 'Telling the Code' in Roy Turner ed. (1974), *Ethnomethodology*.
WILSON, Deidre and SMITH, Neil (1980), Understanding language, *New Society*, 24 July, pp 168–170.
WILSON, Edward O. (1978), Academic vigilantism and the political significance of sociobiology, pp 291–304, in Arthur L. Caplan ed. (1978), *The Sociobiology debate*.
WILSON, Edward O. (1978a), *On Human Nature*, Cambridge, Mass: Harvard University Press.
WILSON, Thomas P. (1971), 'Normative and interpretive paradigms in sociology', pp 57–99 in Jack P. Douglas ed. (1971), *Understanding Everyday Life*, London: Routledge & Kegan Paul.
WILTSHIRE, David (1978), *The Social and Political Thought of Herbert Spencer*, Oxford: Oxford University Press.
WOLFF, Kurt H. (1950), *The Sociology of Georg Simmel*, Glencoe, Illinois: The Free Press.
WORSLEY, Peter (1970), Groote Eylandt Totemism and Le Totémisme aujourd'hui, pp 204–223, in Dorothy Emmet and Alasdair MacIntyre eds. (1970), *Sociological theory and philosophical analysis*.
WORSLEY, P. M. (1980), *Marxism and Culture*, University of Manchester, Department of Sociology, Occasional Paper No. 4, August.
WRONG, Dennis H. (1981), 'Max Weber and Contemporary Sociology', pp 39–59 in B. Rhea ed. (1981), *The Future of the Sociological Classics*.
ZEITLIN, Irving M. (1973), *Rethinking Sociology: a critique of contemporary theory*, Englewood Cliffs, New Jersey: Prentice-Hall.
ZEITLIN, Irving M. (1981), *Ideology and the Development of Sociological Theory*, Englewood Cliffs, New Jersey: Prentice-Hall.
ZEITLIN, Irving M. (1981), 'Karl Marx: aspects of his thought and their contemporary relevance', pp 1–15 in B. Rhea ed. (1981), *The Future of the Sociological Classics*, London: Allen & Unwin.

# Index of Names

Adorno, Theodor, 188, 189
Abercrombie, Nicholas, 121
Aitchison, Jean, 166-7, 168, 169
Albert (case history), 12-13
Althusser, Louis, 171, 187-8, 191-5*passim*, 197-9, 202, 203
Amburgie, Terry, 187
Aristotle, 4, 19, 130

Bachelard, 191, 201
Badcock, C.R., 177
Baldwin, James Mark, 78-9
Ball, Richard, 186
Bandura, Albert, 53
Barstow, Stan, 18
Barthes, Roland, 172-4
Becker, Howard, 124
Beech, H.R., 27
Benjamin, Walter, 188
Bentham, Jeremy, 49, 50
Berger, Brigitte, 76
Berger, Peter, 67, 76, 177-22*passim*, 124, 129, 207
Berlin, Isaiah, 131
Bienkowski, Wladislaw, 151
Bierstedt, Robert, 132
Bilton, Tony, 151
Black, Max, 28, 29

Blau, Peter, 35, 42-6, 47, 108
Blumer, Herbert G., 95, 97-102, 109, 123
Boden, Margaret, 162, 164
Boring, Edwin, 3, 9-10
Bottomore, Tom, 130, 131, 132, 191-2
Boulding, Kenneth, 187
Bowie, Malcolm, 160
Brown, Roger, 166
Bruner, Jerome, 156
Bryant, Peter, 164
Burgess, Anthony, 27

Càbanis, 4
Callinicos, Alex, 160, 109-5*passim*
Canguilhem, 191, 201
Castaneda, Carlos, 154
Charcot, 155
Chein, Isidor, 16
Chomsky, Noam, 29, 164-71
Cicourel, Aaron, 170
Cimino, Michael, 58
Cohen, David, 26, 28, 143
Cohen, Percy, 45-6, 133, 184
Comte, Auguste, 131-6*passim*, 139, 148, 151, 187, 197

## 226 Index

Connolly, William E., 195
Cooley, Charles H., 79–85, 87, 89, 91, 98, 117, 118, 139, 146
Coppolla, F., 82
Coser, Lewis, *xi*, 61
Coulter, Jeff, 94
Cuzzort, Ray, 113

Darwin, Charles, 5, 70, 134–5, 151, 156
Davis, Kingsley, 144
Dawe, Alan, 67–8, 111–12
d'Azyr, 4
De George, Ferdinand, 156
De George, Richard, 156
Dennett, Daniel, 31, 32
Descartes, René, 2–5, 14
Dewey, John, 69, 71–3, 79, 80, 83, 87
Dilthey, Wilhelm, 60–62, 64, 201
Donaldson, Margaret, 162–3, 170
Douglas, Jack D., 137
Durkheim, Emile, 83, 131, 134–42*passim*, 148, 151, 184*bis*

Ellis, Havelock, 156
Engels, Friedrich, 144, 146–53, 202–3
Eysenck, H.J., 49–53

Fancher, Raymond, 5, 6, 8–9, 11, 12, 23, 26, 157
Fletcher, Ronald, 66, 81
Foucault, Michael, *xii*, 45, 195–200
Fowles, John, 106
Fox, Robin, 24
Frayn, Michael, 16
Frazer, Sir James, 37
Freud, Sigmund, *xii*, 83, 90, 155–60, 178, 189, 193

Frisby, David, 61
Fromm, Erich, 188

Gamble, Andrew, 191
Gardner, Howard, 161, 169, 171, 176
Garfinkel, Harold, xii, 114–17
Gerth, Hans, 62, 64
Geuss, Raymond, 189
Giddens, Anthony, *ix*, 117, 175, 190, 196
Gillin, Charles, 94
Glucksmann, Miriam, 141, 191
Goffman, Erving, 45, 108–13, 117
Gonos, G., 94
Gouldner, Alvin, 38, 49, 109, 188–90
Gray, Jeffrey A., 9
Greene, Judith, 167, 168

Habermas, Jürgen, 188, 189–90
Hahn, Frank, 39
Hall, John A., 189
Hamilton, Peter, 118–19
Hawkes, Terence, 154, 171, 173, 176–7
Hawthorn, Geoffrey, 194
Heath, Anthony, 35
Hegel, Georg, 144–6, 152, 187
Held, David, *x*, 189, 190
Hergenhahn, B.R., 8, 20
Hirst, Paul, 193, 194
Hobbes, Thomas, 4, 14
Holbach, Baron, 206
Hollis, Martin, 39
Homans, George C., *ix–x*, 35, 36–7, 39–48*passim*
Horkheimer, Max, 188
Hospers, John, 22
Hughes, Stuart, 156
Hull, David, 187
Hume, David, 22

Husserl, Edmund, 114
Huxley, Aldous, 16

Ions, Edmund, 24, 28, 29

Jahoda, Marie, 156, 158-9
Jakobson, Roman, 171, 172, 175
James, William, 19, 70-73, 78, 79, 82, 83, 90, 98
Jameson, Frederic, 154
Jarvie, Ian, 120
Johnson, Lamont, 112
Joynson, R.B., 14
Jung, Carl Gustav, 158

Kant, Emmanuel, 60-61
Kaplan, David, 24
Keat, Russell, 133, 146, 150
Kiernan, Chris, 27
King, Dave, 59
King, Edith, 113
Koch, Sigmund, 13-14
Koestler, Arthur, 27, 31
Kolb, William, 94
Kuhn, Manford, 95, 102, 123
Kurzweil, Edith, 198

La Mettrie, 1, 2
Lacan, Jacques, 160
Laszlo, Ervin, 186
Leach, Edmund, 131, 174
Lemert, Charles C., 191
Levi-Strauss, Claude, 38, 131, 171*his*, 174-7
Levin, Ira, 1, 2
Lichtman, Richard, 100
Locke, John, 4, 13, 14, 15, 198
Los, Maria, 130
Luckmann, Thomas, 117-21, 122, 124, 207
Lukes, Steven, 47-8
Lyons, John, 170

McCall, George, 105-8, 110, 118, 123
McCarthy, Joe, 29
McGuire, R.J., 52
MacIntyre, Alasdair, 158, 159
McLellan, David, 188, 189
McPartland, Thomas S., 102
McQuarie, Donald, 187
Madge, John, 85
Malinowski, Bronislaw, 37-8, 47, 142-3, 144, 181
Manners, Robert, 24
Martindale, Don, 142, 144
Marx, Karl, *xii*, 28, 62, 63, 119, 131, 134, 144-53, 187-8, 189, 191, 192, 194, 201
Maryanski, Alexandra, 143
Mauss, Marcel, 38, 140-41
Mead, George H., *xii*, 62, 71, 78, 84, 87-95, 97-103*passim*, 118, 119
Meltzer, Bernard, 86, 102
Mennell, Stephen, 117, 139, 175, 176, 194
Merleau-Ponty, Maurice, 114
Merton, Robert, 152, 207
Midgley, Mary, 31, 32
Miel, Jan, 160
Miliband, Ralph, 202-4
Mill, John Stuart, 47, 53
Miller, George, 18
Miller, James, 186
Mills, C Wright, 62, 64, 69, 207
Misiak, Henryk, 14
Mommsen, W.J., 68
Moon, Reverend, 77
Moore, Wilbert E., 144
Mouzelis, Nicos, 188
M'Pherson, P.K., 186-7

Nias, D.K.B., 51-4
Nisbet, Robert, *xi*, 130-31, 132, 134

Nott, Kathleen, 27
Nye, Robert D., 18, 20, 21–2

O'Neil, W.M., 9
O'Neill, John, 61
Ornstein, Robert E., 30
Orwell, George, 16

Packard, Vance, 24–5, 27, 28, 29
Parsons, Talcott, 177–8, 180–88, 194, 202, 207
Pavlov, Ivan P., 5–9, 11, 12, 14, 16, 18, 32
Pettit, Philip, 177
Piaget, Jean, 157, 160–65
Plato, 19, 33, 130
Plummer, Kenneth, 123–6
Podgórecki, Adam, 130
Pompa, Leon, 131
Popper, Karl, 178, 189
Poulantzas, Nicos, 202–4

Rachlin, Howard, 2, 3–4
Rachman, S., 52
Radcliffe-Brown, A.R., 140–43, 150, 184
Raynor, Rosalie, 13
Rex, John, *viii*
Richards, Janet Radcliffe, 30
Rickert, Heinrich, 61, 62, 65
Rieff, Philip, 159
Robinson, Daniel, 4, 19, 30, 156–7
Rock, Paul, *x*, 146

Saint Simon, 132, 133
Sartre, Jean-Paul, 25, 206
Saussure, Ferdinand, 171, 172, 174
Schutz, Alfred, 114, 117*bis*
Sechenov, Ivan, 5
Sexton, Virginia S., 14
Shelley, Mary, 1

Sheridan, Alan, 151, 198–9
Shotter, John, 25, 31
Siegel, A.E., 52
Simmel, Georg, 35–6, 61, 62, 109, 112, 113
Simmons, Jerry, 105–8, 110, 118, 123
Skidmore, William, 39, 46–7
Skinner, B.F., *xii*, 14, 16–30, 41, 48, 57, 60, 86, 166
Sklair, Leslie, 188
Smith, Neil, 167
Sorokin, Patrim, 109
Spencer, Herbert, *xii*, 135–6, 139, 141, 185
Stevenson, Leslie, 16, 29, 157
Stranger, Jack, 30
Strauss, Anselm, 105
Stryker, Sheldon, 102
Sturrock, John, 171, 172
Suggs, R.C., 124
Sulloway, Frank, J., 158
Sutherland, Stuart, 27, 30

Taylor, Daniel, 32
Terrace, H.S., 24
Thomas, M.H., 53
Thomas, William I., 59, 84–6, 88, 92, 95, 98, 100, 110
Thompson, E,P., 194
Thorndike, Edward L., 19–20, 23
Timpanaro, S.Y., 159
Tönnies, Ferdinand, 135–6
Turner, Bryan, 68, 192
Turner, Jonathan, *ix*, 35, 41, 42, 44, 46, 48, 143, 184
Turner, Ralph, 103–5

Urry, John, 133, 146, 150

Van Krafft-Ebing, R., 156
Vico, Giambattista, 130–32, 133, 135–6

von Bertalanffy, Ludwig, 186

Wallace, Ruth, 36*bis*, 47
Walton, Paul, 191
Watson, John B., 9–13, 14, 16, 20, 32, 87
Watson, Robert, 11
Weber, Marianne, 68
Weber, Max, *xii*, 62–70, 73, 87, 89, 100, 114, 120, 182, 199
Weigel, John, 24
Werner, Heinz, 170
Whorf, Benjamin L., 77, 164, 172
Wilson, Deirdre, 167
Wilson, Edward O., 1, 29
Wilson, Thomas, 116, 121
Wolf, Alison, 36*bis*, 47
Wolff, Kurt H., 61
Woolley, Penny, 193, 194
Worsley, Peter, 176, 188
Wundt, 87

Zamyatin, 16
Zeitlin, Irving, 62, 94, 100, 101, 147, 151
Znaniecki, Florian, 59, 84, 85, 86, 92, 110

# Title Index

*A Clockwork Orange*, 27
*A Kind of Loving*, 18
*American Power and the New Mandarins*, 164
*Apocalypse Now*, 82
*Argonauts of the Western Pacific*, 37
*Asylums*, 111

*Beyond Freedom and Dignity*, 17, 25, 28
*Brave New World*, 16

*Capital*, 145, 188, 201, 202

*ET*, 9
*Exchange and Power in Social Life*, 43

*Frankenstein*, 1

*Hamlet*, 26

*Identities and Interactions*, 105

*Knowledge and Human Interests*, 189

*Lipstick*, 112

*Lord of the Flies*, viii

*Madness and Civilization*, 196
*Mirrors and Masks*, 105
*Mythologies*, 173

*Paris Manuscripts*, 188
*Political Power and Social Classes*, 202–4
*Principles of Psychology*, 70

*Republic*, 19

*Science and Human Behaviour*, 17
*Scienza Nuova*, 130
*Sex, Violence and the Media*, 51–4
*Sexual Stigma*, 123
*Social Behaviour*, 40
*Studies in Ethnomethodology*, 114
*Syntactic Structures*, 164

*The Deerhunter*, 58
*The Division of Labour in Society*, 134
*The Dynamics of Bureaucracy*, 43
*The French Lieutenant's Woman*, 106
*The Gift*, 140

*The Human Group*, 40
*The Interpretation of Dreams*, 155
*The Language and Thought of the Child*, 161
*The Making of the Modern Homosexual*, 125
*The Omen*, 52
*The Polish Peasant in Europe and America*, 85
*The Positive Polity*, 132
*The Presentation of the Self in Everyday Life*, 109
*The Protest Ethic and the Spirit of Capitalism*, 62
*The Psychopathology of Everyday Life*, 158
*The Return of the Jedi*, 9
*The Sceptical Feminist*, 30
*The Social Construction of Reality*, 117
*The State in Capitalist Society*, 202
*The Stepford Wives*, 1
*The Structure of Social Action*, 181
*Tristes Tropiques*, 171

*Walden Two*, 17, 25, 33
*We*, 16

# Subject Index

*A prioris*, 61-3
Alienation, 149-50, 152
Autonomy, 95
Axiom, 40-1, 49

Behaviour therapy, 27, 33
Behaviourism, *x-xii*, 1-54, 57-9, 86, 87, 92, 141, 166
Brain processes, 5-9, 32
British Associationism, 3-4, 19, 32
Bureaucracy, 66, 116, 204

Capitalism, 66-8, 148-50, 184, 202-4
Cash nexus, 150
Causes, 18, 22-3, 30-1, 60, 62, 65-6, 73, 74, 83, 90, 102, 139, 143, 158
Chaining, 22
Class, 100-1, 113, 144, 185, 194
Cognitive structure, 154-78
Cognitive development, 160-4
Concepts, *ix*, 14
Conditioning, 7-30, 39, 89, 93
Conflict, 133, 143, 148-50, 157, 185
Consciousness, 10-11, 30-3, 58, 76-95, 119, 147, 151, 189, 197
Contiguity, 4, 14
Controlling humans, 24-33, 97
Creativity, 31, 71-4, 83, 89-90, 95, 102, 111, 139, 144, 149-51, 166, 199, 206
Crime, 137
Critical theory, *x*, 189-91
Culture, 95, 142, 151, 172-8, 185, 193

Darwinism, 70, 134, 151, 156
Definition of the situation, 59, 72, 84-7, 95, 110, 116
Determinism, *xii*, 2-53, 62, 68, 70, 82, 93-5, 99, 102-3, 130, 149-51, 158-9, 187, 190-5, 200
  linguistic, 164
Diachronic analysis, 150, 153
Dialectic, 91, 95, 119, 122, 145-6, 152
Dialetical materialism, 146-7
Discourse, 178, 196-7
Discrimination, 8, 21
Distributive justice, 41, 44
Dualism, 2-5, 14, 187

232

Dynamic, 95, 133, 136, 145, 199

Economics, 35-7
Education, 143, 151, 185, 193-4
Empiricism, 3, 14, 101, 165, 175
Enlightenment, 133
Environment, 26-8, 33, 72, 76, 83, 90-4, 119, 147, 151, 161
Epistemological break, 191-2, 201
Epistemology, 165, 178
Ethnomethodology, 114-17
Exchange theory, 35-54, 72, 108, 183
Explanation, *vii*, 41, 49, *see* Cause

Families, 76-85, 107, 135, 185, 193
Forces of production, 146, 192, 194
Frame of reference, 74
Frankfurt School, 189-91
Free will, *ix-xii*, 1, 57-9, 72, 83, 93, 126, 200, 205
Freedom, 24-33, 83, 90, 94, 118-9, 189-90, 206
Function, 134-5, 152
Functionalism, 134-44, 150, 177, 184, 194

Geist, 145-6
Gemeinschaft, Gesellschaft, 136
General systems theory, 186-7
Generalities, I, II, III, 192, 201, 204
Generalization, 8, 21
Generalized other, 91, 99
Genetic endowment, 1, 3, 33, 70, 90-2

Habit, 11, 71, 89
Hedonism, 39, 49, 157
Hermeneutics, 190, 201

Historical materialism, 144-152, 199
Historicism, 194-5, 201
Holism, 133-52, 180-195
Homosexuality, 124-5
Human-animal comparisons, 23-33, 36-7, 64, 126, 144, 157
Human-machine comparisons, 2-14, 47, 156-7
Human nature, 82, 84, 92, 13, 139, 147, 174
Human needs, 49, 142-3, 144, 157
Humanism, 74, 95, 191

'I' and 'Me', 78, 90, 95, 106, 111-12, 157
Id, ego, superego, 90, 157
Ideal types, 66-8
Idealism, 101, 144-6, 152, 200
Identity, 79, 103-13, 118
Ideological state apparatuses, 193-4, 202-4
Ideology, 150, 173, 185, 187, 189-90, 193-204
Idiographic, 121
Impression management, 108-9
Indeterminacy, 121
Indexicality, 116, 122
Individualism, 49
Instinct, 11, 70, 74, 89, 139, 144, 157
Interactionism, *ix-xii*, 57-126, 129
Interdependence, 135
Interpretative sociology, 60-5, 97-126
Interpretive paradigm, 116, 121
Introspection, 3, 10, 15, 102
Invariance, 74, 139, 140, 162-78

Knowledge, 189-200, 205-6

Kula Ring, 37-8, 143

Language, 12, 24, 77-9, 85-89, 105, 119, 126, 142, 154, 160-74
Law of diminishing returns, 40-1, 44
Laws of history, 130-3, 137, 141, 148-9, 151-2, 158
Libido, 160, 178
Looking glass self, 79, 118, 126

Meaning, 57-65, 77, 140, 187
Means of production, 146, 153
Mechanical solidarity, 136
Metaphysical, 54-5, 146
Methodological individualism, 47-9
Mind, 72, 81-4, 87-95, 131, 139, 144, 154-178
Mode of production, 146-7, 152-3, 192
Models, 15, 66

Nativism, 3, 15, 165, 169, 175
Natural sciences, 60, 70, 74, 131, 141, 156, 189
Neurosis, 178
Nomethetic, 102, 121, 186
Nominalism, 199, 201
Normative paradigm, 116, 121
Norms, 39, 44, 47, 91, 108, 121, 182, 184

Operant conditioning, 18, 33
Organic models of society, 133-40
Organic solidarity, 136
Overdeterminism, 159, 193

Pedophilia, 123-4
Phenomenology, 114, 121
Phenomenon, 74
Philosopher-king, 25, 33

Puzzle box, 19
Pornography, 51-4
Positivism, 4-5, 60, 74, 87, 101-2, 131-2, 135, 141, 146-7, 189
Potlach, 38
Power, 45-6, 110, 113, 117, 119-20, 184-5, 194-200
Pragmatism, 68-74, 90-1, 93, 139
Praxis, 150
Primary groups, 79-83, 85
Problematic, 191, 201
Psychic energies, 90, 141, 157-8
Psychoanalysis, 156-60, 190
Psychopathology, 158, 178
Punishment, 20-1

Radical environmentalism, 13-14, 24-33
Rational action, 65-8
Reciprocity, 37-8, 43-6, 49, 140, 177
Reductionism, 2-14, 23-33, 29-30, 49, 64, 187
Reflection, 77, 79-84, 89, 92, 126
Reflex arc, 15, 72
Reflexes, 7-9, 11-13, 15, 18, 93
Reification, 103, 112-8, 122
Reinforcement, 8-9, 19-33, 37, 78, 166
Relations of production, 146, 194
Relative autonomy, 192-3, 202-4
Religion, 137-8, 141, 148, 151, 185, 193-4, 198
Reproduction, 193, 201
Research, 206-7
Revolution, 42, 144, 150, 185
Reward, 20-46
Role, 103-113, 116
Role-identity model, 106-8
Rules, 67-8, 108, 138
  linguistic, 165-9, 172-4

Sanction, 43, 49
Self, 76-9, 98-100, 102-108, 109-112
Self-indication, 97-9
Semiology (semiotics), 172-4
Sentience, 73, 74
Sexual deviance, 51-4, 59, 123-6
Shaping, 22-3
Signs, 171-4
Skinner box, 22-4, 41
Social change, *x*, 62, 65-8, 73, 83, 87, 91, 120, 133, 144, 146, 148-52, 185, 194, 199-200
Social context, 74, 85-7, 98-9, 108-17, 124-5, 147, 170
Social facts, 133, 136-9, 140, 142
Social organization, 100, 122
Social statics, 133
Socialization, 76-84, 93-4, 99, 107, 112, 118-9, 183-4
Sociobiology, 1, 29
State, 202-4
Stimuli, 5, 11, 17-33, 57, 71-2, 86, 87, 93
Strains, *ix-xii*, 206-8
Structuralism, *ix-xii*, 129-203
Structure, 129-30, 134-5, 141-2, 155-7
Subjective dimensions of society, 60-126
Suicide, 136-7
Symbolic interactionism, 97-121
Symbols, 88-93, 103, 119, 138
Synchronic analysis, 143, 150, 153
Systems, 100, 111, 176, 178, 180-187, 192

Tabula rasa, 4, 13, 15, 61, 198
Teleology, 143, 152
Transformational theory, 165-70

Universals
  cognitive, 174-8
  linguistic, 168-9
Utilitarianism, 35-6, 50

Values, 39, 46-7, 184-5
Verification, 178
Verstehende Sociologie, 64-8, 100
Violence, 51-4
Voluntarism, *xii*, 99-102, 121, 131, 145, 165, 189
Volition, 95, 121

Youth culture, 136

Zeitgeist, 10, 15